CHRISTIANITY'S GREAT DILEMMA

CHRISTIANITY'S GREAT DILEMMA

IS JESUS COMING AGAIN OR IS HE NOT?

One Pastor's Story of
His Search for the Answer

GLENN L. HILL

Moonbeam Publications
Lexington, KY

All Scriptures are from the *King James Version* (KJV) of the Bible unless indicated otherwise.

Scripture quotations marked (NKJV) are taken from the *New King James Version* of the Bible. Copyright 1979, 1980, and 1982 by Thomas Nelson, Inc. Used by permission. All rights reserved.

Scripture quotations marked (NIV) are taken from the Holy Bible, *New International Version*. Copyright 1973, 1978, and 1984 by International Bible Society. Used by permission of Zondervan Bible Publishers.

Scripture quotations marked (NASB) are taken from the *New American Standard Bible*, Copyright 1960, 1962, 1963, 1968, 1971, 1972, 1973, 1975, 1977, and 1995 by The Lockman Foundation. Used by permission.

Scripture quotations marked (ESV) are taken from The Holy Bible, *English Standard Version*, copyright 2001 by Crossway Bibles, a division of Good News Publishers. Used by permission. All rights reserved.

Scripture quotations marked (YLT) are taken from *Young's Literal Translation*.

The Emphatic Diaglott containing the Original Greek Text of what is commonly styled The New Testament, with an interlinear word for word English translation, is designated *The Emphatic Diaglott*, where Scripture quotations are taken from it.

About the cover: In 1902 the famous French sculptor, Auguste Rodin, completed his world-renown bronze masterpiece, "The Thinker." It is used here to represent the author's high hopes that his book will inspire believers to seriously THINK about what they believe and solve the puzzle—the great dilemma facing Christianity.

Copyright © 2010 Glenn L. Hill

All rights reserved. No part of this book may be reproduced, stored in a retrieval system, or transmitted in any form or by any means without the prior written permission of the publishers, except by a reviewer who may quote brief passages in a review to be printed in a newspaper, magazine or journal.

Cover Design: Michael J. Johnson
Editor: Tina Rae Collins
Associate Editor: Jack Gibbert

ISBN / EAN-13: 9-781453-873748
First Printing

MP
Moonbeam*D*Publications
Lexington, KY

TABLE OF CONTENTS

	Dedication	iii
	Acknowledgments	v
	Preface	vii
	Introduction	xi
	Foreword	xv
I.	WHAT A DILEMMA CHRISTIANITY HAS ON ITS HANDS!	1
II.	IN THE GOSPELS WHEN DID JESUS SAY HE WAS COMING?	15
	Matthew 23:36 - 24:35	15
	Matthew 16:27 - 28	34
	John 21:21 - 23	40
	Matthew 26:64	43
	Matthew 10:23	46
	Summary of Chapter II	48
III.	IN THE REVELATION WHEN DID JESUS SAY HE WAS COMING?	51
IV.	THE LAST DAYS	67
V.	THE END OF THE WORLD	81
VI.	THE JUDGMENT	97

	Summary of Chapters IV, V, & VI	120
VII.	WHEN DID THE APOSTLES SAY JESUS WAS COMING?	123
	The Apostle Peter	127
	The Apostle Paul	145
	The Apostle John	181
VIII.	WHEN DID OTHER EARLY CHURCH LEADERS SAY JESUS WAS COMING?	185
	James, Jesus' Half-Brother	185
	The Author of the Book of Hebrews	189
IX.	WHEN DOES THE BIBLE SAY THE COMING OF JESUS WAS IMMINENT?	203
	Increasing Imminence	209
	Closing Summary	215
	Conclusion	221

DEDICATION

This book is dedicated to:

The restoration of
the integrity and credibility of
Jesus,
His Apostles,
and
His Holy Word

And to:

My wonderful wife,
Betty Sue Giddens Hill,
who has been the love and joy of
my life, and my fellow servant in
the work of the Lord for
FIFTY YEARS!

ACKNOWLEDGMENTS

To all of you who read my book and offered your advice, support, and help—**thank you!** You have been a great encouragement to me! I had planned to list all your names here. But dozens of you read my manuscript and I was afraid I would miss someone. It was wonderful to have so many Christian friends all across the country to help me. I am deeply grateful for your assistance and sincerely appreciate all of your suggestions!

To my friend in the Lone Star State, Jack Gibbert, who spent much time and effort editing my book, not once, but twice—**thank you, Jack!** You worked willingly and cheerfully with grace, patience, and good humor. You insisted I discard that "editorial we" and thus made my book a totally new read! I appreciate your help so much and I shall always be grateful to you!

To my friend in Kentucky, Tina Rae Collins, who also spent much time reading and editing my manuscript four times—**thank you, Tina!** You have an incredible knowledge and understanding of the English language and proper grammar. It was just wonderful to have your help! I am most appreciative and grateful to you! (Tina, I take full responsibility for any remaining errors; I may have chosen to do a few things my way, instead of the right way.)

To my professor friend in Tennessee, John S Evans; my Bible scholar brother in Arizona, Tony Denton; my wonderful Baptist brother in the Sunshine State, Evangelist John L. Bray; my good friends in Massachusetts, John and Christine Felisberto; to Don Preston (OK) who wrote my foreword and Arthur Melanson (NJ), Sam Dawson (TX), and Brian Martin (CA) who filled the back cover of my book with their enthusiastic endorsements; and to my local buddies, Steve Temple and Dee Cozart—**thank you so much!** You read and critiqued my manuscript and offered many good suggestions—greatly improving the accuracy and the quality of my work!

To my computer-genius brother in Kentucky, Michael J. Johnson, who created and designed the awesome cover for my book and laid out its pages in an inviting and easy to read format—**thank you, Michael!** Your work has so excited me! I never even dared to dream that my book could look as great as you have made it! You are an incredible talent! I am very grateful to have had the benefit of your many skills!

To my sweet wife, Betty Sue, who read, reread, and then read again each and every word I have written—**thank you, Honey!** You have been wonderful! I have been able to bounce ideas off you, discard the bad ones and keep the good. You helped keep my writing clear, plain, on point, and easy to follow and understand. I am sorry for the countless hours you were left alone while I labored to write. But you were always supportive, patient, kind, and understanding. I cannot imagine having undertaken this project without you by my side. I love and appreciate you very, very much!

Thank all of you for being my friends and my fellow brothers and sisters, my comrades in arms in the work of the Lord. I love you and feel extremely blessed to have you in my life! May the Lord richly bless all of you and repay you for your goodness to me!

In His love,

Glenn

PREFACE

Have you ever wondered what is delaying the return of Jesus—why He does not appear now to rapture His church and destroy this old wicked world? Do you ever ponder about how very long you have been promised that "Jesus is coming soon," but He has not returned? If so, then ***Christianity's Great Dilemma*** may be the most unusual, interesting, and perhaps enlightening Second Coming prophecy book you will ever read!

For most of my fifty years of preaching I taught that Jesus' Second Coming was near, so near that I expected to live to see the Advent. The ministers I listened to as a boy had the same message and the same expectation, but they died without seeing our Lord's coming. The vast majority of ministers for the past hundred years have proclaimed that "Jesus is coming soon," but He has not returned! **Do you ever wonder why?**

Modern-day prophets have kept us in great anticipation as they predicted the imminent coming of the antichrist, along with such things as the great tribulation, the rapture, the end of the world, the end of time, and the battle of Armageddon. Do you ever consider that decades pass, and one century ends and another begins, yet *NONE* of these prophecies come to pass? Do you remember Y2K? As the year 2000 approached, preachers and prophets made many predictions; and *NOTHING* happened! How embarrassing to Christianity! **Could something be wrong with our message?**

But another problem is perhaps even larger. Bible scholars wholeheartedly agree that Jesus promised to return during the lifetime of His contemporaries in that first century. They further agree that His disciples continued to preach that their Master's return was imminent, at hand, and would occur soon. But today, 2,000 years later, the church teaches that Jesus did not come in the first century as He promised! **Now that is a dilemma!**

It is difficult for me and other believers to actually ask the hard questions created by Jesus' perceived failure. We cannot bring ourselves to question the integrity of our Savior. On the other hand, the doubters and unbelievers have no problems pointing out Jesus' apparent false prophecies. In his essay, "The World's Last Night,"[i] the great Christian author, **C. S. Lewis,** wrote exactly what the unbelievers are all saying:

> Say what you like, the apocalyptic beliefs of the first Christians have been proved to be false. It is clear from the New Testament that they all expected the Second Coming in their own lifetime. And, worse still, they had a reason, and one you will find very embarrassing. Their Master had told them so. He shared, and indeed created, their delusion. He said in so many words, "this generation shall not pass till all these things be done." And He was wrong. He clearly knew no more about the end of the world than anyone else.

What terrible accusations against our Lord! Yet, our famous intellectual brother, C. S. Lewis, having no suitable answer to these charges, simply acknowledges in his next paragraph that "It is certainly the most embarrassing verse in the Bible." He was referring to the passage he had quoted where Jesus had promised to return in the "generation" of His contemporaries (Matt. 23:34, Mark 13:30, Luke 21:32).

What a dilemma this is! Jesus told His followers He would come back while some of them were still living, and apparently He did not keep His promise! If I believed Jesus did not do what He said, if I believed He had misled and deceived His first followers, then I could no longer believe in Him. Yet, the conclusion reached by unbelievers, that Jesus "was wrong" about "when" He would return, is exactly what is believed by most of Christianity's leaders today! Were you aware of this? It is shocking! Mainstream Christianity has no credible answer, so they conclude that Jesus must have been wrong! How can it be that the Son of God was mistaken or made a promise He did not keep? What a predicament! **This is indeed a great dilemma!**

For generation after generation we Christian preachers and prophets have been declaring with great emphasis that "Jesus is coming soon." **WE WERE ALL WRONG!** Jesus did not come as we had promised and He surely did not come "soon"! Yet Christianity continues to preach this same message.

Numerous "prophets" have gone so far as to name the date when Jesus would return, but they *ALWAYS* have been wrong! What a blow all of this is to the credibility of Christianity and to the integrity of Jesus and His Holy Word! It is no wonder that atheists and other unbelievers laugh at us and make fun of Christianity. What a great hindrance to the growth of the church! **Indeed, what a great dilemma we Christians face!**

Is there an answer to this huge problem? Yes, thank the Lord! The answer is what my book is all about! In its pages you will find the solution to ***Christianity's Great Dilemma!*** The answer is not some imaginary or hypothetical solution. It is not some invisible and intangible possibility. The answer revealed in this book is firmly and solidly based on the Scriptures themselves! The answer is simple and easy to grasp. It is the truth which, somehow, has been overlooked by most of Christianity. I still wonder how I, too, missed it for so many decades!

This is **A MUST READ BOOK** for every studious, thoughtful, and sincere Christian! I humbly invite you to read it. It is not difficult reading. I tried to write using simple, everyday language and purposely avoided complicated theological terms and words. Yet, I promise you will find it honest, unique, interesting, and even challenging. Most Christians have never heard or even considered the thrilling discoveries found in these pages. Read this book with eagerness! Read with a spirit of expectancy and anticipation! Read with a genuine hunger to find the answer to ***Christianity's Great Dilemma!*** You will not be disappointed! The singular answer runs consistently all the way through the New Testament. **FINDING IT WILL INCREASE YOUR FAITH IN JESUS, AND YOUR WALK WITH HIM WILL NEVER BE THE SAME!**

In His love,

Glenn

INTRODUCTION

For more than four decades I fervently preached "Jesus is coming soon." But when I really faced this dilemma, I just could not preach that message anymore. When I honestly considered that Jesus had told His apostles that when He returned some of them would still be preaching and fleeing from city to city, I wondered if the Lord had misled His disciples (Matt. 10:32). When I took a fresh look at James' promise, "The Lord's coming is near" (James 5:8) and what those words actually meant to the first century Christians, I wondered how I could still be expecting the Second Coming today. When I again studied Hebrews 10:37, "For yet a little while, and He that shall come will come, and will not tarry," I wondered how "a little while" and a promise not to "tarry," could possibly be stretched into 2,000 years. I soon concluded that I did not know enough about the Second Coming of Jesus to be preaching about it! I honestly did not know what to do!

What I finally did was **to stop preaching** about the Second Coming and **to start earnestly studying** it, again. This book is my story! It is about the almost unbelievable transformation in my beliefs, once I found the answer to my dilemma. Here is what I discovered:

1. Jesus had not embarrassed C. S. Lewis and me by failing to keep His promises!
2. Instead, Bro. Lewis and I had terribly misunderstood Jesus and the apostles' teachings about "when" He was coming again!

So, when I began writing this book my vision was to answer this question, **"When does the Bible say Jesus would come again?"** Thus, my book is about eschatology, which is the study of last things, such as the Last Days, the End of the World, the Judgment, and the Second Coming of Jesus.

Since boyhood I have believed in the importance of biblical truth. Whether what I believe is exactly what the Word of God teaches has always mattered to me. To believe something contrary to His Word is to be wrong and I never had any interest in being wrong, especially about my Christian faith. This love for the Bible, and a genuine hunger to know the truth, has often found me at odds with prevailing Christian teachings. So it is again in this book. The interpretations of the Scriptures presented here do not conform to the doctrines preached from most of the pulpits in our land. But, I believe truth is supremely important to God and this means it should be supremely important to Christians. So, throughout my life whenever I have found His truth, I have always felt a great obligation to stand for it. This book is a continuing effort to do just that.

Let me assure you before you begin to read Chapter I, I have not discovered something new that no one else knows or found some new truth no one else has ever seen! In fact, all across America a growing multitude of Christians have found the answer to ***Christianity's Great Dilemma*** and they have been a tremendous help to me. Many, many old and new books and articles have aided me in my search. Also, more web sites are dedicated to answering my dilemma than I can possibly follow. However, I can call no new Scriptures to your attention! They are the same dear verses you and I have read over and over again throughout the years of our lives. What is new is how I, and many others, have now come to understand these same precious passages.

Let me further assure you, I do not "know it all." My experience that resulted in my writing this book proves that. I had to admit I was wrong about many of my beliefs! These were doctrines that were dear and precious to me, things I had believed all my life, and teachings I had preached with great fervor for many years. It was difficult and embarrassing! On the other hand, I was glad to be embarrassed because it meant I had grown in His Word and had come to a better understanding of what the Scriptures teach. Through this experience I learned that, if I will ever be right, sometimes along my journey I will have to admit I am wrong. And, I am sure that there are things about which I am still wrong. I do not "know it all"!

I do hope and pray that people who do not believe in Jesus will read my book! It will answer a lot of their questions about the many dubious Christian teachings concerning the Last Days and the return of Jesus. Hopefully, it will create an opportunity for faith in their lives. That being said, in a very personal way I have addressed my writings to my fellow Christians. I have written to those like me, who love Jesus, believe in Him, and try to serve Him every day. After all, **Christianity's Great Dilemma** is a dilemma within the Christian community and a problem only Christians can solve. I humbly ask you to consider the solution I present here. I do not ask you to believe my words because I say they are true. But, I do hope to challenge you and cause you to begin to study and to really think about the church's teachings about eschatology.

Many of you who know me, including my family, my friends, my fellow ministers, and my brothers and sisters in Christ, think I have left the faith and forsaken the truth. But most of you have never had a good chance to consider the reasons behind the unexpected changes in my beliefs. This book will give you that opportunity. Please read it, study it, and pray for the guidance of the Lord. Do not judge too quickly. Give yourself some time. Changes this big do not occur quickly. It took me a year or two to conclude that what I had discovered, with help from the Lord and others, was indeed the truth. Then it took a little more time for me to admit I was wrong. And yes, it took even more time for me to gather the courage and the strength to take a public stand for the truth I had discovered.

I regret this change has come so late in my life. But, I do thank God it has come in time for me to correct some of my mistakes. All my life as a pastor, whenever I preached I honestly did the very best I knew to do. Now I realize I taught wrong doctrines to many people. I ask for their forgiveness. I hope and pray this book will reach every one of them, and that it will help them to come to a better understanding of God's Word.

Thank you for considering my book! I am honored! Since each chapter is built upon the previous chapters, please begin with Chapter I and read the entire book in order. As you do so, the answer to "the dilemma" will become clearer and clearer to you. I know your time is limited and valuable, but I hope that when you reach the end of *Christianity's Great Dilemma,* you will be glad you took this opportunity to seriously consider the church's end of time teachings. Whatever your final appraisal of my writings, please know that I deeply appreciate your time and consideration!

In His love,

Glenn

FOREWORD

Christianity has a major problem, a problem that many Christians struggle with silently. Believers of all kinds, from professors to those filling the pews, have historically sought answers, with little success. It is a problem that the enemies of Christ are using increasingly against His church. We must confront this problem. We must answer it.

What is this problem? It is the indisputable fact that Jesus, followed by his apostles, predicted for the first century generation, his "Second Coming" in judgment at the end of the age. C. S. Lewis called Jesus' predictions the most embarrassing words in the Bible!

Glenn Hill is a believer who has seen the problem, and like many others has sought to resolve the difficulty. He has struggled with the question of failure or fulfillment. He has spent countless hours in his search to find the answer to this perplexing, challenging, and critical issue.

With an ever increasing number of Bible students, Glenn has found the answer to the problem. And with the tender heart of a teacher he has produced an easy to read, easy to understand book to help other believers find the solution to **Christianity's Great Dilemma.**

In this book, Glenn carefully examines what Jesus, Paul, Peter, John— indeed, all of the NT writers--had to say about the time of the end and Christ's coming. His method of presentation highlights the problem very well, confronting the reader with the reality of what the Bible writers did in fact predict. This method of presentation is very effective, but needless to say, it is challenging for anyone who has not seriously confronted the issue, or anyone who has sought to sweep it under the rug.

If you are one of the countless Bible students who have seen the issue, but had no answers, this book will be a tremendous aid to you. If you have been unaware of what Jesus and his apostles actually predicted, this book will be a true eye-opener!

In **Christianity's Great Dilemma,** you will not be offended by harsh verbiage. You will not be overwhelmed by technical terms. You will be touched by the heart of a teacher, with a true desire to help the reader share in his own personal struggles that have resulted in his own discovery of truth.

I highly recommend Glenn Hill's book to anyone that is willing to think, willing to re-think, willing to confront **Christianity's Great Dilemma**. You will be thrilled at the answers offered in this book.

Don K. Preston

Minister, Author, and President of PRI

www.bibleprophecy.com

www.eschatology.org

I

WHAT A DILEMMA CHRISTIANITY HAS ON ITS HANDS!

Let me get right to the point! Is Jesus coming again or is He not? You and I have been told all of our lives that He is definitely coming again, and that His return will be soon! We hear this message preached regularly in America's pulpits and on radio and TV. I preached it myself for decades! So, it seems almost sacrilegious for me to question whether or not Jesus is actually going to return. I do not mean to be disrespectful in the least! I do not propose this question with anything but the greatest of reverence for Jesus, the Bible, and Christianity. Jesus is my Savior and I love Him with all my heart. **The greatest desire of my life is to please Him** and to live so as to make Him glad that He died to save me!

But back to my question, **"Is Jesus coming again or is He not?"** And if He is coming again, is He indeed coming back soon? For most of my fifty years of preaching I proclaimed again and again, "Jesus is coming again and He is coming soon!" In recent years I have come to realize that the people who heard those sermons really do have plenty of justification for questioning my words. Why? It is simply because Jesus did not come "soon" as I had said He would! In fact it has been a long time and He still has not come! Neither has time ended, nor has the world been destroyed in the great calamity that I had forecast.

So, I spent most of my life preaching that Jesus was coming again and that His coming was very near. I said that He could appear at any moment. Now, I am in the sunset years of my life and His coming, which I declared to be "soon" for over four decades, still has not occurred. Jesus just did not come and He surely did not come "soon"! My sermons were sincere, my heart was honest, and I certainly thought my messages were biblical, but something was wrong.

I have been able to reach only one honest conclusion and that is **that my sermons declaring Jesus was coming soon were just plain wrong!** It did not happen! I confess that I misled the good people who filled the pews and patiently listened to me preach. For my part, I just thank God for His mercy and grace! I thank Him for His love and forgiveness! I thank Him that He is the God of second chances! I thank Him that He has given me another opportunity to get the message right! This book is about my journey, as I tried to learn where I had gone wrong and struggled to find the truth about the great doctrine of the Second Coming of the Lord.

But I have a lot of company! Many other preachers proclaim the message I used to teach. Just recently I saw a famous preacher on TV look straight into the camera and say, "Jesus is coming soon, and in fact He is coming very soon." How long will we Christians just keep accepting these prophecies that never come true? How long before we will begin questioning these failed promises of our Lord's soon return? **The purpose of this book is to get us Christians to think,** to think for ourselves and to study for ourselves, so that we can all find the solution to this dilemma in our Christian doctrine!

Perhaps you, like me, learned the things you believe regarding the Second Coming from those Christians and leaders who came before you. My mother was a wonderful and faithful Christian woman, and she believed that Jesus was coming soon. I was absolutely certain that she was right about this doctrine and it never even crossed my mind to doubt or to question the teaching. **The pastors and preachers in my life were all good, honest, sincere, dedicated, and faithful Christian men.** They were men of great learning and knowledge; and I, without hesitation, believed their words about Jesus' Second Coming. But what they preached and what I preached too, that "soon" the world would end and Jesus would return, never did occur as we had said it would.

These preachers included my father-in-law, perhaps the most wonderful and godly man I ever knew. I cannot tell you how very much I loved and

I. What a Dilemma!

respected him. He was a spiritual father to me and he gave me an angel to be my wife! He was a great preacher of the Gospel! He too declared all his life that Jesus was coming soon. I loved to hear him preach and believed every word he said! He is gone now and I miss him very much. I can still see him preaching his heart out in that old wooden church building. His starched and ironed white shirt would be soaked with sweat, as he warned us to get ready for the soon coming of Jesus. That was many years ago, but Jesus never came and He still has not. It just seems to me that something is obviously wrong here!

My father-in-law's father was a preacher too, and while I never was privileged to hear him preach, from all accounts his message was the same: "Jesus is coming soon." Now that would really go back a long time, perhaps into the late 1800s. Yet today in the twenty-first century, Christianity still waits for the Jesus who was said to be coming "soon" way back in the 1800s! This circle of great ministers who touched my life and I have been telling people for a few generations, well over a hundred years, that Jesus was coming soon. He still has not come! Again, if we will just stop and think, it is not hard to see that something is obviously wrong with this message!

But a hundred years, including three or four generations of preachers, is nothing when compared to the **apparent mistake of the Lord's apostles.** Nearly 2,000 years ago the apostles believed, preached, and wrote Epistles declaring that the coming of the Lord was "near" and "at hand." They too preached that Jesus would be coming "soon." To our knowledge no controversy exists among Bible scholars on this point. Yet now 2,000 years later, if Jesus still has not come, then the apostles seem to have misled and deceived the believers in the early church—as well as all of us who have followed their teachings for the past 2,000 years. **What a problem this is!** Can it get any more evident that something is seriously wrong here? I hope you are beginning to see and to recognize this great dilemma!

As the saying goes, it does not take a rocket scientist to recognize that a major problem prevails in the Christian church's teaching that "Jesus is coming soon." Furthermore, it does not even take a Bible scholar to see the problem! The average Christian can quickly recognize that something is just not right. You may not know the answer to this dilemma, but you cannot help but see that a difficulty exists. So be honest with yourself. No one will know. No one is looking except the Lord. If you are like me and have been secretly wondering why Jesus does not come as He said He would, as His apostles said He would, and as we preachers have said He would, then it is okay for you to reverently and honestly question that part of your faith. As sacred as the teaching is, you will not be committing blasphemy to ask, "Is Jesus coming again or is He not?" It will be okay to ask in your heart, **"If Jesus' coming was imminent in the days of the apostles, can it still be imminent today, 2,000 years later?"**

Having dared to raise these questions, you surely will want to find the answers. That was certainly how I felt. I wanted to know the truth! Obviously, my preaching—and even my singing—that "Jesus is coming soon" turned out not to be true. It did not happen. Yet, the Bible clearly teaches that Jesus was indeed coming soon. What a dilemma! Can we find an answer? Whatever others may do, I hope you will decide to investigate this matter and to find the answer for YOURSELF!

Personally, I was deeply troubled by this problem. After having preached for most of a half-century that Jesus could come at any moment, I just could not preach that message anymore. I was no longer sure and certain that it was indeed true! Yet, I felt like a backslider from the faith to even question such a fundamental, cardinal doctrine of the church. But I was honest before God and He knew it. I desired only the truth. I did not want to be wrong myself, and of great importance, I did not want to mislead others! I did not want to give people hope in Jesus' soon appearing, **if He really was not going to show up right away!**

Thus I began my journey, slowly, quietly, secretly, and fearful of what others would think. I was sincerely looking for an answer to my dilemma. But it is more than just my dilemma! **It is Christianity's dilemma!** The Bible clearly teaches the soon coming of the Lord. The apostles preached it and wrote about it in their Epistles. But, did the Lord come soon as they declared? If not, did the apostles deceive the early church converts? Have they further deceived you and me and the millions of Christians who have followed their teachings? What terrible questions to even think about, let alone to actually ask! But Christianity

I. What a Dilemma!

has a problem here. We Christians do need to face these issues and find the answers!

This problem in Christian doctrine is not overlooked by the atheists and the unbelievers. They are keenly aware of it. They make fun of us and mock us all the time! They have heard Christians set dates for the Lord's coming, only to have the last laugh when our prophecies failed! They have heard us take the latest news headlines and then predict what was going to occur. Then they have made fun of us when nothing happened.

The great British philosopher, **Bertrand Russell,** wrote a book he titled ***Why I Am Not a Christian.*** In it he said that Jesus had made predictions that He would come again in the first century and He did not come. Russell concluded that since Jesus failed to keep this important prophecy, he could not believe anything else Jesus said and therefore could not follow Him. It feels terrible to say this, but this seems like a reasonable conclusion! How embarrassing this is to me as a Christian and especially as a minister of His Word. Go back and read my Preface, where our brother, **C. S. Lewis,** frankly admitted that a Scripture teaching that Jesus would return in the lifetime of some of His followers was "certainly the most embarrassing verse in the Bible." What a dilemma! We Christians must get this problem solved and bring an end to this embarrassing and detrimental situation!

In spite of all their failed prophecies, our modern-day prophets keep on making new prophecies and writing more books. Based on the latest news headlines they keep updating, revising, and adjusting their predictions. And, we Christians keep buying their books and making them rich. We believe their latest predictions as if they were the Gospel. But our memories are short, so we forget about all the times they previously have been wrong. We forgiving believers feel certain that the prophets have it right this time, and that their latest predictions will surely come to pass! **But they never do!** Something is wrong here and I hope you will be stirred to begin to think about this and to study these issues!

In 1926 **Oswald J. Smith** wrote a book titled *Is the Antichrist at Hand*, in which he said the Italian dictator Benito Mussolini was the antichrist. When

Mussolini died in 1943, Mr. Smith realized he had been wrong. He asked people who had purchased his books to please return them and he would buy them back! He had made a false prophecy! He was wrong, but at least he was honest and admitted his mistake! To support their new prophecies, today's writers, prophets, and preachers are using the **SAME** Scriptures and the **SAME** arguments that Oswald Smith used. And like Smith, they are ALL wrong too! I do not remember any of our modern authors and preachers apologizing for their false prophecies or admitting they had been wrong, though some may have. But, I surely never have heard of any of them offering refunds to the millions of us who purchased their false and worthless books. **Think, Christians, think!** When will we begin to hold our preachers and prophets accountable for what they say and what they write? It is high time the mass of Christianity stood up and said, **"Enough is enough!"** This book is written to get us to stop being so gullible and to begin to seriously think and study for ourselves!

In my lifetime, perhaps the most significant event in the eyes of most Christians was **the establishment of the State of Israel in 1948.** Our modern-day prophets immediately began the countdown to "the end." They said we, who were living in the twentieth century, were the last "generation" spoken of in Matthew 24:34. This passage reads, "This generation shall not pass, till all these things be fulfilled." We were told that since a biblical generation was forty years, Jesus would return and the world would end no later than forty years from 1948, which would be 1988. **Obviously, the prophets were wrong!** Next we were told, because of a calendar miscalculation, it would be 1989. **Wrong again!** Then they decided that perhaps a generation was sixty years, so "the end" would come in 2008. **Wrong again!** Recently I saw a very famous TV preacher still clinging to these wrong ideas and declaring that we who live in the twenty-first century are the last "generation" and we will see "the end." He pretended to quote Matthew 24:34, but he twisted the Scripture to make it read as he desired. He said, *"The generation that lives to see these things* shall not pass, till all these things be fulfilled." What sacrilege! That is not what the Scripture says! Will men ever realize that their prophecies have failed because their interpretations of the Scriptures are wrong? **Is it any wonder Americans have drifted away from Christianity?**

You will remember all the excitement among all of us as the year 2000 approached. Many books were written and many predictions were made about what was going to happen. We were told the Lord was finally going to come and the world was going to end! The prophets and book publishers were having quite a field day! A preacher in my city wrote a book declaring that Jesus was coming on January 1, 2000! (I wish I had saved the big newspaper article.) It is 2010 as I write and edit and none, let me repeat, **NONE of their prophecies came to pass!** What an embarrassment all of this is to the cause of Christ! We just give unbelievers all the reasons they need to make fun of us! It is a wonder anyone believes anything we preachers say. Our failed predictions have made such a mockery of the Bible! Our credibility in the eyes of the world is shot! Can you see that problems exist in Christianity's doctrines about Jesus' Second Coming, the Last Days, the End of the World, and prophecy in general? We believers in Christ must face these issues; and for the sake of Christ and His church, we must find where we are wrong, make corrections, and restore the integrity of Christian teachings.

Again, for the sake of Jesus, for the credibility of the Bible and the church, and for your own peace and satisfaction, I urge you to pursue this matter! Do not just blindly say, "Well, my mother believed Jesus was coming soon, my grandmother believed it, and my great-grandmother believed it; therefore, I know it is true." Actually, this is all the more reason to question the church's doctrine. After all, how far can you stretch the word "soon" and it honestly still be "soon"? If three previous generations of your ancestors each expected the Lord to come soon, and if after all this time He has not come yet, obviously something is wrong! Please at least, like me, admit it and then quietly and secretly begin your search for the answer and for the truth about our Lord Jesus' Second Coming.

We Christians call Jesus' promise to come again the "Second Coming." But it may surprise you to learn that the term is not found in our Bibles. Nevertheless, it is the commonly used phrase when describing the Advent of our Savior and so I shall use the term "Second Coming" freely in my writings to avoid any confusion.

I do not have to prove that the Bible teaches Jesus would come again. If any doctrine is clearly taught in the New Testament, it is that Jesus would return again after He had left Earth. To my knowledge, no argument exists among

Bible scholars on this issue. We find many passages regarding His return in the New Testament! I have seen estimates that as much as forty percent of the New Testament Scriptures are related to the Second Coming of Jesus. The abundance of Scripture about the subject leaves no doubt that the apostles believed, preached, and wrote that Jesus was coming back. Not only do scholars agree that the Second Coming is biblical, but also they agree the Bible teaches that His coming was at hand and near in the days of the apostles. The New Testament is full of Scriptures telling us His coming was imminent in the days of the early church. As we said, Bible scholars generally agree on these points. The multitude of evidence would make it hard to disagree!

All the controversy seems to revolve around whether our Lord kept His many promises to return. Did Jesus come again in the days of the early church as they expected? If not, has He come back sometime in the centuries since those early days? Finally, if He has not yet returned, is He coming sometime in our future? The mockers and unbelievers say that since the apostles taught His coming was at hand in their day, and since Jesus apparently did not come in the first century, the apostles were all fakes and phonies! They say the Bible is just another book and has no credibility! In other words, you cannot believe what it says because what it says has turned out to be a bunch of lies! What an indictment! What a dilemma! **The sad thing is—Christianity has done virtually nothing to refute these charges.** Again, we have a problem here and you and I must find the solution!

Some believers trying to get around this problem have concluded that indeed the apostles did think, believe, and preach that Jesus was coming soon. But, they have further concluded **these chosen men of God were mistaken about the time of their Lord's return.** This is amazing! There goes divine inspiration out the window! What a totally unacceptable answer to the problem! It is no better than that of the unbelievers. It too destroys the credibility of the Bible, admitting that it is full of lies. If the apostles were mistaken about such a crucial doctrine as the Second Coming of Jesus, about what else do you suppose they were wrong? Our faith in their words is shaken! Can we trust anything they have said? If the apostles and Jesus were indeed mistaken, then we Christians may as well lay our Bibles on the shelves! We should forget them because they are, as Bertrand Russell concluded, not trustworthy! What a dilemma!

I. What a Dilemma!

Then some Christians somehow make themselves believe that words like "soon," when referring to the Second Coming, mean something other than what they normally and customarily mean when used in our language. This is their solution to the problem: "Near" does not mean near, "at hand" does not mean at hand, "quickly" does not mean quickly, and "nigh" does not mean nigh when they are referring to the Second Coming! For example, when James 5:8 said, "The coming of the Lord draweth nigh," this **DID NOT** mean that His coming was getting close. However, when John 11:55 said, "The Jews' Passover was nigh," this **DID** mean that the Passover was getting close. You and I know this is not right and is no way to ever get a proper understanding of the Scriptures. But it is amazing the lengths to which we Christians will go to try to make the Bible support our views!

Other believers trying to get around the problem have concluded that the answer lies in the fact that the Bible says:

> But, beloved, be not ignorant of this one thing, that one day is with the Lord as a thousand years, and a thousand years as one day. (II Peter 3:8)

Here, the solution to Jesus' non-appearance is that one day with Jesus is the same as 1,000 years is with man. Man has been looking for Jesus to come for about 2,000 years, but in God's time, it has been only a couple of days. So whenever Jesus comes, He will still be coming "soon," as far as He is concerned. This seems very deceptive on the part of God, but that is what I used to preach. It was the only excuse I could find for Jesus' long, long delay in returning. **But I was wrong!** We shall study this verse at length in Chapter VII, under the heading of "The Apostle Peter," so I refer you to that section.

Others say that Jesus has not returned during the past 2,000 years because He is waiting to get as many people saved as possible. In all sincerity they quote II Peter 3:9:

> The Lord is not slack concerning His promise [to come again], as some men count slackness, but is longsuffering toward us, not

willing that any should perish but that all should come to repentance. (NKJV)

Most Christians, who believe that Jesus is delaying His coming in order to get more people saved, also believe that lost souls will spend eternity writhing in the fires of hell. Of all the new babies born every week, we know that the vast majority of them will die without ever accepting Jesus. This means that a great many more people are going into eternity lost, than are being saved. Yet, Jesus does not want any to "perish"! But by delaying His coming Jesus is losing vastly more than He is saving. This scenario just does not make sense. This passage refers to the time in the days of the early church when Jesus was indeed waiting as long as He could for His people (the Jews) to accept Him as their Messiah and be spared from the coming destruction of their nation. We shall also study this verse in more detail in Chapter VII under "The Apostle Peter."

All these efforts trying to explain Jesus' failure to come again in the first century, as He and His apostles said He would, are without merit. They do not solve Christianity's problem of the non-performance and non-appearance of our Savior. These supposed answers neither satisfy the skeptics, nor bring any comfort to the believers who are hungry for the truth. In fact some of these ideas, as shown, discredit our own Holy Bible. Others make us look foolish in the eyes of those who do not believe in our Jesus.

All these ideas and interpretations of the Scriptures are the result of our trying to support and protect Jesus whom we love so much, and that is commendable. He was supposed to come in the first century AD, but apparently He did not. We have to come up with some excuse as to why He did not do as He promised. Otherwise, people will continue to use this issue as an excuse to scorn and laugh at Jesus and His followers. We know Jesus is real! We know He has saved us from our sins! We know He has turned our lives around and made new people out of us. We have personally experienced all of this. We know His Word is true. We do not doubt our salvation or our God! So, when some mocker calls our Jesus a phony and a fraud, we have to rise up and defend Him, and we should! We feel we must show that Jesus did not fail and that He does keep His promises. But when the explanations we use in defense of our

I. What a Dilemma!

Lord's integrity are not true, then we make Jesus and Christianity look even more foolish to the world.

Truth is its own greatest defender. The truth stands on its own feet and protects itself! **Personally, I have come to believe that our problem as Christians, with the doctrine of the Second Coming of Christ, is that we have misunderstood what Jesus and the apostles taught about it!** Once we can come to understand what they said and what they meant by what they said, then this big dilemma for Christianity will go away. The scoffers and mockers will be left with mud on their faces! The credibility of the Bible will be restored! Jesus will be shown as the true Son of God who never lied, never failed, and always did exactly as He promised! Now is that not a goal worth earnestly pursuing?

So is Jesus coming soon or is He not? I believe I have found the answer in the Word of God, the Bible. Of course, for most of my life I thought I knew the answer to this question. But as I have already explained, my position was shaky and eventually fell apart. So is Jesus coming soon? I used to think that the answer was "yes," but now I am sure that the answer is "no"! This has obviously been a very difficult and an emotional change for me. But when I saw the light, only one option was available to me, **and that was to admit I had been wrong and to embrace the truth!** I did that! The loss of intimate fellowship with Christians who are dear and precious to me has certainly made my journey very, very painful. On the other hand, finding the answer to my dilemma has been more exciting and more rewarding than I could ever describe!

I invite you, I beg you, and I plead with you to please come with me as I go through the Scriptures trying to explain, with the Lord's help, the answer I found to my dilemma. Again, I beg you to please read and study for yourself! Do not just take my word! Taking someone else's word is the reason Christianity has this big dilemma on its hands! Be like the Bereans, of whom Paul said, they "searched the scriptures daily" with regard to what Paul was preaching. They made an honest effort to determine "whether those things were so" (Acts 17:11). Many preachers do not want you to check behind them or to question what they say. Not Paul! He was proud of the Bereans for searching behind him to make sure that he was preaching the truth! I feel the same way!

Read and study behind me! If what I am saying is true, believe it! If you find me in error, if I misinterpret the Scripture, if I take a passage out of context, or if I twist the Word to make it say what I want it to say—tell me, show me, and explain it to me! **If I am wrong I will change! I just want to be right! I cherish biblical truth! I live to find and to understand the truth of God's Word!**

As I said in the Introduction, I have not discovered something new that no one else knows, or found some new truth that no one else has ever seen. In fact, a growing multitude of people have found the answer to this dilemma. A multitude of old books, new books, articles, and Web sites have helped me to see the light. However, I have no new scriptures! I have no new verses to tell you about! They are the same ones you and I have read over and over again throughout the years of our lives. What is new is how I have come to understand these same old verses in a totally new and wonderful light. I had to be honest with myself and with my God! I had to be willing to be wrong! I had to proceed with an open mind if I was ever to find the answer to *Christianity's Great Dilemma*.

Always when I studied the Scriptures I knew that a proper understanding required me to ask certain questions about a passage as I began to dig into it. Questions like:

> **Who was the writer?**
> **To whom was he writing?**
> **About what was he writing?**
> **Why was he writing?**
> **When was the writing?**
> **What was the setting?**
> **What was the context?**
> **What were the circumstances at the time?**
> **What did the words mean to the original recipients?**

These "W" questions, as I call them, would help to get me into the proper setting to begin to understand what the Scripture was about, what it meant, and how to apply it. But, the honest truth is that when it came to passages about the Second Coming, I had never done a very good job of applying these principles of study. When I did begin to apply them, the Second Coming Scriptures began to come alive with new meanings that I had never seen before. And the wonderful thing was, this new understanding began to solve my dilemma about the Second Coming of Jesus.

First let us look at what Jesus said about coming back. He surely promised that He would return on many occasions in the Gospels:

> Be ye therefore ready also: for the Son of man cometh at an hour when ye think not. (Luke 12:40)

At His ascension, this promise was repeated and reaffirmed to Jesus' followers by two seemingly supernatural men dressed in white:

> Ye men of Galilee, why stand ye gazing up into heaven? This same Jesus, which is taken up from you into heaven, shall so come in like manner, as ye have seen Him go into heaven. (Acts 1:11)

So Jesus promised to return. You and I have no doubts about that! **But "when" did Jesus and His apostles say He was going to come? This is the big question!** So I will begin our study by looking at some of the things that Jesus said that contribute to this question of "when."

But before I get started, let me tell you at the beginning, my Bible knowledge is limited and a very long way from being perfect. I am still trying to understand multitudes of passages. Without hesitation, I say that two things are certain. First, I still have questions, and second, I do not know all the answers! At one time in my life I thought I knew it all; I thought I had "the whole truth." Thank God I have been delivered from that attitude! Over the years I discovered, by the goodness of God, that I was mistaken about some things. So I did not know it all! Whenever these mistakes were revealed to me and I saw my error, I gladly changed my position. I have come to realize that **UNLESS I AM WILLING TO BE WRONG I WILL NEVER BE RIGHT!** And the Lord knows I want to be right!

I pray that whenever I am wrong, God will continue to give me the grace to admit it. Then, I pray He will give me the strength and courage I need to stand for whatever is right! My pastor used to say, "There is no honor in being wrong." I hope and pray that all the way down to my last days I will keep growing in the grace of my Lord, keep learning more and more about His Book, and keep bringing what I believe into conformity with His Word! I again invite you to join me in my journey. Let it become our journey as together we seek the answers to ***Christianity's Great Dilemma***!

II

IN THE GOSPELS
WHEN DID JESUS SAY HE WAS COMING?

We begin with a passage where the apostles actually asked Jesus our question about "when" He would be coming back. Not only did they ask the question, but Jesus gave them the answer. You may be surprised to learn that Jesus narrowly limited and defined the period of time in which He would be returning. So, let us begin our search for **"when"** Jesus said He was coming again and see if we can identify and understand His answer.

Matthew 23:36 and Matthew 24:1-3 & 30-35

23:36. Verily I say unto you, All these things shall come upon this generation.
24:1. And Jesus went out, and departed from the temple: and His disciples came to Him for to shew Him the buildings of the temple.
2. And Jesus said unto them, See ye not all these things? verily I say unto you, There shall not be left here one stone upon another, that shall not be thrown down.
3. And as He sat upon the mount of Olives, the disciples came unto Him privately, saying, Tell us, when shall these things be? and what shall be the sign of Thy coming, and of the end of the world?
30. And then shall appear the sign of the Son of Man in heaven . . . and they shall see the Son of Man coming in the clouds of heaven with power and great glory.

31. And He shall send His angels with a great sound of a trumpet, and they shall gather together His elect from the four winds, from one end of heaven to the other.
32. Now learn a parable of the fig tree; When his branch is yet tender, and putteth forth leaves, ye know that summer is nigh:
33. So likewise ye, when ye shall see all these things, know that it is near, even at the doors.
34. Verily I say unto you, This generation shall not pass, till all these things be fulfilled.
35. Heaven and earth shall pass away, but my words shall not pass away.

To understand these verses you and I must see the larger picture surrounding them. Then we must do a good job of asking and properly applying the "W" questions: who, what, when, where, and why.

The story in Matthew 24 started back in chapter 21 when Jesus made His triumphal entry into Jerusalem. He went into the temple and drove out the sellers, the buyers, and the moneychangers. He then retreated to Bethany overnight and came back in the morning and began to teach in the temple (chapters 21-23). In chapter 23 he denounced the scribes and Pharisees in perhaps the most scathing sermon of His ministry, calling them hypocrites, serpents, even a generation of vipers! He ended by pronouncing a coming Judgment upon them and Jerusalem. He said in Matthew 23:35, "That upon you may come all the righteous blood shed upon the earth." The religious leaders and the Jewish people would pay dearly for their sins and for the wickedness of their fathers too.

Then, in verse 36 above, He said about that Judgment, "Verily I say unto you, all these things shall come upon this generation." Bible scholars agree that "this generation" referred to the people listening to Him speak. It referred to His contemporaries, the people then alive in Jesus' day. Jesus continued to pronounce Judgment, and in verse 38 He declared, "Your house is left unto you desolate." This "house" was not only the very temple in which Jesus stood, but also everything Judaic, including all that was the house of Judah, their lives, families, land, nation, religious system, priesthood, and way of life. All of it, according to Jesus' words, was destined for complete desolation! What horrible prophecies these were!

Then Matthew 24 begins with Jesus and His disciples leaving the temple. As they exited, the disciples tried to make sure Jesus saw all of the magnificent buildings of the temple complex. Instead of being impressed Jesus made another stunning prophecy. In chapter 23 Jesus had just predicted a terrible Judgment on the Jewish nation. Now in chapter 24 He predicted the utter destruction of their beautiful temple:

> See ye not all these things? verily I say unto you, There shall not be left here one stone upon another, that shall not be thrown down. (Matt. 24:2)

From the temple the group proceeded, perhaps stunned and in silence, to the Mount of Olives. The sermon Jesus delivered to His apostles here is known as the Olivet Discourse because He gave it on the Mount of Olives. Mark 13 and Luke 21 also record this sermon, and each gives us a little additional insight into what Jesus said.

Once seated on the Mount of Olives, the shocked and shaken disciples began to ask Jesus about these terrible prophecies of Judgment coming upon their people, Jerusalem, and the temple. Remember, Matthew's original writings contained no chapter divisions. Therefore, the Judgment prophecies that began in Matthew 23:32 continue into our story in Matthew 24. The disciples were concerned about all of the things their Master had just predicted. In Matthew 24:3 they asked Him three questions, although all three were connected and related:

1. When shall these things be?
2. What shall be the sign of Thy Coming?
3. What shall be the sign of the End of the World?

Of course our interest is primarily in question number 2 since we are searching for answers to our question, **"When did Jesus say that He was coming?"** But we cannot grasp that answer unless we also understand the other questions. You may find it helpful to open your Bible to Matthew 23 and 24.

We can imagine the disciples were very disturbed about the terrible prophecies of doom and destruction Jesus had just pronounced upon their nation and beloved temple. They wanted to know more about them and, particularly, they wanted to know "when" all of these things were going to happen. They wanted to know if any signs from God would let them know when this Judgment would be near.

The disciples knew that in the Old Testament, when God brought Judgment upon a nation, the prophets often spoke of Him as having come down, of His having arrived on the scene to execute justice. We do not know all that Jesus told the apostles about His coming back, but they associated these current prophecies of the coming Judgment on their nation with Jesus' coming. So they asked Him for signs of His coming (2).

They also knew if their nation were destroyed and left desolate, and if their temple were leveled to the ground, that would be the end of their world (3). The word "world," in their third question in the KJV, is a poor translation of the original Greek word *aion*. It should have been translated "age," and the newer versions of the Bible have made this correction. They include the NKJV, the NASB, the NIV, and the ESV, just to name a few. So we have the disciples wanting to know when their "age" would end. Their age was the Mosaic age, the age of the Old Covenant, the Law of Moses, and the prophets. If their temple was going to be torn down, if their nation and way of life were going to be totally destroyed, they recognized that would end their age. They were not asking for signs about the end of the natural world as we know it today. They had no reason even to be interested in that!

All these questions related to the disciples' desires to know "when" this awful Judgment was going to come. In response to Jesus' prophecies they asked, "When shall these things be?" They wanted to know:

When will this Judgment of God come upon our nation for "all the righteous blood shed upon the earth" (23:35)?

When will Jerusalem's house be "left unto you desolate" (23:37-38)?

II. The Gospels

Regarding the temple's demise, when will there "not be left here one stone upon another, that shall not be thrown down" (24:2)?

When was Jesus coming back?

And when was their world (age) going to end?

Jesus' answers to the apostles' questions are what Matthew 24 is all about. If we can see this basic fact, then we can understand this chapter. Matthew 24 is all about the Judgment Jesus had pronounced upon His people. From history we know the Roman armies completely destroyed Judea, Jerusalem, and the temple by AD 70. Matthew 24 is about the things that would be happening in the coming years from the time Jesus made these prophecies in AD 30 until the end came in AD 70. This will become clearer as we continue our study.

Let me inject some historical facts here that will help to strengthen our faith. It was AD 30 when Jesus made this prophecy of the temple's destruction. As we shall see, He said it would happen before the generation of His day had passed away. A generation in the Bible was forty years, so this gave Jesus a maximum of forty years for His prophecy to come to pass.

Are you ready for this? Forty years later, in AD 70, the Roman army completely destroyed the temple, just as Jesus had prophesied! That is amazing! Jesus had further prophesied that not one stone would be left upon another. Well, this prophecy was so completely fulfilled that an Old Testament prophecy of Micah was also fulfilled. It says: "Therefore, on account of you, Zion will be plowed as a field, Jerusalem will become a heap of ruins" (Micah 3:12 NASB). On page 43 of *The Destruction of Jerusalem* by **George Peter Holford,** he said: "It is recorded in the Talmud and by Maimonides, that Terentius Rufus, captain of the army of Titus, absolutely ploughed up the foundation of the temple with a ploughshare." Is this not totally incredible?

And that is not all! **Flavius Josephus** in his book *The Wars of the Jews* said the Roman general, Titus, decided to spare the temple from destruction.

Titus felt that the temple was such a magnificent building that it should not be destroyed. He wanted to preserve it for the glory of the Roman Empire and as a monument to his and Rome's success. His order was for the temple not to be damaged. However, one of Titus' soldiers threw a firebrand through one of the temple's windows and set the holy structure ablaze. When word came to Titus, "He rose up in great haste and . . . ran to the holy house in order to have a stop put to the fire." He gave orders "with a loud voice" and gave signals "with his right hand" for his soldiers "to quench the fire." But the normally highly trained and well-disciplined Roman legions were like wild madmen, and "made as if they did not so much as hear Caesar's orders," and with great passion continued "to set it on fire"![ii] How awesome this history is! Does it not amaze you? The great Roman general and his tens of thousands of soldiers could not save the temple! Why? Because one greater than Titus, one greater than Caesar, even Jesus Christ, the Son of God, had said forty years earlier, "There shall not be left here one stone upon another, that shall not be thrown down" (Matt. 24:3). **God had spoken, and General Titus could do nothing but follow His orders!**

This was indeed the Judgment of God upon His people, not just the power of Rome to conquer. In ***Josephus: The Essential Writings,*** page 365, we find the following: "As Titus entered the city [Sept. 26, AD 70], he was astonished at its strength, and especially the towers which the tyrants had abandoned. Indeed, when he saw how high and massive they were, and the size of each huge block, he exclaimed, 'Surely God was with us in the war, who brought the Jews down from these strongholds, for what could hand or engine do against these towers?'"

Christians, do not let anyone cause you to doubt your faith! Just as Jesus had said, not only was the temple utterly destroyed in spite of Titus' desires to save it, but also it was destroyed within the limited time period Jesus had prophesied! Titus was as helpless as an ant to save it! Our Jesus had already sealed its doom! Just as Micah prophesied, the ground of the Holy City was ploughed like a field! OUR BIBLE IS TRUE! OUR GOD IS REAL! JESUS IS THE SON OF GOD and we can believe in Him and trust what He has said! Yet unbelievers and some Christians are telling you and me that Jesus did not do what He said He would do, that His prophecies did not come to pass! That is why I am writing this book! I want to restore in the minds of doubters the integrity, the credibility, and the authenticity of Jesus and the Bible! The complete fulfillment of Jesus' prophecy of the destruction of the temple and that destruction's coming within the exact time period He had stated, are two perfect examples that His words are true, and that He was indeed the Son of God! Hallelujah!

Jesus began in Matthew 24:4 to answer the apostles' questions. The balance of this chapter deals with Jesus' reply and His words of counsel to the men He had chosen to carry on His work. He told them they would have to endure many things before all of the things about which they had asked would come to pass. He gave signs for which to look and advice on how they should react to the coming events. Among other things, in Matthew 24 He told them:

> Verses 4, 5, 11, 12, & 23-26, Many false prophets and false Christs would arise, deceiving many;
> Verses 6 & 7, wars, famines, pestilences, and earthquakes would abound;
> Verses 9 & 10, they would be afflicted, betrayed, hated, and killed;
> Verse 12, many would leave the faith;
> Verse 14, the Gospel would be preached in all the world;
> Verses 15-20, when they saw the abomination of desolation, they should hurriedly flee from Judea to the mountains; and
> Verses 21 & 22, there would be great tribulations, such as they had never known.

The verse 15 reference to the "abomination of desolation" is presented by Luke in clearer words. Luke actually interprets for us how to recognize this "abomination of desolation." Luke 21:20-21 says:

> When ye shall see Jerusalem compassed about with armies, then know that the desolation thereof is nigh. Then let them which are in Judea flee to the mountains.

Among the many things for which Jesus told His apostles to watch, **the army surrounding Jerusalem was surely the major sign.** When that began to occur, they would know that the desolations and Judgment He had prophesied were near. They should quickly flee from Jerusalem and Judea so as not to be caught in the coming tragedy. History tells us that in the mid 60s AD the Romans attacked Judea and Jerusalem and by AD 70 utterly destroyed them both along with the temple. More than 1,000,000 Jews died, and the Romans took the survivors as slaves and prisoners of war. Their holy city, their houses and land, their holy temple, and their way of life as Jews were all totally and utterly destroyed! This was the Judgment that Jesus had prophesied would come upon "this generation" (Matt. 23:35-36). This was the utter desolation He had predicted (Matt. 23:37-38). The horrors and sufferings endured by the Jewish people during the years of this war fulfilled Jesus' prophecy of a time of "great tribulation" such as never had been known (Matt. 24:16-22). The history books about Jerusalem's fall attest to the unbelievable torments suffered by the Jewish people.

This horrible calamity coming on His beloved city and on His own people is what moved Jesus to tears right in the middle of His triumphal entry into the city. Luke records it for us in chapter 19:

> And when He was come near, He beheld the city, and wept over it, Saying, if thou hadst known, even thou, at least in this thy day, the things which belong unto thy peace! but now they are hid from thine eyes. For the days shall come upon thee, that thine enemies shall cast a trench about thee, and keep thee in on every side, And shall lay thee even with the ground, and thy children within thee; and they shall not leave in thee one stone upon another. (Luke 19:41-44)

No wonder Jesus wept! Later in Jerusalem, as they led Him away to be crucified, a great company of people followed Him including many weeping women. Knowing the horrors awaiting His people, Jesus made the following comment, recorded by Luke:

> But Jesus turning unto them said, Daughters of Jerusalem, weep not for me, but weep for yourselves, and for your children. For behold, the days are coming, in which they shall say, Blessed are the barren, and the wombs that never bare, and the paps which never gave suck.

II. The Gospels

Then shall they begin to say to the mountains, Fall on us; and to the hills, Cover us. (Luke 23:28-30)

Notice the similarity in what Jesus said to the "Daughters of Jerusalem," and what He said in verse 19 of Matthew 24, "Woe to them that are with child, and to them that give suck in those days!" This verse in Matthew was a reference to the difficulty of fleeing into the mountains that a woman with small children would have. Here in Luke, "Blessed are the barren" was a reference to the great tribulation coming on "Jerusalem," a time so severe that it would be better not to have children, who would also have to suffer through the misery.

"Then shall they begin to say to the mountains, Fall on us; and to the hills, Cover us," referred to the same time, a time of such tremendous stress on the people, a time in which they would long to die. As we shall learn later, the book of Revelation is also about this same period of time in the nation of the Jewish people. In Revelation 6:15-17, John even used Jesus' own words in describing this same time and the desperate feeling among the people: "And said to the mountains and rocks, Fall on us and hide us from the face of Him that sitteth on the throne, and from the wrath of the Lamb." All these references were about the coming Judgment of God on the Jewish people. It was coming soon, in the lifetime of those women who were weeping for Jesus!

Knowing all the terrible things that were coming on His people crushed the heart of Jesus. Even as He made His triumphal entry into Jerusalem, He broke down and began to weep. Days later on His way to Calvary, He was filled with great compassion for the weeping women. Oh, how Jesus loved His people! Oh, how much He wanted to save them from the coming disaster! But the nation just would not listen to Him! For those who did believe, who did follow Jesus, Paul said they would be saved "from the wrath to come" (I Thess. 1:10). Their deliverance from the calamities coming upon Judah certainly would begin with their obeying Jesus' command to hastily "flee into the mountains" when they saw "armies" begin to surround Jerusalem.

I hope you are beginning to understand what Matthew 24 is all about. Yet most Christians have been taught and believe that these signs and events in Mathew 24, Mark 13, and Luke 21 have not yet occurred. They are looking to see them happen any day now in the twenty-first century. But please, we must let the Scriptures speak for themselves! Ask those "W" questions! To whom was Jesus talking? Whom was He warning about things to come? About whom were the prophecies made in Matthew 23 and 24? To whom did the apostles' questions pertain? If we will honestly do this, we will see that this chapter is not at all about you and me, but entirely about the apostles and their day. Consider how specifically and **PERSONALLY** Jesus spoke to **THEM**, not to us today! In the verses below from Matthew 24, see how **personally everything related to the apostles, not to you and me living 2,000 years later:**

> Verse 4, Take heed that no man deceive **YOU**;
> Verse 6, And **YE** shall hear of wars and rumors of wars: see that **YE** be not troubled;
> Verse 9, Then shall they deliver **YOU** up to be afflicted, and shall kill **YOU**, and **YE** shall be hated of all nations;
> Verse 15, When **YE** therefore shall see the abomination of desolation;
> Verse 16, Then let **THEM WHICH BE IN JUDEA** [not us in America] flee unto the mountains; and
> Verse 33, So likewise **YE**, when **YE** shall see all these things, know that it is near, even at the doors.

Look again at the words above in capital letters and bold print (my emphasis). What else could Jesus have said to have made these statements any more personally related to His apostles, to their lives, and to their age? His words were **ALL ABOUT THEM!**

He did say one other thing, which is not properly translated in our King James Version. In verse 6, Jesus used the Greek word *mello,* which means "about to" or "about to be." (We will look at this word in more detail later.) The version of the New Testament known as *The Emphatic Diaglott* presents the original Greek text and a word-for-word English translation in side-by-side columns. In that version verse 6 in the Greek reads, "You shall be about . . . to hear wars and reports of wars." The accompanying English translation says, "And you will soon hear of conflicts and reports of battles." **Therefore, the wars would be occurring in their day, not ours!** Here is further proof that

II. The Gospels

Matthew 24 was about the days and times of the apostles. Yet today, every time a new conflict begins preachers begin to quote this verse 6 and to say, "The signs of the Lord's coming are being fulfilled right before our eyes." As I hope you can see, this is an obvious and terrible misuse of this text! Oh what great confusion and needless anxiety we preachers do cause!

It is really easy to see that all **this related personally to the disciples of Jesus and to their day.** Nothing anywhere in this chapter makes any reference to us and to our days in the twenty-first century. It was all about them and their age! Jesus was telling His disciples about many things that would happen, either to them, or around them, prior to the occurrence of the specific things about which they had asked Him.

Then in Matthew 24:32-33 Jesus gave His disciples a very short parable. He said that when they saw a fig tree begin to put out tender leaves, they knew summer was near. We can all relate to this. Then Jesus told His disciples that "likewise," when they began to see these signs come to pass, then they would know "it is near, even at the doors." What would be at the doors? What would be near to happening? The answer is, all the things about which the disciples had questioned Jesus:

The Judgment on Judah would be near.
The desolation of their nation would be near.
The destruction of their temple would be near.
The end of the Old Covenant age, which was the world about which they asked, would be near.
And the return of Jesus, His Second Coming, would be near!

Well, I have finally mentioned Jesus' coming again! But some understanding of what Matthew 24 is all about is essential if we are to find the answer to our question. Now that we have been introduced to Matthew 23 and 24, we can get back to our text Scriptures and to our search for the answer to **"When did Jesus say He was coming?"**

In Matthew 24 Jesus gave the disciples, and us, two specific answers about when He would be returning. The two answers agree, but they give us two different ways in which to identify the time frame—that is the period of time during which Jesus said that He would return.

If we look back at the Scriptures with which we began, we see Jesus' **FIRST ANSWER** in verse 30. He said, "Then . . . they shall see the Son of Man coming in the clouds of heaven with power and great glory." Jesus was in the midst of talking about:

> The signs that would precede the destruction of Jerusalem,
> The armies that would destroy the city and the temple,
> The misery and sufferings of the people in these times, and
> The arising of false Christs and false prophets.

While talking about these things, Jesus said, "then," meaning in the time frame of all these other events, **HE WOULD COME BACK (v. 30).** We have found the answer to our question! Jesus said He would come in the time of the fulfillment of the prophecies He had made about the Judgment of God on the nation of Judah! In the time when these other events were occurring, or had occurred, "then" **He would return!** The word "then" puts His coming in the same time frame as the coming of the armies that destroyed the temple, which He had foretold in Matthew 24. Again, we know from history that the temple was destroyed by the Romans in AD 70. **This means that Jesus would have come back by that time too, by AD 70!** This is our **FIRST ANSWER!** That may come as quite a surprise to you and perhaps is an unexpected answer to our question! But just keep reading, please! **The entire New Testament agrees with this answer!**

Let me say it again. Here in Matthew 24, Jesus listed a series of events that would happen in connection with Jerusalem's being "compassed with armies" (Luke 21:20). He specifically and often used the word **THEN** to indicate that these other events would come in close proximity to the desolation of the city:

Verse 16, Then, let them which be in Judea flee into the mountains.
Verse 21, For then shall be great tribulation.
Verses 23-24, Then . . . there shall arise false Christs.
Verse 30, Then . . . they shall see the Son of man coming in the clouds.

How much clearer could Jesus have been as He endeavored to tell His apostles "when" His prophecies would occur and "when" He would return? The major thing for which to look were the armies surrounding Jerusalem. **ONCE THEY SAW THESE ARMIES, THEY WOULD KNOW:**

THEN, they should flee to the mountains (v. 16).
THEN, would be great tribulations, "such as was not since the beginning" (v. 21).
THEN, would be false prophets and "if it were possible, they shall deceive the very elect" (v. 24).
THEN, Jesus would come again "with power and great glory" (v. 30).

Here clearly is the answer to our question, "When did Jesus say He was coming again?" **Once the Roman armies arrived, THEN would begin a series of events culminating with Jesus' Second Coming!** These armies arrived in the 60s and finished their destruction in AD 70. So, Jesus returned during this time too! This was an amazing discovery for me! In Matthew 24 this is our **FIRST ANSWER!** But Jesus continued to teach!

Jesus was not yet content to leave this matter of "when" He would be returning. He gave the apostles a **SECOND ANSWER** that further identified the time frame in which He would return. In case any questions remained among His apostles about "when" He would come back, Jesus added a final, all inclusive, and plain time statement. In verse 34 He said:

Verily I say unto you, This generation shall not pass, till all these things be fulfilled. (Matt. 24:34)

So here we have Jesus' **SECOND ANSWER** to the apostles' questions, and to our question, about "when" He would be coming back. Jesus said "all these things" which He had prophesied would be "fulfilled" in "this generation." "All these things" included the prophecy of His coming in verses 30 and 31: "they shall see the Son of Man coming in the clouds." "This generation" was the generation of people to whom Jesus had given these prophecies. **Therefore, He had to return during the generation of people who were alive THEN!** Both of Jesus' answers about when He would be coming were in the same period of time:

> **FIRST**, He would come in the time of the Judgment on the Jewish people, which was accomplished by AD 70.
> **SECOND**, He said He would come back during the present generation of people.

Again, both these answers cover the same general period of time in the first century AD! Wow!

A generation in the Bible is considered by scholars to be forty years. So all the things Jesus had prophesied had forty years in which to come to pass, or else He would be a false prophet. This included all the prophecies in Matthew 23 and 24: the wars, the famines, the earthquakes, the armies compassing Jerusalem, the Christians fleeing Judea, the great tribulation among the Jews, the destruction of the temple, the desolation of Jerusalem and the house of Judah, the end of the Mosaic age (world), and the coming of Jesus "with power and great glory." Since Jesus made these prophecies in AD 30, a generation (forty years) would have given Him until AD 70 for everything to come to pass. Here is a tremendously important fact! History verifies that all of Jesus' physical and natural prophecies came to pass by AD 70! This is incredible and it leaves us with no reasons to doubt that the spiritual events, perhaps most unseen by the natural eye, also came to pass by AD 70 just as Jesus had predicted. Among other spiritual things, "heaven and earth" (the world of Judaism) passed away, the age of Moses ended, the Law passed, and Jesus came "in the clouds of heaven" as He had said. Otherwise, He deceived His apostles. We know that Jesus is not a liar and a deceiver! The **only other option is that He returned as He had promised, and I have come to believe that He did.**

II. The Gospels

Jesus went to great lengths to be sure that His apostles knew "when" His prophecies would come to pass. When He began prophesying in Matthew 23, He said in verse 36: "All of these things shall come upon this generation." As He ended the prophecies in Matthew 24, He said the same thing again in verse 34: "This generation shall not pass, till all these things be fulfilled." These two verses are like a giant pair of bookends, holding and enclosing the prophecies, and limiting the time of their fulfillment to "this generation." That generation was the generation of people living in the days of Jesus, His apostles, and the early church. The disciples wanted to know "When shall these things be?" How much plainer could Jesus have been? Jesus did not name dates, but He did give them a period of forty years in which everything He had predicted would come to pass. He gave them signs for which to watch to help them know when "the end" would be near, and when His coming would be "at hand." Throughout the New Testament, we will find that the apostles used all of this information. They used it to warn the people and to prepare the church as Jesus' return approached, and as the Judgment on the nation of Judah became more and more imminent.

Considering how specifically Jesus named the time frame for the fulfilling of His prophecies, it is difficult for me to understand why most Christians are still waiting for all, or some part, of Matthew 24 to come to pass. Today many great and famous Bible teachers, who say Jesus has not yet returned, try to get around the impact of Matthew 24:34 by claiming that "this generation" was not referring to the people alive in Jesus' day. They say it refers to our generation today. They find themselves "between a rock and a hard place" and have to come up with some kind of answer! First, they cannot deny that Jesus prophesied in Matthew 24:30 that He would come again. Second, they cannot deny Jesus said four verses later, in verse 34, that everything He had prophesied, which included His coming, would come to pass before "this generation" passed away. So the only solution they can find is to say that "this generation" did not mean the generation of people who were living then. Instead, it meant our generation, nearly 2,000 years later. This makes the Scripture fit their message. Now it supports what they preach. They say Jesus said He would come in "this generation" and that means you and me, the people living today. So, we are the last generation, and our generation will "not pass" before Jesus comes. What a sad and mistaken interpretation of the Scripture this is. **It does not seem to matter that absolutely no scriptural passages support this idea.**

To my knowledge no disagreement exists among Bible scholars that Jesus' **first** use of the phrase "this generation" in Matthew 23:36 referred to the people living then, the people to whom Jesus was preaching. But, when most preachers come to His **second** use of the term in Matthew 24:34, they say that "this generation" means our generation today, 2,000 years later! **Nothing in this Scripture, or anywhere else in the Bible, supports such an idea!** In Matthew 23 and 24 Jesus was talking about the same subject, the Judgment that was coming upon His contemporaries, whom He called "this generation." In both chapters He was talking about the same people, His contemporaries, the Jews, whom He called "this generation." Nothing changes from chapter 23 to chapter 24 that would allow "this generation" to mean one group of people in Matthew 23:36 and a different group in Matthew 24:34. Please do not manipulate the Scriptures! It is so easy to see that Jesus was referring to the people to whom He was speaking, those whom He knew, and those with whom He lived in the first century! Our Lord's meaning is obvious! Nothing even remotely indicates that He was talking about a generation of people 2,000 years in the future! **NOTHING!**

Consider this. The term "this generation" is used more than twenty times in the New Testament, and for **ALL** of these other times, **EVERYBODY** agrees the term refers to the people alive and living then in Bible times. But the same term, "this generation," in Matthew 24:34 refers, they say, to people who are living today, thousands of years later. Can you see how wrong this is? In the past 2,000 years many generations of people have lived. I am made to wonder how many of those generations also decided that "this generation" meant their generation. I hope you can see this is nothing but a misuse and an abuse of the Scriptures. As I have said before, "Oh the lengths to which we preachers will go to try to make the Scriptures conform to what we believe!" We can easily solve the problem by just believing what Jesus plainly said! That is what I have decided to do!

Over the years, before I came to a better understanding of Matthew 24, I taught that this coming of Jesus was indeed His coming in Judgment on

Jerusalem and the Jewish nation. But I also maintained that Jesus would still be coming again sometime in my future and gather his faithful people to Himself. But Matthew 24:31, which I always passed over because I did not understand it, says that Jesus would be coming for His saints too, at this same time! Now that I understand that this Matthew 24 coming is the same coming the entire New Testament talks about, verse 31 falls right into place. Here it is:

> And He shall send His angels with a great sound of a trumpet, and they shall gather together His elect from the four winds, from one end of heaven to the other. (Matt. 24:31)

This gathering of "His elect" was what I was expecting to happen at a future coming of Jesus. But Jesus said it would happen in the same age as the Judgment on Jerusalem. So the coming of Jesus that was going to occur in the first generation of Christians, was the Second Coming for which I was still looking. This will become clearer and more easily understood as we proceed through this study. His coming described in Matthew 24 was indeed a coming in Judgment, but He would judge both the good and the bad. He would bring rewards for both (Matt. 16:27-28), just as I had always expected Him to do in a future coming. His "reward" for the wicked nation was destruction, but He would "gather together" (v. 31) those who believed in Him, and they would "ever be with the Lord" (I Thess. 4:17).

So in these Matthew 24 prophecies, we have already found an answer to our question, **"When did say Jesus say He would come again?"** Here it is:

FIRST, Jesus promised to come again during the time of the Judgment, the destruction of Jerusalem and the temple, which was completed by AD 70.

SECOND, Jesus promised to return before the generation in which He lived had passed away. That would have given Him forty years to about AD 70.

Is this not amazing? How did I miss this for so long? But the excitement keeps growing! We are in for more incredible discoveries! **ALL THE**

GOSPELS AND THE ENTIRE NEW TESTAMENT SAY THE SAME THING! They all agree with Jesus' prophecy in Matthew 24.

Before we leave Matthew 24, let us look briefly at the verse following the "this generation" statement. After having made many prophecies, in verse 35 Jesus makes one more:

> Heaven and earth shall pass away, but my words shall not pass away. (Matt. 24:35)

Perhaps it is a little early in our study to introduce a verse like this one. But we are right here at it, and it will help us greatly if we can understand what Jesus was saying. So what was He saying? First, Jesus did not change the subject about which He had been prophesying. He had just predicted the utter destruction of the Jewish world, even saying about the temple, "There shall not be left here one stone upon another, that shall not be thrown down" (v. 2). Here in verse 35 Jesus meant that this world of the Jewish people, their "heaven and earth," would "pass away." In contrast, His words, His prophecy, would "not pass away," but would come true just as He had said. His words did not fail! Within forty years the magnificent temple was destroyed and Jerusalem was ravaged and burned. The residents died, fled, or were carried away to become slaves. Can you see it? The "heaven and earth," that had been the world of the Jews and Judaism, did indeed "pass away." But Jesus' words, His prophecies about all of this, stood the test of time and were all fulfilled! We will study more about all of this later.

So we have reached the end of our study of Matthew 23 and 24. Jesus said nothing at all about coming in our day, in the twenty-first century. Yet, we have found some answers to our question, **"In the Gospels when did Jesus say He was coming?"** I repeat, Jesus said He would come back:

1. During the time frame of God's Judgment on the nation of Judah, which judgments reached their climax in AD 70, and
2. During the generation of people living at the time when Jesus was on Earth.

II. The Gospels

It has not been my purpose in this study to explain all the various signs and events prophesied by Jesus in Matthew 24. That would require a book in itself. I was just looking for any statements that would tell you and me when Jesus would be coming again. I did not even mention all the prophecies He made in the Olivet Discourse. I just used some for examples. Whatever those prophecies were, all of them, including His coming, were fulfilled in that first-century generation. Perhaps this is different from anything you have ever heard, but Jesus either returned within forty years of AD 30 or else He gave a false prophecy. What a dilemma this is for Christianity! That our Jesus is a false prophet is an unacceptable option! He surely came back as He said He would!

For a thorough verse by verse explanation of Matthew 24, I highly recommend a great book by a Baptist minister, Evangelist John L. Bray, titled **Matthew 24 Fulfilled**. This book is available from American Vision, P.O. Box 220, Powder Springs, GA 30127, and from www.AmericanVision.org.

Matthew 16:27 & 28

As we continue to look for things Jesus said that could give us some insight as to "when" He would come again, let us consider the following two verses in Matthew:

> For the Son of man shall come in the glory of His Father with His angels; and then He shall reward every man according to His works. (Matt. 16:27)

> Verily I say unto you, There be some standing here, which shall not taste of death, till they see the Son of man coming in His kingdom. (Matt. 16:28)

The conversation that ended with these two verses had its beginning in verse 21. Jesus told His disciples He must go to Jerusalem and suffer, be killed, and rise again. Peter, out of love for his Lord, declared that such a thing would not be! Jesus then rather harshly rebuked Peter, saying that Peter did not understand the things of God, which included Calvary and the sufferings of Jesus.

Then Jesus told the disciples that if they would indeed follow Him, they must deny themselves and take up their crosses. But He assured them that the way to find the best life was to give up their natural lives for His sake. Then He asked if there was any profit and gain in the world for which it would be worth losing their souls. He was saying they could ignore Him and pursue their own goals, but they would lose out on their relationship with Him and eternal life. He was trying to get them to understand that while gains and profits were to be had in the world, they were as nothing in comparison to what they would have if they would deny themselves in their present life and follow Him.

Then the conversation flowed very smoothly into verse 27, where Jesus continued with the same thoughts. He told them about the rewards He would bring for every man when He returned. Remember, He had just been talking to them about gains and profits, about rewards they could have in the world if they

II. The Gospels

so chose, versus the rewards they could have for turning their backs on the world and following Him. But as we saw in Matthew 24, to follow Jesus they would go through great persecution and suffering. So Jesus was trying to solidify their allegiance. First He assured them that He would pay better wages than this world. Secondly, He assured them that they would indeed get paid, though not at that time. He promised to pay them when He came again.

But this verse 27 does not seem to help us in our pursuit of an answer to our question, **"When did Jesus say He was coming?"** At first glance, we find no indication as to "when" that would be, or how long the disciples were going to have to wait to get their rewards. The truth is, this verse does give us some indication! However, here again our King James Version of the Bible does not reveal that fact to us! Where the word "shall" appears in the KJV, the original word is not a word for "shall," but the Greek word *mello,* which means "about to be." Whether this error was made by mistake or because of the biases of the translators, only God knows! As we shall find, it does happen quite often! In verse 27 in ***The Emphatic Diaglott*** of the New Testament the word *mello* appears in the Greek text, and the accompanying English translation reads:

> For the Son of Man is about to come in the glory of His Father, with his angels; and then he will recompense to each one according to his conduct. (Matt. 16:27)

Young's Literal Translation also properly translates *mello* and reads:

> For the Son of man is about to come. (Matt. 16:27)

So this verse does give us some indication of "when" Jesus was coming, saying that His return was "about to" happen. But Jesus had not even finished His work on Earth yet, much less ascended to the Father. However, Jesus knew, that in contrast to all the previous generations of Israel, it was "this generation" to whom He was preaching that would see His Second Coming. So in relation to the centuries of Jewish history, to be now in the generation that would witness His return, Jesus could rightly refer to it as being "about to be" *(mello)*. In this verse Jesus did not get any more specific, but He did so in the next one. As we shall see, Jesus was assuring these men, whom He was trying to get to give up their lives for Him, that at the most it would not be a long, long time before He returned and brought their rewards with Him!

By the use of *mello* Jesus made His disciples to know that His return and their payday would not be centuries and millennia away. If after nearly 2,000 years He still has not returned, then Jesus just lied to these men! He recruited them under false pretense! He tricked them into joining His army and sacrificing their lives for His sake! If Jesus has not yet come, then His promises of better wages and a payday "about to" come were just a bunch of lies! The only other alternative, which I hope you are beginning to discover, is that He did come in that "generation" (Matt. 24:34) and rewarded His faithful servants exactly as He had promised them!

We now come to the next verse, Matthew 16:28, which is the last verse in the chapter and is also the last verse in the conversation that began in verse 21. Reread verse 28, above. Jesus continued to talk about His coming so this verse is relevant to our study, as we seek to find what Jesus said about "when" He was coming. In the previous verse (27) Jesus gives the disciples some sense of when He was coming by saying it was "about" (*mello*) time for it to occur. In verse 28 He was more specific and put a kind of limit or maximum, as to the most distant time His coming could be. He drew a rather distinct boundary and said His coming would not be delayed beyond this point in time. To His followers He said that some of them standing and listening to Him would "not taste of death," that is, would not die, before He came back. In other words, for some of them He would come during their lifetime! **This is quite a clue in our search for "when."**

Jesus' ministry lasted three and a half years, ending in AD 30. So this statement about when He was coming was made sometime during those three and a half years, probably toward the end of that period. At any rate, these were grown men and He had told them that some of them would still be alive when He came back! Let us look at what this means. For the purpose of our example, let us assume a man's life expectancy was seventy years and that Jesus spoke these words in AD 30. If it was "about" time for Jesus to come, and if He was coming before "some" of them died, then the disciples could calculate the

II. The Gospels

approximate longest time that they might have to wait for His return. The chart below is a little demonstration of what they might conclude:

IF THEIR AGE WAS	AND THEY LIVED TO BE	TO COME BEFORE THEY DIED JESUS MUST COME WITHIN THE NEXT	ADDED TO AD 30 THAT WOULD BE
50	70	20 YEARS	AD 50
40	70	30 YEARS	AD 60
30	70	40 YEARS	AD 70
20	70	50 YEARS	AD 80

These examples serve to illustrate for us what kind of possibilities existed as to when Jesus might come. Some of the older men probably would die before He came. However, a man who was twenty to thirty years old probably would be among those who had the best chance to still be alive when Jesus returned. But some of these disciples, being encouraged by their Master to give up their lives for His sake, would surely die before He came back at the last day, at the end of the Old Covenant age. Should they die, what about their rewards? They had no need to worry. Jesus had promised them in John 6:39-59 that He would resurrect them at the last day. So they would be there too, along with those still living when He returned.

The Thessalonian Christians were also concerned about this potential problem of dying before Jesus came back, and consequently missing out on that great event and on their rewards. Paul reassured them in I Thessalonians 4:13-18 that they had nothing about which to worry. If they were still living when He came, great! But if they had died or, as the case likely would be, if they had been martyred, then Jesus would raise them back to life again. They would miss nothing! We will look at this passage in more detail later.

Back to Matthew 16:28. It is easy to see how this verse helps us with our question about "when" Jesus said He was coming. He stated very plainly that His coming would be during the lifetime of some of those to whom He was speaking. So you can see that Jesus locked Himself into a time frame! He must come back, at the latest, in the next fifty years or so in order to return while some of these men were still living. If He did not come before all of them died, then here again He would have deceived His followers and lied to them. He would have been guilty of using treachery to get them to deny themselves and follow Him. But Jesus neither lied nor deceived His disciples! He came as He promised, before they all died!

So again, Jesus is not coming soon in our day in the twenty-first century. We have not yet found any promise or prophecy of Jesus that says He would come in our day. We have not found anything He said that even faintly hints at the possibility that His coming would be hundreds and thousands of years in the future. **We will not find any! They do not exist!** He did promise to return in the days of the early church while some of His original followers were still alive, and I believe He did. If today in the twenty-first century Jesus still has not returned, then in order for Him to keep His word some of those first-century disciples must still be alive. They would be around 2,000 years old! We know that is not true! So we are left again with only two alternatives. Either Jesus lied and was a false prophet or He has already come again the second time, centuries and centuries ago. He did not lie! I believe He did come just as He promised!

Consider how perfectly these verses in Matthew 16:27-28 harmonize with our study of Matthew 24:34. In Matthew 16 we have learned that Jesus said He was coming in approximately twenty to fifty years. In Matthew 24 Jesus said His coming would be before the generation to whom He preached had passed away. We learned that a generation is forty years, which falls within the twenty to fifty years of Matthew 16. So we are getting a picture of the approximate period of time in which Jesus made His second appearance. **We could say, just on the authority of the Scriptures we have already studied, that Jesus' return occurred somewhere in the last half of the first century, probably between AD 50 and AD 80!** This is amazing! Something else is amazing—**the whole New Testament agrees and supports this same time frame for Jesus' Second Coming!**

Most of my life I believed this passage in Matthew 16:27-28 was fulfilled on the day of Pentecost in Acts 2. Now I can see that Jesus did not come at Pentecost in all of His "glory." Long after Pentecost the Epistles

II. The Gospels

portray a church still looking for Jesus to come in His glory. For example, consider Titus 2:13: "Looking for that blessed hope, and the glorious appearing of our great God and our Savior Jesus Christ." Neither was Pentecost in Acts 2 the Judgment Day. We find no indication that He rewarded every man according to his works at Pentecost. Besides, it was not time for rewards—the church was just beginning its journey! Rewards day comes after a person has been faithful and endured to the end. At Pentecost the new church had just begun to fight! It would be some thirty-five years later before Peter would write that the Lord "is ready to judge the quick and the dead" (I Peter 4:5). So my designation of Pentecost just did not fit!

Also in Matthew 16:27-28 Pentecost was not very far away, perhaps a few months to a year or so. Jesus had said some of them would not die before He came back. If He was talking about Pentecost, then His statement was a little meaningless. Of course in a mere year some of them would still be living! In fact most of them would still be living. So it does not make any sense to say Jesus was speaking of His coming on the day of Pentecost. He was speaking of a time much farther away, about forty years or so, as we have seen in this study. Now His statement makes sense. In that period, perhaps most of them would be dead, but some would still be living.

No, Jesus is not coming soon in our age today! He never promised to come in our day. **But He did promise the first Christians that He would come in their day!** And as we shall see, His apostles continued to make this same promise to all those who would do as they had done, deny themselves, shoulder their crosses, and follow Jesus.

I can hardly believe that most of my life I was looking for Jesus to come each and every day, until by His grace my eyes were opened to see this truth. He has already come! That is why all the many times preachers and prophets have set dates for His coming, it never happened. That is why all the thousands of times preachers, including me, have said "Jesus is coming soon," it never happened! It had already happened! He had already come! You will see this more and more clearly as we continue our study.

John 21:21-23

Let us look next at a conversation Jesus had with some of His disciples. Something Jesus said appears, on the surface, not to give us any help with our question about "when" Jesus said He was coming. But if we examine the passage closely, we will find some thoughts that may help us:

> Peter seeing him saith to Jesus, Lord, and what shall this man do? Jesus saith unto him, If I will that He tarry till I come, what is that to thee? follow thou me. Then went this saying abroad among the brethren that, that disciple should not die: yet Jesus said not unto him, he shall not die; but if I will that he tarry till I come, what is that to thee? (John 21:21-23)

This was the last account of Jesus that John recorded. It was the third time Jesus had shown Himself to His disciples since His resurrection. They had been fishing all night without any luck. Jesus appeared on the shore and apparently yelled to them to cast their net on the right side of the ship. They did so and filled their net. Then the apostles realized the man on the shore must be Jesus. Peter went overboard and waded quickly to shore, and the others came with the boat and the big catch of fish.

When the disciples landed they saw that Jesus already had bread and fish on a fire, and He bade them to "Come and dine." After eating, in verses 15-17 Jesus questioned Peter's love for Him. Peter affirmed his love for his Lord but was rather disturbed that Jesus would question him in this manner, perhaps especially in front of other disciples. Jesus did not stop, but kept on questioning Peter! Then in verses 18 and 19 the Lord made a prophecy about Peter's death. He said that Peter was young then and went where he liked; but, when he got older, because of his love for his Lord, others would bind him and carry him where he did not want to go and would take his life.

Peter was probably feeling like he had been singled out by the Lord for some tough questioning and for a rather disturbing prophecy of his death. We can imagine that Peter was wondering, "What about the rest of these guys?" Not being one to keep his thoughts to himself, Peter asked Jesus, "Lord, and what

II. The Gospels

shall this man do?" "This man" was not identified by name, but we have always thought that Peter was referring to John. However, some Bible scholars think "this man" and "the disciple whom Jesus loved" was Lazarus (John 21:20). That may be true, but that is a study for another time. For our study we will assume this man was John. Paraphrasing, the Lord's answer to Peter was something like this: "If I want John to live till I come again, that is none of your business; you just follow me!" The Lord seemed to be rather blunt with this leader of His apostles!

Now, we get to see if we can find anything here about our "when" question. If Jesus was planning to come back in our day in the twenty-first century, what a foolish statement He made about John! John would now be about 2,000 years old, still having birthdays, and still waiting for the Lord to come! This makes no sense at all! But Jesus knew He would be returning within a few decades. So now His statement makes sense!

As we have seen earlier, Jesus had promised to return during the current generation. He had further promised to come back while some of His disciples were still living. And here, in my own words, He said to Peter: "If I want John to be among those still living when I return, that has nothing to do with you." Now Jesus' words are reasonable and clear! Before I saw this truth, I was always puzzled by Jesus' statement. It seemed foolish and made no sense to me! Now I see it fits perfectly! It plainly portrays the fact that Jesus would be returning while some of His followers were still living. I mean, of course, living to a normal age!

But we have more evidence! In verse 23 a rumor began to spread among the brethren that John would not die! But Jesus had not said definitely that John would not die. He only proposed the possibility by saying, if He wanted John to live till He came, that had nothing to do with Peter. Now think about this rumor. Word was going around that John would not die. Verse 23 does not include "till Jesus comes" but this is implied, because that is what Jesus had said. The rumor then was that John would not die before Jesus came back. Now if the disciples thought it was going to be hundreds and thousands of years before Jesus came again, then this rumor was really crazy! John would live to be hundreds and thousands of years old, waiting for the Lord to come. This makes no sense! Who would believe and spread a rumor like that?

But the disciples knew Jesus was coming back in their "generation." They already knew "some" of them would still be living at His coming. So the rumor was that Jesus had chosen John to be among those "some" to live till He came. Now you can see the rumor is reasonable. Now it makes sense and you can see how it could have been believed by the brethren and quickly spread among them. Here is the point! **This rumor reinforces the fact that the disciples were looking for Jesus to return in their lifetime.** They believed this because that was what their Lord had taught them! No other conclusion is reasonable!

So here in these three verses in John's last chapter is a little "gem" that speaks to us plainly about "when" Jesus was going to return. It does not contradict what we have already learned. Instead it supports and agrees with Jesus' promises that He would be returning in the generation of the early church age, and that He would come back before all of His disciples had died.

Matthew 26:64

We come now to another event in the life of Jesus where He makes a prophecy relating to our question, **"When did Jesus say He would return?"** Here it is:

> Jesus said to him, You have said it yourself; nevertheless I tell you, hereafter you will see the Son of Man sitting at the right hand of power, and coming on the clouds of heaven. (Matt. 26:64, NASB)

Earlier in this chapter Jesus had eaten His last Passover with His apostles. Afterwards they all went to the Mount of Olives. There our Lord retreated to the garden of Gethsemane to pray. Then He prophesied that His hour was "at hand" and His prophecy was true. Just as He spoke the words, Judas and the Roman soldiers came upon them. The soldiers arrested Jesus and led Him away. They took Him to Caiaphas, the high priest, and to the Sanhedrin, which was assembled at the high priest's palace.

They brought false witnesses to testify against Jesus. Through it all He remained quiet. Jesus' silence seemed to rile the high priest and he railed at Jesus, who still held His peace. Then Caiaphas, in apparent anger, commanded Jesus by the living God to tell them whether or not He was "the Christ, the Son of God" (v. 63). Jesus finally broke His silence by saying, "You have said it yourself," in effect confirming that He was the Christ, the Son of God. Then Jesus spoke additional words that further infuriated the high priest and those with him. In the mind of Caiaphas these words were a declaration by Jesus that He was God, that He was deity! Jesus said, "Hereafter you will see the Son of Man sitting at the right hand of power, and coming on the clouds of heaven."

Whatever the full meaning and nature of this prophecy may be, for our study we do have Jesus making another prediction about His coming. But does it in any way give us any idea about "when" Jesus would come? Well, previously I never thought that it did. Jesus had simply said, "You will see the Son of Man . . . coming on the clouds of heaven." I always read the verse as if Jesus had been speaking to me in my day. I thought I would see Jesus coming because He said "you" will see Me coming. What a poor interpretation of the Scriptures! I failed to ask my "W" questions, especially the one that asks, "To whom was Jesus speaking?" Once I put this statement of Jesus in its proper setting, a totally new light shone upon this prophecy. As you will see, the same is true of many other Scriptures throughout the New Testament.

But again, does this verse help us with our "when" question? Yes, it does! What did Jesus tell the high priest and the Sanhedrin? Jesus told them that they would see Him "coming on the clouds of heaven." He said, "You will see the Son of Man . . . coming on the clouds of heaven." He was speaking to the high priest and the members of the Sanhedrin in AD 30, not to you and me in the twenty-first century! So for Jesus' prophecy to be true, some of the people in this gathering would have to still be alive when Jesus came. Here is the answer to our "when" question! **We have Jesus AGAIN telling His contemporaries they would not die before they saw His return!** This time it was not His disciples, but His enemies, the high priest and the Sanhedrin. Caiaphas shortly concluded Jesus was guilty of blasphemy and that He should die, and the majority agreed.

Jesus again limited the time of His coming to the lifetime of some of the persons who were living when He was on Earth. Here He said the high priest and members of the Jewish high council would see His coming. It is unlikely that all of these men lived to AD 70, but surely some of them did. So Jesus limited His return to sometime during their lifetime. Is this not within the same period of time that Jesus had been saying previously? Yes, absolutely! He did not contradict His other prophecies at all! This prophecy agrees with everything else He had said about "when" He would come. In fact nowhere did Jesus ever make the slightest reference to His coming as being in the far distant future, hundreds and thousands of years away. **NOWHERE!** Always, let me repeat, **ALWAYS** He said that He would come in "this generation," during the lifetime of His contemporaries. Not only did Jesus promise to come before all of His followers died, but also, in this verse, before all of His enemies had died!

We began this portion of our study asking, "When did Jesus say He would come?" You have seen some of what Jesus said on the subject. Did He say anything that would make you believe He is coming "soon" today? Not one thing, nothing at all! In this verse, Matthew 26:64, you again have only two alternatives. Either Jesus came back before all of the Sanhedrin died, or He lied! **What a dilemma!**

1. If we insist on continuing to say, "Jesus has not come yet, but He is coming soon," then we are saying Jesus lied and thus was a false prophet.
2. If we see this truth and say, "Jesus is not coming in our day because He came in the days of the Sanhedrin," then we take a stand against a cardinal teaching of today's church.

I cannot accept that Jesus was a liar, a deceiver, and a false prophet, and thus certainly not the Son of God! The only truth here is Jesus came as He had promised over and over again, in the days and lifetime of His contemporaries in the first century AD.

Which will you choose to believe, the creeds, traditions, and doctrines of men or the plain words of Jesus? I hope you are beginning to see why I had to change my views about the Second Coming of our Lord Jesus. But you and I have only begun in our studies, and many, many more Scriptures support what we have already found regarding our question of **"When did Jesus say He was Coming Again?"**

Matthew 10:23

Here we have another place where Jesus mentioned the timing of His coming and showed that His coming was not a far distant event, but would occur in the lifetime of His first disciples:

> But when they persecute you in this city, flee ye into another; for verily I say unto you, Ye shall not have gone over the cities of Israel, till the Son of man be come. (Matt. 10:23)

Earlier in this chapter Jesus sent His twelve apostles to preach to "the lost sheep of the house of Israel" saying, "The kingdom of heaven is at hand" (verses 6-7). But most of the chapter seems to deal with the resistance they would encounter and the persecution and suffering they would have to endure. He told them they would have to flee from city to city, being chased by their persecutors. Then He made the statement which draws us to this verse: "Ye shall not have gone over the cities of Israel, till the Son of man be come."

I do not understand this verse as well as I would like. Of course this is just one of many. But I certainly believe I understand it better now than I did at one time. I used to believe that this coming of Jesus occurred at Pentecost in Acts 2. But that does not fit. The apostles did not have to begin fleeing from city to city until well after Pentecost. So Pentecost does not fit. Let us see if we can find a time that does.

For our purposes in our search for an answer to, **"When did Jesus say He would come?"** this passage plainly seems to have something to contribute. Jesus said, in effect, that His apostles would still be fleeing from city to city when He returned. So what can we conclude here? For one thing Jesus would be returning while at least some of the apostles were still preaching, still being persecuted, and still fleeing from city to city. I have taken the position that His Second Coming happened by AD 70, occurring in conjunction with the destruction of Jerusalem and the end of the Old Covenant age. Christians were undergoing difficult persecutions right up to this ending, as portrayed in the Epistles. In fact the Epistles reveal that the believers were eagerly anticipating their Lord's coming because they were expecting Jesus to bring them relief from their terrible persecutions.

But the point for our study is that some of His apostles would still be alive when Jesus came back. So here again Jesus' coming would occur during the lifetime of some of His followers! This is consistent with everything else we have found! Whatever the full and correct interpretation of this verse is, it cannot mean that Jesus was saying, "I will be coming back in a couple thousand years." Instead **He was saying He was coming again while some of His apostles were still preaching and still fleeing!** We are left with only one acceptable option. His coming had to have been during the first century AD, while some of His disciples were still alive! So again, Jesus is not coming soon in the twenty-first century because **He came in the days of the early church, exactly as He promised over and over again!**

SUMMARY OF CHAPTER II

You and I certainly have not exhausted the passages in the Gospels related to the Second Coming of the Lord. But in this chapter I think we have considered most of the words of Jesus that give us any hints as to "when" He might come again. In several other passages Jesus mentioned His coming but He did not give us any specific information as to the time He would be returning. We have therefore not dealt with these verses, since our search is for those passages that plainly tell us "when" Jesus said He would be coming.

Let us recap what we found in Matthew, Mark, Luke, and John:

In Matthew 24, Mark 13, and Luke 21 Jesus said:

1. He would come during the time frame of God's Judgment on the nation of Judah, which judgments reached their climax in AD 70; and

2. His coming would occur in the generation of the people to whom He preached when He was on Earth.

In Matthew 16 Jesus said it was about time for His coming and that some of the people to whom He was preaching would still be alive when He came back.

In John 21 Jesus again left the impression upon His disciples that they would not all die before He returned, beginning a rumor that John would live to see His coming.

In Matthew 26 Jesus told Caiaphas, the high priest, and the Sanhedrin that they would see His coming. Therefore, some of them would still be alive at the time of His return.

In Matthew 10 Jesus told His disciples that at the time of His coming, some of them would still be preaching and fleeing from city to city because of persecution.

II. The Gospels

Based on these Scriptures, we can reach only one conclusion: **Jesus returned in the first century!** Otherwise, He was a liar, deceiver, and the worst kind of false prophet! What a dilemma! But, it is a dilemma we can easily solve. You and I just have to lay aside our wrong beliefs about "when" the Second Coming would occur and accept what Jesus said about "when" He would be returning. This will solve the problem!

With regard to Jesus' being a false prophet, consider what the famous minister, **Rev. R. C. Sproul,** said in 1993 at the Covenant Eschatology Symposium in Mt. Dora, Florida. To my knowledge Rev. Sproul has not said that the Second Coming is history, but he has been open and honest in recognizing the dilemma Christianity faces. He said:

> Maybe some church fathers made a mistake. Maybe our favorite theologians have made mistakes. I can abide with that. I can't abide with Jesus being a false prophet, because if I am to understand that Jesus is a false prophet, my faith is in vain.

The verses we have considered **ALL AGREE** as to the period of time during which Jesus would be returning. Not one single conflict exists among all of them! No other passages in the Gospels give any other time frame than what we have seen. Nowhere, not once in any of the Gospels, do we find the least reference to Jesus' coming being an event that was a long, long way off, in the far distant future! **Not one!** So we have no reasons, based on the Gospels, to believe anything other than what we have found!

Would you use any of the following reasons as an excuse not to accept and not to believe what Jesus said about "when" He was coming?

> It is not like I have always believed.
> It is not like my parents, family, and friends believe.
> It is not the way my preacher preaches the Second Coming.
> My grandmother could not have been wrong.
> My church and Christianity in general do not believe this way.
> I would not be welcome in the fellowship if I espoused these ideas.

None of these statements are justifiable reasons at all for not believing what JESUS PLAINLY SAID IN THE GOSPELS! Do you want truth or traditions? Would you rather be right or continue to be wrong in order to be accepted by your peers? What does your conscience tell you? What does your brain say? Does your capacity to reason and to understand tell you that what you have just read could be true? Do you recognize now that Christianity does have a great dilemma on its hands and problems do exist with its teachings about the Second Coming?

Can you see that the continual promises by preachers today that "Jesus is coming soon" are beginning to get rather pathetic? Obviously all of those promises have failed! Can you see that they have failed because they are wrong and unscriptural? It is not the Bible that is mistaken, but rather man! I pray you will have the courage to do the right thing! At the least, because you love Jesus and because you love His word, you should by now be deeply moved to pursue this matter. **Read, study, and pray until you understand it for yourself!** Keep on until you are satisfied in your own heart and mind as to whether or not what you have read here is the truth!

As we shall see, the balance of the New Testament agrees with the Gospels. We find no conflict! The apostles preached and taught the people exactly what Jesus had taught them. We would expect to find a kind of divine unity between the apostles' messages and Jesus' words, and praise God, we do! Read on!

III

IN THE REVELATION
WHEN DID JESUS SAY HE WAS COMING?

It will be interesting to see whether Jesus reveals anything about the time of His return in the last book of the Bible, the great mystery book, Revelation. We may find more help with our "when" question than we ever imagined. It is not my purpose here to try to explain the multitude of signs and symbols of Revelation, even if I could. However, I do hope to lay some groundwork for a proper understanding of those things. So before we begin our search for **"When did Jesus say He was coming?"** it is necessary that we understand some important fundamentals and basic guidelines for interpreting this book. Understanding Revelation is mainly a matter of finding the answers to some of our "W" questions. The book opens like this:

> The Revelation of Jesus Christ, which God gave unto Him, to shew unto His servants things which must shortly come to pass; and He sent and signified it by His angel unto His servant John. (Rev. 1:1)

I believe the proper title for the book of Revelation is found in these opening words, "The Revelation of Jesus Christ." To most Christians the book is a dark mystery and a source of great confusion. For preachers and prophets, it is the source of many false prophecies! However, it is called "Revelation" because it is a revealing of God's plans and purposes for those to whom it was written in the first century. The word "revelation" means "a revealing or disclosing of something." So if the book is just mystery and darkness, then the Lord gave it the wrong name. The first verse should read something like this: "The never to be revealed secrets of Jesus Christ."

Note the words in verse 1: "which God gave unto Him [Jesus], to shew unto His servants [the early Christians] things which must shortly come to pass; and He sent and signified it by His angel unto His servant John." This is the apostle John, who wrote it down in a letter and sent it to his fellow believers. Here in the opening verse it is plainly stated that the words of Jesus to John were for the purpose of **SHOWING** Jesus' servants some things that were **SHORTLY** coming to pass. The book, or letter, was plainly given to reveal things, not to hide them! This is further shown in the third verse of the book where Jesus says:

> Blessed is he that readeth, and they that hear the words of this prophecy, and keep those things which are written therein: for the time is at hand. (Rev.1:3)

I suppose in a very limited sense of the word "readeth," the early Christians could have read the letter from John without having any idea what it was all about. But they were also supposed to "hear" the words of the prophecy. In the Bible, to hear the word of the Lord means to obey the word of the Lord. However, they could not have obeyed the book of Revelation if they did not understand what it was saying. Further, they were to "keep" the things that were written in the letter. How could they have kept the things written in the book if the entire book was one big mystery to them? Obviously they could not! The churches then, of necessity, had to understand (and they did) the symbolism with which John wrote in order to know what messages the letter was bringing to them. Only then would they know how it applied to their lives, and how they should respond.

So I believe that in just the first three verses, with Jesus dictating and John writing it down, Jesus has established beyond question that this letter is indeed "The Revelation of Jesus Christ." Jesus was not hiding anything from His servants but instead He was showing, revealing, and disclosing to **THEM** things He wanted **THEM** to read, hear, obey, and keep! We must keep these things in our minds as we study this book! It was not written to you and me, but to **THEM!**

III. The Revelation

To a limited degree we have answered our "what" and our "whom" questions. But, let us look a little further at "to whom" the Revelation was written. If we go back to the very first verse again, Jesus tells us. He said, "to shew unto His servants." His servants would have been the first-century believers. So John was writing to his contemporaries, his fellow Christians in the first century. They were perhaps people he knew and to whom he had preached and ministered.

In the fourth verse John gave a greeting that is similar to the opening greetings in other Epistles. Revelation is an Epistle too! As we are about to see, it is a letter to some churches. In his opening John stated plainly to whom he was writing his letter, and it was not to us in the twenty-first century!

> John to the seven churches which are in Asia: Grace be unto you, and peace, from Him which is, and which was, and which is to come. (Rev. 1:4)

And then more specifically, in verse 11 Jesus dictated and John wrote the names of the churches to which this letter was written:

> What thou seest, write in a book, and send it unto the seven churches which are in Asia; unto **EPHESUS,** and unto **SMYRNA,** and unto **PERGAMOS**, and unto **THYATIRA**, and unto **SARDIS**, and unto **PHILADELPHIA,** and unto **LAODICEA.** (Rev.1:11, emphasis mine)

In the early church age churches existed in these seven cities in Asia. So this Epistle written by the apostle John was written to the Lord's servants in these seven churches! Now it is essential that we keep this in mind if we are ever to understand Revelation. It was not written to us living now in the twenty-first century! Yes, certainly, like the rest of the Old and New Testaments, we can learn lessons and discover eternal truths from Revelation. But the first and primary application was exclusively to the Christians living in the first century AD. No doubt this letter and the other Epistles addressed to specific churches were passed around among the other churches so that all the believers could benefit from the writings of the apostles and leaders of the early church.

When Jesus and John were writing Revelation, I think it is safe to say that neither one was thinking about you and me, living 2,000 years later. Their attention was totally on those early servants of the Lord and **THEIR** great needs! It was addressed to **THEM!** The letter was about them and their lives. It was about the problems and difficulties they were facing and would yet face. It was about encouraging them to hold on and to be faithful until the end. It was about what Jesus was going to do to give them relief from their sufferings. It was about how Jesus was going to bring justice and Judgment upon their persecutors and usher in a better day for His church! Remember, in verse 1 Jesus was showing things to His servants **THEN**, not now! He was revealing things to Christians **THEN**, not today! He was showing **THEM**, not us, things that were "shortly" going to come to pass **THEN**, not thousands of years later!

So let us look at another "W" question that is equally important! "When" were all of these great and notable events in Revelation going to happen? When were all of these prophecies, all of these strange things John saw, going to come to pass? Can we find any clues? Did Jesus tell these early followers anything that gave them any ideas as to when it would all happen? And most importantly for our study, if Jesus said anything to them in Revelation about His Second Coming, did He give them (and us) any ideas or close estimates as to "when" that coming would occur?

So far all of our answers seem to come from the first few verses. That is the sign of a well-written letter, is it not? Go back to verse 1. Jesus said that He was showing His servants things which **MUST SHORTLY** come to pass. That is quite a hint! He was saying to these seven churches that the things about which they would be reading in their letter were things that would happen "shortly." And He put even more emphasis on "shortly" by adding "must"! Jesus was saying that the things in this book were not going to be stretched out over centuries and millennia. **They MUST come to pass SHORTLY!**

Can you believe that? Virtually all we see, hear, and read today is how all these prophecies in Revelation are either happening right now or they are on the verge of happening in the near future! Something is wrong here! Jesus told these churches in Asia in the first century AD that these things "must shortly

III. The Revelation

come to pass"! **That was nearly 2,000 years ago!** Either the events prophesied in Revelation have long since been fulfilled or Jesus and John deceived, misled, and lied to the saints at Sardis, Ephesus, and the other churches! What a dilemma this is for Christianity and for its teachings that the prophecies in Revelation are still waiting to be fulfilled—2,000 years later!

Well, we have quite a problem here! But how do preachers get around this problem and this plain English—**MUST SHORTLY COME TO PASS?** I mentioned things like this in our first chapter. They say, among other things, that "shortly" here does not mean what "shortly" usually means. Can you believe that? Or they may say that "time" does not mean anything to God since He is eternal. So "shortly" does not mean that God is going to get in a hurry. He has all the time in the world! Again, can you believe that? Are you interested in following a God who is that slick, sly, misleading, and deceitful? Neither am I! But our God is not deceitful and He communicates with His people in words we can understand. Otherwise, what is the point in His telling us anything at all?

The problem is that the majority of Christians today have been taught that the events in Revelation are yet to occur sometime in the future. Thus, that is what they believe. So when they come upon a passage like Revelation 1:1, that plainly says something different, they try to make the verse fit what they already believe and teach. **This is certainly what I used to do in my studies.** However, what you and I should do is change what we believe to conform to the Scriptures! It is high time that we do just that! We must stand up, be strong, admit we are wrong, and get today's church on the right road to finding God's truth about the book of Revelation!

What do you suppose "shortly" meant to these early Christians when they read the word, not once but two times in their letter? What would it have meant to you? **This is a vital question** for a proper understanding of any of these Scriptures! Regarding any verse always ask, "What did the words and the verse mean to the people to whom they were originally written?" We all know what "shortly" meant to these believers! It meant that the prophecies about which they were reading would be fulfilled soon—in the not-too-distant future. Jesus even put a little extra emphasis on "shortly" by adding the word "must." **These prophecies in Revelation MUST SHORTLY happen!**

"Shortly" meant the same thing that it meant in all the other Epistles. It meant the same thing it meant when Paul told the Philippians in 2:19, "But I trust in the Lord Jesus to send Timotheus shortly unto you." We all know what Paul meant and we all know the Philippians were excitedly looking for Timothy to come soon. This is not complicated unless we do not want to believe the obvious truth! Peter said in II Peter 1:14, "Knowing that shortly I must put off this my tabernacle, even as our Lord Jesus hath shewed me." No argument is found here! Do we not all agree that Peter was saying he did not have very much longer to live? Oh, the lengths to which men will go to try to make the Bible agree with what they already believe! The truth here is plain and clear! "Shortly" in Revelation 1:1 means the same thing it always does, the same thing it does in these verses from Paul and Peter!

But we have more, much more! Look back at Revelation 1:3, above. Jesus was determined to make certain that everyone clearly understood **WHEN all of the events in Revelation would occur.** So in verse 3, He stated **AGAIN** when it was all going to happen! He said, "For the time is at hand." Jesus emphasized the nearness of these events, not once but two times in the first three verses of the book! **Do you think He might have been trying to make a point?** Yes, absolutely He was! In case anyone was not sure what "shortly" meant in verse 1, He further explained it in verse 3 by saying the things He was about to show them were "at hand." The NKJV and the NASB both translate verse 3 to read "for the time is near." This is what "at hand" means—"near."

John 2:13 says, "And the Jews' Passover was at hand." Obviously, this verse meant that the time for the Passover was near. Paul said in II Timothy 4:6, "For I am now ready to be offered, and the time of my departure is at hand." Again everyone agrees! Paul was saying that his death was near and soon he would die! Now please tell me, how could the events in Revelation have been "at hand" and "near" to the people receiving this letter in the first century, and still not have happened nearly 2,000 years later? Either Jesus was wrong, or the preaching and teaching we hear today is wrong! With a choice like that we should not have much difficulty making our decision! Of course Jesus was right! It is today's preachers and prophets who are wrong!

III. The Revelation

The events in Revelation ALL must have occurred in the first century AD or else Jesus was wrong! What a dilemma this is! Any events being fulfilled in the far distant future would not fit into Jesus' time frame of being "near," "at hand," and "shortly" coming to pass. **MY DEAR READER, THE KEY TO UNDERSTANDING THE BOOK OF REVELATION IS FOUND IN THE FIRST THREE VERSES OF THE BOOK!** It has been there all the time! How did I ever overlook it for so many years? What is Christianity going to do about its teachings? What are you and I going to do about what we believe?

As we continue to look at "when" the awesome events in Revelation would occur, let us leave the first three verses and go to verse 19.

> Write the things which thou hast seen, and the things which are, and the things which shall be hereafter. (Rev.1:19)

This verse talks about the past, "the things which thou hast seen"; the present, "the things which are"; and the future, "the things which shall be hereafter." The KJV expresses no sense of timing as to when the future things would occur. But Jesus was more specific than that! How so? As we have seen before, here we have it again. The Greek word *mello* is in this verse, but the KJV writers did not properly translate it in our English version. Jesus actually said in the original Greek, "the things about to *[mello]* occur." This gives a whole new meaning to the verse. John was not just writing of things which were going to happen "hereafter," sometime by and by, but they were events that were "about to occur" **THEN!** So verse 19 is in harmony with the first three verses. They all agree! The fulfillment of the prophecies in Revelation was "at hand" and "about to occur" "shortly"! In *The Emphatic Diaglott,* accompanying the Greek text is an English translation of verse 19 that reads, "the things which are about to transpire." That is just beautiful and it gives further support to everything we are finding!

So the first chapter of Revelation, without any conflict or question, declares emphatically that the things John was writing about would be occurring soon. They would not be happening 100 years, 500 years, or 2,000 years later. They were events that were "near," "at hand," and "about to occur" "shortly" in the days and times of these seven first-century churches! Yet all you and I see, hear, and read today is that the prophecies in Revelation have still not been fulfilled. However, we are told we should look for them to be fulfilled any day now! How can something so opposite to what Jesus said be such a major Christian teaching? The answer lies partly in the fact that we Christians have not studied these issues for ourselves! Instead we have been as gullible as little children. We have just believed what we have been told by those whom we trust without searching the Scriptures! My great desire in writing this book is to help move all of us to study our Bibles, to read, to investigate, to find, and to ultimately know for OURSELVES what is true and what is false!

We shall get to the verses about Jesus' coming "shortly." (The way I used to define "shortly," that could be a really long time!) But Revelation reveals much more about "when" its prophecies would be fulfilled. Jesus, dictating to John, took no chances of creating any misunderstandings about "when" these events would happen. We have seen how thoroughly He covered the matter in the first chapter. But did you know that in the last chapter, Jesus was equally as thorough about "when" the prophecies in Revelation would be fulfilled? Well, He was! **After** Jesus had shown all the amazing signs and symbols, which make up most of Revelation, **He ended the letter just as He had started it, emphasizing and reemphasizing that it would ALL TAKE PLACE SOON!** He said even more about "when" in the last chapter than He did in the first! And as we have seen, He covered it really well in the first chapter. Look at chapter 22:

> And He [Jesus] said unto me [John], These sayings [everything in this letter] are faithful and true: and the Lord God of the holy prophets sent His angel to shew unto His servants [in the seven churches] the things which must shortly be done. (Rev. 22:6)

This is amazing! It is the same thing Jesus said in the first verse of the book! He even used some of the exact words! Again, do you get the feeling that Jesus wanted to emphasize this point, "shortly be done"? Do you get the feeling He really meant what He was saying? He started this letter to the seven churches emphasizing that these **prophecies must shortly come to pass!** Now He ends the letter with the same emphasis, **saying these events must shortly be**

done! How can Christians continue to believe something totally different from what Jesus said over and over again?

But we have still more!

> And He saith unto me, Seal not the sayings of the prophecy of this book: for the time is at hand. (Rev. 22:10)

This time Jesus used the exact same words that He used in verse 3 in the first chapter—"for the time is at hand." What else could Jesus have said in order to get His point across? How much plainer could He have been? How could He have been clearer? We can believe, without any doubts, that the first-century followers of Jesus got the point, understood the message, and realized that **THEY WOULD SOON SEE** the fulfillments of the prophecies in their Epistle—Revelation!

And consider this: Jesus said to John, "seal not," meaning not to close up or keep hidden the prophecies in Revelation, "for the time is at hand" for their fulfillment. An Old Testament example in the book of Daniel will help us to better understand what Jesus meant by "seal not." In Revelation this command to "seal not" the book is in the last chapter, after the prophecies had been given. Likewise, in the last chapter of Daniel, some 600 years before Christ, God gave Daniel an exact opposite command. He said:

> But thou, O Daniel, shut up the words, and seal the book, even to the time of the end. (Daniel 12:4)

We obviously cannot get into Daniel's prophecies in this study, but many of Daniel's prophecies were about 600 years away from the time of their fulfillment, all the way to the time of Christ. So since it was **hundreds of years** before some of Daniel's prophecies would come to pass, he was told to "shut up the words, and seal the book." In contrast, John was told by Jesus some **2,000 years ago,** to "Seal not the sayings of the prophecy" in Revelation, "for the time is at hand" for their fulfillment. Can you see the problem here? If Revelation's prophecies still have not been fulfilled after 2,000 years, why did Jesus not tell John to seal up his book too? He told Daniel to seal up his book, when some of his prophecies had only a mere 600 years to wait! The reason is obvious! The time for the fulfillment of Revelation's prophecies was "at hand"! This point further supports the fact that the prophecies in Revelation would be fulfilled in the days of the early church in the first century AD. **Jesus went to great lengths to make certain the early church clearly understood that Revelation was about events that would occur in their day and time, not 2,000 years later as we are told today.**

(Here is a little side note. The "time of the end" in Daniel 12:4, above, came in the time of Jesus and His apostles. In the New Testament it is called the Last Days and the End of the World [Age]. It was the time of the ending of the Old Covenant age and the final days of the world of Moses and the Law! We will study these things in the following chapters.)

Hopefully, we are now a little better prepared to look at the verses about the Second Coming found in Revelation. We know the book was written to the Christians living back then, not to you and me. It was about things that would happen soon in their lifetime, not today. They, not you and I, were to read, obey, and keep what was written in this letter to them. And finally, we know all the prophecies in the book were to come to pass shortly because the time was at hand and near. The first chapter and the last chapter are like **a giant pair of bookends** enclosing this letter to the churches. Chapter 1 and chapter 22 confine to the first-century age, the time period for all of Revelation's events to occur! This is just amazing! This is so important, let me say it again! In this special prophetic letter "unto the seven churches which are in Asia," Jesus' opening words and His closing words are like a giant pair of bookends, holding and limiting the fulfillment of **ALL THE PROPHECIES** to a time that was "near," "at hand," and "shortly" coming to pass! Wow! How did I ever miss this for such a long, long time? **This is the key to understanding the book of Revelation!**

We, of course, are not going to study the book of Revelation as such. But if you wished to pursue such a study, with what we have just learned, you would already be far ahead of most Christians. As you would look for the fulfillments of prophecy and as you would try to understand the wild symbols, you would not waste your efforts looking at history 500, 1,000, or 2,000 years later. You now know to study the history of the first century, because only that age fits within the giant bookends, and within the period of time that our Lord absolutely set in stone! What a new day it would be in Christianity if all Christians could see this! Remember, the **key to the book of Revelation** is found in the first three verses of the book. Those verses tell us "when" ALL of the prophecies were to be fulfilled.

Finally now, we can get back to our study of **"When did Jesus say He was coming?"** Let us see if some of the passages in Revelation can help us. We go back to the first chapter, verse 7.

Behold, He cometh with clouds; and every eye shall see Him, they also which pierced Him. (Rev.1:7)

In this verse we find a plain clue that helps us in our search for **"When did Jesus say He was coming?"** It says "they also which pierced Him" shall see Him when He comes. Actually, no "they" pierced Jesus. Literally and physically it was, I suppose, just one Roman soldier. But the "they" refers to those who were responsible for His being pierced, to those who caused His death. Obviously, "they" were the Jewish people who screamed "Crucify Him" and the Sanhedrin, which condemned Him to death (Acts 2:36). So if those who had Jesus crucified were going to see His coming in the clouds, then some of that same generation of Jews who "pierced Him" had to still be living when He returned. The book of Revelation was written some thirty-five to thirty-nine years after the crucifixion. Time was running out for that generation of Jewish people, if they were going to see His coming. The people who "pierced Him" were getting elderly and were approaching the end of their lives. **Therefore, Jesus had to have returned rather "shortly" after this Scripture was written! AMAZING!**

Do you remember our study of Matthew 26:64? That verse says the same thing that Revelation 1:7 says! In Matthew, Jesus told the high priest and the members of the Sanhedrin, who were certainly among those who "pierced Him," that they would see His "coming in the clouds." Can you see how perfectly these two verses agree, one from the first book of the New Testament

(Matthew) and one from the last (Revelation)? OH, THE HARMONY IN THE BIBLE IS SO BEAUTIFUL!

But even if this verse in Revelation 1:7 had no clues as to "when" Jesus was coming, the saints in the seven churches knew the answer to that question anyway! His coming would be soon and shortly, because the time for the fulfillment of Revelation's many prophecies was near and at hand! Further, Revelation 1:7 says the same thing as Matthew 24:30, "they shall see the Son of man coming in the clouds of heaven." Jesus had said in Matthew 24:34 that His coming was going to happen in "this generation" and some of that same generation were still alive at the time of Revelation. Some of them were the "they" in Revelation who would see His coming. I say again, "How beautiful is the harmony of the Bible!" When Jesus prophesied His coming in Matthew, the event was some forty years away, but when Revelation was given His coming was very near. Let us move on.

Jesus told the church at Thyatira:

But that which ye have already, hold fast till I come. (Rev. 2:25)

Jesus did not say "when" He was coming, but the church there, as we have learned, knew it would be "shortly"! Think about this point. If Jesus' return was not going to happen "shortly" and instead was going to be hundreds and thousands of years in the future, was it not rather deceitful for Him to say, "Hold fast till I come"? Absolutely it was! But Jesus knew the Thyatirans did not have to hold fast much longer because He knew He was coming soon. He was not teasing them or giving them false hope just to try to keep them faithful! His exhortation was genuine and sincere!

And further, please notice that Jesus did not encourage the Christians at Thyatira to hold fast until they died. That would have been the proper exhortation if it were going to be thousands of years before He returned! Jesus knew His coming was nearer than the likelihood of all their deaths, so He encouraged them to "hold fast till I come." What a thought!

To the church at Philadelphia, He was a little more specific:

III. The Revelation

> Behold, I come quickly: hold fast that which thou hast, that no man take thy crown. (Rev. 3:11)

Here we have the same message but to another church. Jesus again said He was coming, but this time He gave a little more information, saying He was coming "quickly." Jesus was saying His coming was near and at hand, and that He was coming soon! The Philadelphia saints would not have to "hold fast" for much longer for their Savior was coming "quickly." What do you suppose "quickly" meant to these Philadelphia saints? Put yourselves in their shoes. "Quickly" meant that their Lord was coming soon, right away, before very much longer. It meant the same thing it meant when Jesus told Judas, "That thou doest, do quickly" (John 13:27). We all know what "quickly" means. We can easily see the truth in this verse if we just accept the normal definition of the word.

Now let us go back to the last chapter, where Jesus closed His letter to His people, delivered through His servant John. Remember our quest has been to see if the book of Revelation gives us any information about "when" Jesus said He was coming again. We have found some helpful passages already. Do you wonder what kind of emphasis Jesus put on **"WHEN"** He would be coming, as He ended His message to the seven churches of Asia? Let us look again at the last and final chapter in the Bible, Revelation 22:

> Behold I come quickly: blessed is he that keepeth the sayings of the prophecy of this book. **(VERSE 7)**

> And, behold I come quickly; and My reward is with Me, to give every man according as his work shall be. **(VERSE 12)**

> He which testifieth these things saith, surely I come quickly. Amen. Even so, come, Lord Jesus. **(VERSE 20)**

What message do you think Jesus was trying to get across to these saints of God who were suffering awful things at the hands of the Jews and the Romans? **What promise** was He making over and over again? In these final words of God's Holy Book, about what did Jesus want everyone to be absolutely sure and certain? Is His message not crystal clear? Is it not very plain? Did He emphasize any one point? And what was that point? **You and I know the answer!** In this last chapter of the Bible, in simple, easy to understand words, Jesus promised His people, **NOT ONCE, BUT THREE TIMES,** that He would be returning right away! In our plain English, He assured them:

**LOOK, I AM COMING QUICKLY!
LOOK, I AM COMING QUICKLY!
ABSOLUTELY, I AM COMING QUICKLY!**

What else could Jesus have said to convince and reassure His saints that **He was on the verge of returning?** What else could He have said to make His suffering people know that **the time of their waiting for His return was nearly over?** He could not have been any clearer! **How did I miss this for so very long?** If Jesus did not come shortly after He sent this letter to the seven churches, if He did not soon make His "glorious appearing," then surely you and I cannot trust Him or His words! If He did not keep these promises to these early believers, then we can just forget about all of His promises of salvation for us! Why? Because He is a Jesus who does not keep His promises! But, I know that cannot be! Yet today's most respected and distinguished Christian leaders tell us Jesus did not keep His promises to come quickly and that to this day He still has not come! What a dilemma Christianity has on its hands! **The church today says Jesus is coming again and coming soon but its Holy Book, the Bible, says He promised to come centuries and centuries ago!**

In our studies so far, **EVERYTHING** we have found says Jesus returned a long, long time ago! In contrast, we have found **NOTHING** that says He is coming today! We Christians must begin to accept and to believe what our own Holy Book says instead of believing the mistaken traditions we have inherited from others! We know that Jesus was not a liar and a deceiver! Why then should it be so difficult for us to believe He kept His word, did what He said He would do, and returned in the generation of those first Christians?

III. The Revelation

Many times in my life I have preached "Jesus is coming soon" and quoted these verses from chapter 22 as my "proof"! **How wrong and mistaken I was!** Thank God for a second chance to get it right! These promises were made about 2,000 years ago to people living **THEN!** Jesus was coming quickly **THEN, IN THEIR DAY!** As we are discovering in our study, **HE NEVER ONCE** promised to come back in our age in the twenty-first century!

So, the book of Revelation has revealed to us several more of Jesus' statements and promises as to "when" He would be returning. And all of them agree with **everything** else Jesus said in the Gospels. Look above again at Revelation 22:12. In this verse Jesus promised to come with a "reward." This is the same thing He promised His followers earlier when He was on Earth: "And then He shall reward every man according to his works" (Matt. 16:27-28). In both passages Jesus was talking about the same event, His Second Coming. You will also remember in this passage in Matthew, Jesus said some of those persons to whom He was speaking would not die before He came back with their rewards. That promise is in complete harmony with verse 12, in the last chapter of the Bible. In Revelation Jesus was promising to "come quickly" with rewards—"quickly" so as to keep His promises in the Gospels to return while some of them were still living! Amazing! As He spoke in Revelation, it had been probably thirty-five years or more since His words in Matthew. Some of those people, to whom He spoke in Matthew, were still living—but now it was no longer a few decades before His coming. In Revelation, nearly four decades later, His coming was "near," "at hand," and "about to" occur! He would be coming "shortly" and "quickly"! This is really amazing! Let me say this again:

At the time of the Revelation Jesus promised to come quickly so as to return before all of His first followers died and before the generation of which He had been a part had all passed away!

Wow! When I first saw this truth I was ecstatic! For me this was an incredible discovery! All my life I had believed that Jesus was about to come in my lifetime. Now I know that He returned in the lifetime of those first believers, **just as He had promised them.**

OH, HOW BEAUTIFUL IS THE HARMONY OF THE WORD OF GOD! If the atheists could but see this harmony, they might believe! Instead they laugh at us saying, "Your Jesus is a fraud! You are still looking for His return but He said that He was coming 'quickly,' and that was 2,000 years ago!" Oh, how great is the need for Christianity to get its doctrines corrected, to solve this great dilemma, and to shut the mouths of all those who make mockery of our Savior, our Bible, and our way of life!

Heavenly Father, please help us your preachers, and help us your people, to pursue your word, to find your truth, and to deliver your church from this great dilemma! In the name of Jesus, Amen!

The next verse is the last verse in the Bible so we may as well include it! This verse contains the apostle John's closing words of this Epistle to his beloved saints in Asia. It reads much like the closing words of the other Epistles:

The grace of our Lord Jesus Christ be with you all. Amen. (Rev. 22:21)

For a chapter by chapter commentary that honors the time statements given by the Lord in the Revelation, I highly recommend ***The Consummation of the Ages*** by Kurt M. Simmons.

IV

THE LAST DAYS

I am anxious for us to continue our search for "when" the Scriptures say that Jesus was, or is, coming again. We have looked at Jesus' own words about His coming, first in the Gospels and then in Revelation. Next I want us to look at what His apostles believed, what they wrote, and what they taught the people. But before we do that, it is important for us to have a good understanding of what God was doing in the early age of the church. Comprehending this necessitates a proper understanding of some important terms found in the New Testament. Among those terms are the **Last Days**, the **End of the World**, and the **Judgment**.

Actually, we still will be studying the Second Coming of Jesus because all three of these phrases describe things we all associate with His Second Coming. If you are like I was, you believe that sometime during the Last Days, the last day would finally come. At that point Jesus would return and execute Judgment. His saints, dead and alive, would go to be with Him as their eternal reward. The physical world and all the wicked people left on it would be utterly annihilated in the great and terrible fires of the last day. I suppose most Christians hold similar views of the End of the World. I further suppose these three events are things all Christians associate with the Second Coming of our Lord. We all believe Jesus was coming in the Last Days. We believe He was coming at the End of the World. We believe He was coming on Judgment Day. So if we can find "when" these events occurred, or will be occurring, then that will help us with our "when" question regarding His coming. These three events are so interrelated it is difficult to separate them. So as we study one of these subjects, we shall be continually overlapping the other two.

Are we living in the Last Days today in the twenty-first century? Well, just recently I saw a famous preacher on TV look directly into the camera and say, "We are living in the Last Days!" Almost everyone you hear speaking says that we are living in the Last Days. This is exactly what I preached for decades! But "when" does the Bible say the Last Days were, or will be? And of equal importance, the Last Days were, or are, the last and final days of what? Let us see what answers we can find.

The Old Testament contains many prophecies about the Last Days, but none of them indicate that any days in the Old Testament were the Last Days. The prophecies all refer to sometime beyond the days of the Old Testament. While we can read several Old Testament prophecies about the Last Days, I will use just one of them. I use this one because its fulfillment is beyond questioning, since it is plainly stated in the New Testament. It is a rather famous passage from the prophet Joel:

> And it shall come to pass afterward, that I will pour out my spirit upon all flesh; and your sons and your daughters shall prophesy, your old men shall dream dreams, your young men shall see visions: And also upon the servants and upon the handmaids in those days will I pour out my spirit. (Joel 2:28-29)

On the day of Pentecost the Spirit was poured out on those in the upper room. The onlookers mocked the believers and accused them of being drunk. Peter came to their defense and went on to preach the first sermon of the newly founded church. He quoted Joel:

> For these are not drunken, as ye suppose, seeing it is but the third hour of the day. But this is that which was spoken by the prophet Joel; And it shall come to pass in the last days, saith God, I will pour out of my Spirit upon all flesh: and your sons and your daughters shall prophesy, and your young men shall see visions, and your old men shall dream dreams. (Acts 2:15-17)

So in his first sermon, Peter used a text from Joel. He declared that the pouring out of the Spirit on that Pentecost day was the fulfillment of Joel's

IV. The Last Days

prophecy. He further declared that this event had happened in the Last Days. Therefore, Peter plainly stated that the Last Days were in existence at the Feast of Pentecost in AD 30.

Some people do not believe the Last Days were in existence in Peter's day and time. They believe Peter was mistaken when he said, "But this [the outpouring of the Spirit] is that which was spoken by the prophet Joel." They further say Peter was wrong when he called that time the Last Days. Now this is a dilemma! Those who say Peter was wrong are still looking today for the fulfillment of Joel's prophecy. They are expecting a great outpouring today of the Holy Spirit, followed by the soon coming of Jesus.

If the foremost of the apostles, the one with the keys to the kingdom of God, made that kind of serious blunder on the very day the Lord founded His church, can we believe anything else Peter said or wrote? Peter may have been wrong about a lot of other things too! And if Peter was mistaken in his first sermon, what does that say about the credibility and the wisdom of Jesus, to put such a man in charge of His new church? And what about the powerful Holy Ghost that Peter and the others had just received? It must not have been working very well! Was it not supposed to "guide" them, the apostles, "into all truth" (John 16:13)? Oh the lengths to which we preachers will go to try to make the Bible agree with what we believe! If Peter was wrong, we can just throw away our Bibles and forget about Christianity for we cannot trust the Word of God! But Peter was right! Peter was telling the truth! He did understand Joel's prophecy! And the church was indeed founded in the Last Days, just as Peter said! This will all become even more obvious to us as we continue our study.

Let us now look at another verse that will help us to understand when the Last days were:

> God, who at sundry times and in divers manners spake in time past unto the fathers by the prophets, Hath in these last days spoken unto us by His Son. (Heb. 1:1-2)

We all know God spoke to the fathers by the prophets in the days of the Old Testament. We also know that He spoke nearly 2,000 years ago by His Son in the days of the New Testament! So this verse says when God sent His Son, Jesus, to speak to His people, it was in the time of the Last Days! This means the Last Days were in existence when Jesus preached and, as we heard from Peter, were still in existence when the apostles began to preach at Pentecost.

So if the Last Days were in existence nearly 2,000 years ago, how can we be living in the Last Days today in the twenty-first century? All my life I thought I had that all worked out! As we have just seen, I always knew and believed the Last Days were in the time of the New Testament. I could not deny the plain truth in the two verses above! But I thought I was still living in the Last Days today. I just stretched those Last Days far, far out and I said, "The Last Days began in Jesus' day and I am still in those same Last Days today." **I did not have any Bible at all to support that position,** but I believed Jesus was supposed to come in the Last Days. At that time in my life, I did not believe He had yet come. I had to do something! Extending the Last Days for thousands of years was the best answer I could find. As I have said again and again, it is amazing the lengths to which we preachers will go to try to make the Scriptures support what we already believe! **I was quite guilty of this!** The good thing was—I did not even realize it! Had I realized it, and then knowingly twisted the Scriptures to fit my preconceived ideas, I would have been a hypocrite of the lowest order. Perhaps many of you are in this same situation and are honestly unaware of it. Like me, you just believe what you have been taught. And every time you study the Bible, you try to understand it in a way that supports your beliefs. That was my story; and if this is how it is with you, I do hope my little book will make you aware of that situation.

It was indeed quite a stretch for me to say we are still in the Last Days today in the twenty-first century! I said the church had been living in the Last Days for nearly 2,000 years, but the Last Days would surely be ending soon. Consider this! The whole age of Moses and the Old Covenant lasted only about 1,500 years! How unreasonable then it was of me to say the Last Days had extended or stretched nearly 2,000 years and still counting. The Last Days were in the days and times of Jesus and His apostles. Peter and Hebrews clearly and plainly tell us that! So we are not living in the Last Days today. This will become clearer as we continue to look at the Scriptures.

IV. The Last Days

Another verse that will help is found in one of John's Epistles:

Little children, it is the last hour; and as you have heard that the Antichrist is coming, even now many antichrists have come, by which we know it is the last hour. (I John 2:18 NKJV)

We have a new term here, "the last hour." Whenever the period of the Last Days would arrive, eventually the last day would finally come. It follows that on the last day, the last hour would come, as the clock would count down to zero. So what is John saying? Just like Peter, John also understood the Last Days. He knew to what the Last Days pertained! He knew what signs Jesus had given to him and to the other apostles regarding these Last Days (Matthew 24). And as John looked around at the signs occurring in his world, he knew the time of the ending of the Last Days was getting very, very close. **So seeing the Last Days were about to end,** he abandoned that term for the more imminent term "the last hour."

John was warning his children, his followers, that the Last Days were about over! He was really encouraging them to hold on a little longer! They were so near to the ending of the Last Days that he said, "It is the last hour!" **AND TO BE SURE THEY GOT HIS POINT, HE SAID IT AGAIN:** "It is the last hour"! So if in John's day, it was "the last hour" of the Last Days, it is impossible that 2,000 years later we are still living in the Last Days! If we are still in the Last Days, then no longer are we talking about just stretching out the Last Days for 2,000 years. Now we are talking about stretching out "the last hour" for 2,000 years! That is totally unreasonable! The Last Days must have ended shortly after John wrote his Epistles. If they did not, then we have another dilemma. John would have been misleading his "little children." He did not do that, however! We shall see as we continue our study that the Last Days did end soon! Later, we shall look at I John 2:18 again and find much more there to help us with our "when" question.

So we have found that the Last Days were in the time of Jesus (Heb.1:1-2) and His apostles (Acts 2:15-17). As these days neared their end, John stopped talking about the Last Days and began to speak of "the last hour" (I John 2:18 NKJV).

Let us now turn our attention to another question regarding the Last Days. **The Last Days were the last and final days of what?** What exactly was in its final, closing days in the New Testament? At that time was anything coming to its end? Was anything in the days of the early church passing away? If we could find the answer to these questions, then that would help us to further understand (1) what the Bible means when it speaks of the Last Days and (2) when those Last Days were in existence.

Almost all Christians will readily agree that many things were indeed in their last and final days, when Jesus was on Earth and when His apostles were preaching. Many things were passing away in those early years of the church. Among them were the following:

> The age of Moses and the prophets was in its last days and passing away, making way for the age of Christ and His church!

> The age of the Old Covenant was in its last days and passing away, making room for the New Covenant (Heb. 8:13)!

> The age of being in God's family, by virtue of being born a natural descendant of Abraham, was ending! In the coming age anyone could be in the family of God through faith in Jesus!

> The age of natural Jerusalem being "the place where men ought to worship," was giving way to the time "when ye shall neither in this mountain, nor yet at Jerusalem worship the Father." Instead, men would be able to worship God anywhere in the world, "in spirit and in truth" (John 4:20-24).

> The Levitical priesthood was in its last days and being replaced by the followers of Jesus, who were "a royal priesthood" (I Peter 2:9).

> The old physical Jerusalem was in its last days and soon would be gone! In its place was coming a new spiritual city, the "Jerusalem which is above . . . the mother of us all," "the city of the living God,

the heavenly Jerusalem" that was "about to come" (*mello*) (Gal. 4:26; Heb. 12:22, 13:14).

The Law of Moses, with its harshness and condemnation, was in its last days! It was being replaced by the grace of Jesus Christ with its love and forgiveness!

Jesus had said "Heaven and earth shall pass away" in "this generation" (Matt. 24:34-35). That was exactly what was happening to everything pertaining to the world of Judaism. The way was being made for the promised "new heavens and a new earth, wherein dwelleth righteousness," the world of Christ and His church (Isa. 65:17; II Peter 3:13).

Hallelujah! Understanding this was wonderful for me! I rejoice not in the Judgment that came on the people and the land, but in the arrival of His grace—replacing the old age of condemnation and death! And this list could go on and on! But the SUM OF THIS LIST is that **all things** from the world and times of old natural Israel were in their last days and fading away. Most of natural Israel was already gone, scattered among their captors centuries earlier. All that remained were, primarily, the Jewish people in Judea and Jerusalem. They maintained the old order of things: the Law, the priesthood, the sacrifices, the feast days, and the rituals. **ALL OF THESE THINGS were in their last days and passing away!** Even the physical city of Jerusalem and the temple were in their last days, destined shortly for destruction as part of God's Judgment on the nation. The whole world of Judaism was on the verge of tumbling down and coming to an end. **This is what the biblical Last Days were about!**

Are you beginning to see what things were in their last and final days in the apostolic age? If you are, then you are beginning to see what the Last Days were all about! They have nothing at all to do with us today! The Last Days were about the things in New Testament times that were literally in their last and final days of existence and on the verge of passing away. The Last Days were all about the times and days of the early church, the age of Jesus and the apostles! The Last Days were all about the ending of the age of Moses and the establishment of the age of Christ! It all happened nearly 2,000 years ago! **The biblical Last Days are over and done!** How did I ever miss this for most of my life? It is very clear and plain to me now! But let us look at some more Scriptures:

> But I am the Lord thy God, that divided the sea, whose waves roared: The Lord of hosts is His name. And I have put My words in thy mouth, and I have covered thee in the shadow of mine hand, that I may plant the heavens, and lay the foundations of the earth, and say unto Zion, Thou art My people. (Isa. 51:15-16)

Here God is saying He brought Israel across the Red Sea, and then at Mount Sinai put His words in their mouths by giving them His law and establishing them as His people. I call this verse to your attention because, in establishing Israel as a nation of His people, God said that He had created a heavens and an earth. Obviously, He was not speaking of the natural heavens and earth, as they already existed. He was referring to this new nation of Israel, with its Law and its unique system of religion, as a new heavens and earth which He had created.

Now when Jesus said in Matthew 24:35, "Heaven and earth shall pass away," He was speaking of the heaven and earth He had created when He established Israel at Sinai. This is plain! You will remember from our study of Matthew 23 and 24, Jesus had just prophesied about all of those terrible things that were coming upon that generation, including the destruction of Jerusalem and the temple. Then He made His statement "heaven and earth shall pass away." Is it not easy to see He was referring not to the natural heaven and earth, but to the heaven and earth that was the world of the Jewish people? That "heaven and earth," that world, was in its last and final days, and by AD 70, the world of Judaism into which Christ was born was completely gone, utterly destroyed by the Romans! **These times were the biblical Last Days!**

Listen to Paul:

> For the fashion of this world passeth away. (I Cor. 7:31 KJV)
> For the form of this world is passing away. (NKJV & NASB)

Paul was saying the thing that was the fashion and the form of their world was passing away. Notice the present tense of this verse, "is passing away." **It was an ongoing process as Paul wrote.** The only thing in "fashion" in that day was Judaism. Paul was saying the world of Judaism was coming to its end. Judaism was in its final days and in the process of passing away! Meanwhile, Christianity was in its first days! The apostle John said the same thing as Paul:

> And the world passeth away. (I John 2:17 KJV)
> The world is passing away. (NKJV & NASB)

Again, it was a **PRESENTLY** occurring event in John's day: "The world is passing away." The world of the Jews and Jerusalem was in its last and final days and passing away! **This was the time of the Last Days!** Paul and John could not in the least be talking about our natural world. If so, that would mean the world has been passing away for nearly 2,000 years and counting. That makes no sense! Even if they had been talking about the natural world, John and Paul had absolutely no reason to warn the Christians living then! A world that would be passing away thousands of years later would not have affected them at all! Can you see the obvious truth here?

As we have looked at the Last Days, we have purposely not mentioned the End of the World. But as you can readily see from the above verses, the world that was coming to an end was not our natural heavens and earth; it was not our globe; it was not our planet Earth with all of its inhabitants. But the world, "the heavens and earth" where the Jews and Judaism lived, was in its closing days, was dying, and would soon be gone! In its place was arising Christianity, "the new heavens and earth," where all men could live and dwell spiritually, where all men could worship and please God from anywhere on Earth! Oh can you see this? It is so beautiful!

> For if what is passing away was glorious, what remains is much more glorious. (II Cor. 3:11 NKJV)
> For if that which fades away was with glory, much more that which remains is in glory. (NASB)

In the earlier verses in this chapter, II Corinthians 3:7-10, Paul compared the "ministration of death," the Law of Moses, with the "ministration of the spirit," the grace of Christ. He said the Law had its glory, but its glory was as nothing when compared to the glory of the grace we now have in Jesus! He then added verse 11 above. It is easy to see that Paul is saying the Law, the Old Covenant, the "ministration of death," was in its closing days, fading away, and "passing away"! But the thing that remains, the grace of Jesus, the New Covenant, "the ministration of righteousness," is much better and much more glorious! Praise the Lord! Can the truth about the Last Days get any clearer? Later in the Epistles, John says essentially the same thing as Paul:

> The darkness is passing away, and the true light is already shining. (I John 2:8)

Oh how beautiful this is! Can you see that the darkness, which was in its last days and in the process of passing away, was the Old Covenant, the old system of condemnation and death? In its place already was shining the true light, the Gospel of Jesus Christ. Hallelujah:

> Light was replacing darkness!
> Grace was replacing the Law!
> Forgiveness was replacing condemnation!
> Life was replacing death!

All this was an ongoing process in the days of the apostles. The Law of Moses was in its last days, fading away and dying out. But the Gospel of Jesus Christ was rising and filling all of the land! Praise the Lord! Just one more point and we shall try to move on:

> I will make a new covenant. (Heb. 8:8)
> In that He saith, A new covenant, He hath made the first old. Now that which decayeth and waxeth old is ready to vanish away. (Heb. 8:13)

What can be added to these words? They are as plain as day! The Old Covenant was in its last days, old, decaying, in the throes of death, and "ready to vanish away"! The Greek text says that it was "near disappearing"! **These Bible times were the Last Days!**

TODAY WE ARE NOT LIVING IN THE LAST DAYS! We have seen from the Bible that the Last Days were in the times of the early church age in the first century AD. We have seen that the Last Days were all about the ending of the Old Covenant world. The Last Days have nothing to do with the days and times in which we live. They were in the days and times of Jesus and the apostles! The Last Days existed during the period of the transition from the Law of Moses to the grace of Jesus Christ. **The Last Days are over and done!** They reached their end when that transition was fully completed in AD 70 with the destruction of Jerusalem, the temple, the Jewish people, their religious system, and their way of life. We can conclude from what we have learned that the Last Days had a lifespan of about seven decades, lasting from the birth of Christ to the destruction of Jerusalem by the Roman army in AD 70.

In this book we are searching for the answer to the question, **"When does the Bible say Jesus would come again?"** Virtually all Christians believe Jesus was going to return in the Last Days. We have seen that the Last Days were in the days and times of the early church. So in order for Him to return in the Last Days, Jesus had to come in that first century AD. Wow! But we should not be shocked! **This is exactly the same period of time in which Jesus said He would return!** This is **exactly** what we found in the four Gospels and in Revelation, all of which we have already studied! The Bible agrees with itself! This is just wonderful!

Nothing in the Bible in any way says the Last Days are still going on today! Let me repeat, **NOTHING!** Instead, we have looked at multiple Scriptures that have shown us that the Last Days were in the days of Jesus and the apostles. And we have looked at numerous Scriptures that have revealed to us exactly what the Last Days were all about. The Bible has shown us the things that were coming to their end, fading away and therefore in their final days. We have not begun to exhaust the verses that say exactly what we have already found. We could keep on and on! Do not ever again be alarmed by preachers who pound their pulpits and tell us, "We are living in the Last Days." **IT IS NOT TRUE!**

The Resurrection

If we Christians have associated any one subject with the Last Days and the Second Coming of Jesus, it is the resurrection of the dead. While the resurrection as a subject is not a part of the matter being studied in this book, we know that the resurrection and the Last Days are completely intertwined in the Bible. So before we leave the Last Days let me share with you how I now see Jesus' many promises to raise up his followers at "the last day." My new understanding of the Last Days has brought me to a different view and perception of the resurrection. Nobody denies that Jesus taught the resurrection would occur at the last day. In our study of the Last Days, we have found that these days were in the first century, ending with the events of AD 70. So the biblical Last Days, and thus "the last day," have come and gone. This means the resurrection also came. Whenever the last day of the Last Days arrived, by AD 70, the resurrection came. This is what Jesus promised many times:

> Whoso eateth my flesh, and drinketh my blood, hath eternal life; and I will raise him up at the last day. (John 6:54)

As is evident from the words of the apostle Paul, the hope of resurrection was the hope of Israel:

> And now I stand and am judged for the hope of the promise made of God unto our fathers: Unto which promise our twelve tribes, instantly serving God day and night, hope to come. For which hope's sake, King Agrippa, I am accused of the Jews. Why should it be thought a thing incredible with you, that God should raise the dead? (Acts 26:6-8)

It is obvious from these verses that the hope of the fathers, which Paul was preaching, was their hope of resurrection. Paul was arrested for preaching that hope:

> I am a Pharisee, the son of a Pharisee: of the hope and resurrection of the dead I am called in question. (Acts 23:6)

IV. The Last Days

Where did Paul get this doctrine of the resurrection? He told us in a couple of passages. He said he believed "all things which are written in the law and in the prophets" (Acts 24:14). Then he further declared that in his preaching he said "none other things than those which the prophets and Moses did say should come" (Acts 26:22). So the hope of the resurrection that Paul preached (1) definitely came from the Law and the Prophets and (2) was the hope of Israel.

The question could be asked, "If the hope of the resurrection was Israel's hope, and if that hope came straight out of the Law and the Prophets, then why was Paul arrested for preaching it?" Only one reason exists and it is the same reason the apostles were arrested in Acts 4. Just as did the apostles in Acts 4:2, I believe Paul preached "through Jesus the resurrection of the dead." The religious leaders wanted nothing, not even a resurrection, if it had to come "through Jesus." So, this is why they had Paul arrested. If he had left "Jesus" out of his resurrection sermons, he could have stayed out of jail!

I have come to believe that the Old Testament saints and the New Testament saints who had died were resurrected with the return of Christ by AD 70. I no longer believe Abraham and the other Old Testament faithful are still waiting for their Messiah to come and resurrect them. He came as they expected and ushered them into eternity with Him. If Abraham is still waiting to be resurrected, then the coming of the Baby in a manger did nothing for him. He had waited hundreds and hundreds of years for Jesus to come and bring his reward, and now he has waited 2,000 more years, and still counting. How unfair is this on God's part. But if you can grasp the facts (1) that Abraham would be resurrected at the last day, and (2) that the last day has come, then it should also be easy to see that the resurrection has come. Paul said in Acts 24:15 "that there shall be a resurrection." The Greek word *mello* is used in this verse, and what Paul really said was "that there is about to be a resurrection." And that was 2,000 years ago! The Greek text says, "A resurrection about to be." How can the Bible be true and the resurrection, that was "about to be" in Paul's day, still not have come to pass today?

The resurrection is certainly a subject for another book and a topic for a more learned writer. Nevertheless, with the return of Christ by AD 70, I see the resurrection of all the dead in Christ. With the work of salvation complete, Jesus has no need to come again to do anything else. He raised all of His dead saints at the last day and ushered in a new day in which His followers no longer need such a resurrection. Why? Because I believe today under the New Covenant, the dead no longer wait in their graves for centuries for a resurrection. I believe Jesus fixed all of that with His death, burial, resurrection, and Second Coming. If Abraham is still awaiting resurrection and if when we die we join him in waiting, then the New Covenant offers nothing better than the Old. But it does offer something better! I now believe at the end of this earthly life, Christians are immediately brought into eternity with God. It was not that way in Old Testament days. But now that Jesus has accomplished all of the work of redemption, we hear Him say:

> Blessed are the dead which die in the Lord from henceforth. (Rev.14:13)

Yes, the Old Testament saints did have to wait for their reward, but now we have a better hope! With the return of Christ by AD 70, He brought an end to the way things were under the Old Covenant, and ushered in a better way under the New Covenant. So from then on, that is "from henceforth," when we die we no longer have to wait, but immediately begin to enjoy the blessings of eternal life with Jesus. IS THIS NOT A HOPE AND A FUTURE MORE WONDERFUL THAN MY MERE WORDS CAN DESCRIBE? INDEED IT IS!

I have touched on only a few of the many Scriptures about the Last Days. For a full treatment of this subject, I highly recommend a great book by Don K. Preston titled ***THE LAST DAYS IDENTIFIED!*** This book is available from Don Preston, 1405 4th Ave. NW #109, Ardmore, OK 73401, and from www.eschatology.org.

V

THE END OF THE WORLD

This study is a continuation of our look at the Last Days. Why is this true? Because in popular Christian theology, at the end of the Last Days will come the End of the World and the end of time. The fires of the Last Days will burn up our planet Earth, and everything on it, including all the people who have not been raptured. The fires will be so intense that even the heavens will be destroyed! This is similar to what I also believed and preached for many years.

Christianity is looking for these events to occur at any moment, preceded by the rapture of the church. Many preachers and prophets have predicted the date when these events would occur. They told us when the world would end and when time would be no more. It is obvious that all these "prophets" had two things in common: (1) They were all positive their predictions were correct and (2) they were all wrong! **But I was equally wrong!** I never was foolish enough to name a date. But I did preach, "The world could end at any time, and if not today, it will surely end soon." But it did not! Yet the church continues to teach this same doctrine, believing and hoping that the next prophet will have his figures and dates correct. I can tell you now, his prophecy will fail too! I can say that because the church's teachings about the End of the World and the end of time are **totally without any biblical foundation!** Now that is a dilemma of huge proportions for Christianity!

The truth is, not only is the teaching of the end of the physical earth unbiblical, but it is a direct contradiction of the Bible! Consider these passages:

Neither will I again smite anymore every living thing, as I have done. (Gen. 8:21)

And He built His sanctuary, like high palaces, like the earth which He hath established forever. (Ps. 78:69)

The world also is stablished, that it cannot be moved. (Ps. 93:1)

Who laid the foundations of the earth, that it should not be removed forever. (Ps. 104:5)

Thy faithfulness is unto all generations: thou hast established the earth, and it abideth. (Ps. 119:90)

One generation passeth away, and another generation cometh: but the earth abideth forever. (Eccl. 1:4)

Unto Him be glory in the church by Christ Jesus throughout all ages, world without end. Amen. (Eph. 3:21)

So we have God's promise to **Noah** after the flood that He would never again destroy every living thing on Earth. We have the words of the **Psalmist,** the words of the wise man, **Solomon,** and the words of the apostle **Paul.** All of these passages contradict the teaching that Earth and its people will soon come to a fiery end! Instead, these verses tell us that God will never do such a thing! They tell us that Earth's existence is forever and we live in a world without end! However, the King James Version of the Bible does speak of the End of the World. So, since God has promised not to "smite every living thing" again, what do these Scriptures mean? Let us see if we can find some answers!

The phrase "the end of the world" appears five times in the King James Version. The phrases "the end of this world" and "the ends of the world" each appears one time. In all seven verses the word translated "world" is from the Greek word *aion,* which means "age." Thus the KJV tends to mislead us in our efforts to understand these passages. Properly translated, these verses would all read "the end of the age," "the end of this age," and "the ends of the age." I am

V. End of the World

not saying this because it helps support my position. In reading my book, I hope you have come to know me well enough to realize that I am no longer interested in trying to make the Scriptures support my beliefs. I just want the truth and only the truth! I will change my position to conform to whatever the Scriptures teach! However, it is true that the word "world" should be "age" and is translated "age" in the newer Bible translations. I have checked the following versions and **ALL** of them have made this correction in **ALL** seven verses:

New King James Version (NKJV)
New American Standard Bible (NASB)
English Standard Version (ESV)
New International Version (NIV)

So the truth is, neither Jesus nor any of His apostles ever used the term "the end of the world." They said "the end of the age." Of course they could have used the word "world." As we have learned in our studies, a "world" was coming to its end in the first century. We saw this especially in our look at the Last Days. But the world that was ending was not our literal planet Earth. It was the world of the Jewish people that spiritually and physically collapsed into a pile of rubble by AD 70. This is the end of the "world" (age) to which all seven of these verses refer! The secret to understanding these seven verses, and MOST of the New Testament, is to be able to see that, with the fall of Jerusalem in AD 70, the old Mosaic age came to its end. And this is "the end" foretold in Old Testament prophecy and mentioned so often in the New Testament!

Bible scholars are unanimous that the Jewish people believed in two ages. First was the age in which they were living when Christ came. This period was called "this age," and it was the Mosaic age—the age of Moses, the Law, and the prophets. They looked forward to another age, which was referred to as "the age to come" and was the Messianic age, the age of the Messiah. Jesus uses this terminology in Matthew 12:32: "it shall not be forgiven him, neither in this world [age], neither in the world [age] to come." We know that the Jews' Messiah came and His name was Jesus. But His people failed to recognize and accept Him. However, their failure did not stop the march of time or God's plans. The age of Moses still came to its end, and the age of Christ still had its beginning. All of this, both the ending and the beginning, reached its climax in AD 70!

Jesus' people would not acknowledge or accept Him. Their insistence on holding onto the things of their old Mosaic age became great obstacles and hindrances to the advancement of the new Messianic age of Jesus. This is well documented in the book of Acts, where the believers were under continual and severe persecutions by the Jews. Hebrews 9:8 says, "that the way into the holiest of all was not yet made manifest, while as the first tabernacle was yet standing." The writer is saying that the Messianic age, the age of Christ and His church, would not realize its full potential as long as the tabernacle, the temple, that great symbol of the old age, was still standing. It had to be removed, along with everything it represented, and it was! In AD 70, when the Romans destroyed Judea, Jerusalem, and the magnificent temple, the age (world) of Moses ended and the major obstacle to the advancement of the age of Christ was removed. **This was the biblical End of the World [Age].** It was the end of the age and the end of the Law of Moses and all that pertained to it! In contrast, the Bible **NEVER** speaks of the end of our physical world and planet Earth!

Further, the Bible **NEVER** speaks of the **END OF TIME!** Can you believe that? As much as we preachers have preached about the end of time, yet the phrase **CANNOT BE FOUND IN THE KING JAMES BIBLE!** The Bible does speak of "the time of the end" (Dan. 12:4). But the end of time means something totally different from "the time of the end"! Any "time of the end" would be the time of the ending of something. In the Bible "the time of the end" is the time about which we have been studying, and "the time of the end" of which Daniel prophesied. Daniel's "time of the end" was the time of the Last Days, in which the Jews' world came to its end, with the destruction of their holy city and their holy temple. "The time of the end" was the time of the ending of the age of Moses and the Law. "The time of the end" was the time of Jesus and His apostles, when "this age" was coming to its end and "the age to come" was having its beginning! But **NOTHING** in the Bible teaches the end of time as we know time in our world! **NOTHING!**

While the term "the end of time" is not in the Bible, a phrase in Revelation 10:6 says: "that there should be time no longer." This verse is often used to teach the ending of time, as we know it, but this passage is not referring to the ending of time. It refers to a time when no "time" will be left for the nation of the Jews to repent and accept their Messiah. It speaks of the Judgment about to come upon the Jews and Jerusalem in AD 70. In this Revelation passage John is prophesying a time—"which must shortly come" (Rev. 1:1)—when Judah's time will be exhausted, time will have run out, the day of opportunity will have ended and God will wait (delay) no longer. The longsuffering and patience of God with His people will have come to its end. We have learned that a time soon came in Jewish history when their time was exhausted, when "time no longer" existed for the nation to repent. The end and the time for Judgment had come! It was the same time in their history as prophesied in Revelation 22:11: "He that is unjust, let him be unjust still: and he which is filthy, let him be filthy still." Judgment Day would have come and it would be too late for the Jewish nation to repent. God would have proclaimed "time no longer"! The "filthy" and the "unjust" would just have to remain "filthy" and "unjust." Time for getting right would be gone! It would be too late! For Revelation 10:6, the Revised Version expresses this as "delay no longer," which is what I have said the verse means—**Judgment Day would be delayed no longer!** The NASB says "that there will be delay no longer." I rest my case! Revelation 10:6 does not teach the end of time, but the end of opportunity for the nation to get right with God! Nothing, I repeat, **NOTHING,** in the Bible speaks about the end of time or about the end of our natural world and planet!

Let us get back to our seven verses. Five of them are found in the Gospel of Matthew. Here are the first three:

> The harvest is the end of the world [age]. (Matt. 13:39)
> So shall it be at the end of this world [age]. (13:40)
> So shall it be at the end of the world [age]. (13:49)

All three of these verses are parts of parables Jesus was using as He taught the people. The first two are in the parable of the wheat and the tares, and the third is in the parable of the fishing net. Both parables teach the same thing—the good and the bad are left together until the end of the age and then separated. With our preceding studies, you know the end of the age came at the destruction of Jerusalem. Matthew 13:39 mentions "the harvest." In John 4:35 Jesus says, "Lift up your eyes, and look on the fields; for they are white already to harvest." Notice the words "white already to harvest." Harvesting was a present need! The harvest in Matthew and John was an ongoing harvest of souls in THAT age. It was the great effort by Jesus and His apostles to convert the Jews from Moses to Christ, from Judaism to Christianity, and thus to save them from the impending disaster. Notice Matthew 13:40 says, "At the end of this world." **THIS WORLD was the world of Matthew's day.** It was "this age," the age in which the people were then living. The ending of both parables came at the end of that age, AD 70!

In the parables, the good and bad would be separated at the end of the age. The good would receive their rewards and the bad would be destroyed or cast away. This sounds like Judgment Day, does it not? It was indeed Judgment Day! The followers of Christ were "delivered" from His "wrath" (I Thess. 1:10), because they obeyed His words, escaped, and fled to the mountains (Matt. 24:16). The others endured the ravages of the "great tribulation" (Matt. 24:21)—hunger, starvation, death, and captivity—as the Roman army besieged Jerusalem for years and then finally burned it to the ground!

You will remember in our study of Matthew 16:27-28, that Jesus promised to come again and "reward every man according to his works." He further promised to come while some of them were still living! Those verses and these verses in chapter 13 all speak of this same time, "at the end of this world [age]." ALL of these passages are speaking of the same Judgment Day! I hope you are now seeing that the Last Days, the End of the World (Age), and the Judgment were all events of the early age of the church and occupied approximately the first seventy years of that first century AD.

Here are the next two times "the end of the world" appears in Matthew:

Tell us, when shall these things be? and what shall be the sign of thy coming, and of the end of the world [age]? (Matt. 24:3)
And lo, I am with you always, even unto the end of the world [age]. (Matt. 28:20)

V. End of the World

Recall that in our study of Matthew 23-24, we saw that the End of the World (Age) was the end, naturally and spiritually, of the world of Judaism. So after what we have learned, the second passage should be easy to understand. Jesus said these words to His apostles just before His ascension. It would be some forty years before the End of the World, that is, the destruction of Jerusalem and Judaism. As we know, during these forty years His apostles would have it very, very rough. Fleeing from "city to city," persecutions, beatings, imprisonments, and even death would be their way of life. These words of Jesus (Matt. 28:20) near the end of His ministry were a promise to be with His disciples through it all. He did not promise to deliver them from their sufferings, but to be with them all the way "even unto the end of the world [age]." I believe that the supernatural powers of the apostles during this time to heal the sick, to raise the dead, and to perform untold miracles were the fulfillment of Jesus' promise to be with them "unto the end of the world [age]." This is not to say that our Lord is not with His people today; but the truth is, since the days of the apostles, no one, to my knowledge, has ever had the power to work such miracles. At the end of the age these Jewish persecutions would cease because Jesus would return in Judgment of these persecutors and destroy them and their city! **That Jewish world was the world that would end!** Are you getting the picture? Is this all coming together for you? I do pray so!

> Now all these things happened unto them for ensamples: and they are written for our admonition, upon whom the ends of the world [age] are come. (I Cor. 10:11)

This is our sixth verse. Paul was exhorting the Corinthians to be good and faithful Christians, not to sin and thus be destroyed, as were some of the children of Israel in their forty years of wilderness wanderings. He said their ancestors' history was written for "our admonition," that is, for the admonition of Paul and the Corinthians. Then he added that he and the Corinthians were living at a time when the ends of the world, or age, had come! Notice the present tense of the verb! Paul said the ends of the world (age) "are come." The end was not coming hundreds or thousands of years later! Paul said it was upon them at that time! Paul was warning **THEM** that they could not take any chances with their faithfulness; the end was too near! This verse could not have been written to David, Daniel, or Jeremiah! Yes, they lived in "this age" of

Moses too, but they did not live in "the end of this age," and they did not live in the Last Days of that age. However, Paul and the Corinthians did! Can you see this? This letter to the church was written in about AD 56-57. In a little more than a decade that world, that age, came to its end! I have preached from this verse many times, and always wrongly applied it. But properly interpreted, this verse cannot be made to apply to the end of our world today! Thank God for this light!

The seventh and last time "the end of the world" appears in the Bible is in Hebrews. If you have any doubts about what you have just read, this verse should take them all away:

But now once in the end of the world [age] hath He appeared to put away sin by the sacrifice of Himself. (Heb. 9:26)

This verse does not need much interpreting! It tells us that Jesus had come and died on the cross for our sins. We already knew that. The amazing thing is, the writer tells us that when Jesus "appeared" and sacrificed "Himself" for our sins, it was in the time of "the end of the world [age]." **Jesus died in the End of the World!** Did you catch that? But how can that be? We know when Jesus was crucified. It was nearly 2,000 years ago and the natural world has not ended! But the writer says Jesus sacrificed Himself at the End of the World! Obviously, it was not the end of planet Earth, as it still endures 2,000 years later! Oh, is not the truth here so plain? Jesus came to Earth and was crucified in the time of the ending of the world, the world of Moses and the prophets in which Judah lived. When Jesus came that world, that age, which was called "this age" by those then living, was in its last and final days and would soon end. The world of the Jews and Judaism—the world of the priests, the temple and the rituals of the Law—was the world into which Jesus was born and later crucified. And that world, having existed for about 1,500 years, was near its end when Jesus came and died for all mankind! Can the truth get any clearer? The end of our world is not approaching today! **The End of the World was the time when Jesus came and died for us (Heb. 9:26)!** Can you now see and understand to what the End of the World in our Bible is referring? I do pray you can see this!

V. End of the World

Let us move on to other passages that will further help us get a firm grasp on the meaning of the End of the World.

> But the end of all things is at hand: be ye therefore sober, and watch unto prayer. (I Peter 4:7)

Again, our world and planet were not among the "all things" of which Peter wrote. They have not ended 2,000 years later! Yet the end of the things of which Peter spoke was "at hand," or "near," as the NASB says! We know what did end and what ending was "at hand" when Peter wrote these words around AD 65! This is the very same kind of warning Paul gave to the Corinthians above in I Corinthians 10:11! Peter said to be sober, watch, pray, do not fall away, because the end was so near! Peter's "all things" included all the Old Testament prophecies of Israel's end and Judgment. Hear what Jesus said: "For these be the days of vengeance, that all things which are written [in the prophets] may be fulfilled" (Luke 21:22). Jesus spoke those words some thirty-five years earlier. By the time of Peter's Epistle around AD 65 the end was "at hand" **THEN, not today!** This verse has nothing to do with the ending of our natural world, as we hear preached so often. What was "near" was the end of the "heavens and earth" that God had created when He made Israel His special people and gave them His Law at Mount Sinai (Isa. 51:16). "All things" pertaining to that old world of Israel, both their physical things and their spiritual things, were very near to ending and forever passing away! **This was the biblical End of the World!**

This End of the World was so close that Paul once said:

> Brethren, the time is short. (I Cor. 7:29)

I used to abuse this verse, preaching that the Second Coming was near and therefore everyone had better get ready to meet the Lord because "time" was "short." This verse is part of a passage in which Paul counseled his people at Corinth not to get married (I Cor. 7:25-28). Did I preach that part too? Of course not!

Paul did not know exactly when the wrath of God would fall on the nation; but when he wrote this letter to the Corinthians in about AD 56-57, he believed the end was so near that it was not a time to be getting married and starting a family. Persecutions were bad and would get worse. All-out war with Rome was in the making. The great tribulation prophesied by the Lord loomed on the horizon. The time when the believers would have to leave everything and flee to the mountains was getting nearer every day (Matt. 24). Times were bad and they would get worse before they got better!

So, Paul said if a person was single then that was "good." If he had a wife that was fine too, but if he did not have a wife then not to "seek" one. If a person did get married he would not have "sinned." However, he would be setting himself up for "trouble," from which Paul was trying to "spare" them (7:25-28). Why would Paul give such counsel? He stated his reason in verse 26: "I suppose therefore that this is good [advice] for the present distress." What "present distress"? Reread the previous paragraph. Their world was in a mess and near its end—"time" was "short." It was not a good time to get married and start a new family!

"The time is short" has nothing at all to do with us today! This was a situation in the early church 2,000 years ago! The biblical End of the World—the world of Judaism—was nearby and the Judgment of God would not be delayed much longer. I hope this explanation makes sense to you!

These verses are a perfect example to show how very important it is to be sure we know the context and setting when we are trying to understand a passage. Otherwise, we could quote I Corinthians 7:25-28 and preach that Paul said people should not get married. We would be totally misrepresenting Paul. It was only because of the current situation that Paul recommended celibacy. Do you see this?

We continue our study of the End of the World with another verse from the apostle Peter. Many times I have used this verse to preach that in the Last Days when Christ comes, the natural earth and heavens will all be burned up:

> But the day of the Lord will come as a thief in the night; in the which the heavens shall pass away with a great noise, and the elements shall melt with fervent heat, the earth also and the works therein shall be burned up. (II Peter 3:10)

V. End of the World

Where in the world did Peter get a sermon like this? After reading this far in my book, you probably know the answer! He heard it from His Savior, Jesus! This is exactly what Jesus preached and taught to His disciples: "Heaven and earth shall pass away" (Matt. 5:18, 24:35). But as we have seen in our studies, Jesus was not talking about the passing of the physical world or the natural heavens and earth. He spoke of the ending of their world, "the heavens and earth" of the Jewish people. Their government, their politics, their religious system, their holy city, and their sacred temple would all soon come to an end—and did so, as we have learned!

In Matthew 24:35, Jesus simply said that the heavens and earth would pass away. Peter got much more descriptive, using symbolic imagery to enhance the awfulness, the completeness, and the finality of this destruction. But in Matthew 24:29 Jesus also used symbolic words to describe this great calamity, saying, "The sun shall be darkened and the moon shall not give her light and the stars shall fall from heaven." But neither Peter nor Jesus was talking about the natural sky and Earth. To do so would have been to contradict the Word of God, as we saw at the beginning of this chapter. **They were both talking about the coming end of the world of Judaism** and all that pertained to it! I do hope that you can see this!

Earlier in II Peter 3, Peter had compared what was about to happen to the present "heavens and earth," with what had happened in Noah's day (verses 5-6). He mentioned the heavens and earth of Noah's time and said, "The world that then was" perished. But the natural earth was not destroyed, for the ark soon came to rest on the top of a mountain. When Noah opened a window of the ark and looked out, the natural heavens were still there! But Peter said the "world" of Noah perished! Well, if it was not the natural "heavens and earth" that were destroyed, what perished? In II Peter 2:5 Peter said what perished was "the world of the ungodly." The wicked and sinful people of Noah's day perished, and their carnal and idolatrous works were destroyed by the flood waters! It was the end of their world!

Likewise in II Peter 3:10, another world was going to perish; but as in Noah's day, it would not be the natural heavens and earth! This time it would be Jesus' own "ungodly" people, whom He had called "Ye serpents, ye generation of vipers" (Matt. 23:33). They had killed their prophets, crucified their Messiah, and persecuted and killed His followers! This Judgment and wrath of God was upon them, not upon literal Earth! **What had the natural heavens and planet done to offend the Almighty and to deserve to be destroyed?** Nothing, nothing at all! But His people had offended their God, and the promised day of the Lord's wrath was quickly coming upon them. It is indelibly written in the pages of history that the guilty land of Judah was overwhelmed with a fiery deluge of wrath and Judgment, ordained by God and executed by the Roman armies. The Jewish people's earthly things and their heavenly things, that is to say their civil institutions and their spiritual institutions, were all utterly destroyed! This was the coming conflagration of which Peter prophesied! **It was the biblical End of the World!** This verse in II Peter 3:10 has **absolutely nothing** to do with the end of our natural world today in the twenty-first century!

Looking at history, we now know that this destruction of Jerusalem was just two to three years away when Peter wrote these words to the church. But Peter did not know that! He did not know exactly how much time was left. But he did know the signs of "the end" that Jesus had given him and the other apostles (Matt. 24). Seeing these signs being fulfilled all around him, Peter could tell "the end" was very close! In fact "the end" was so near when Peter wrote that he exhorted the saints to look for it and hasten its coming (verse 12)! If this event has not yet occurred, then Peter was being rather deceitful to his readers! But Peter was not misleading the church! This great Day of the Lord was near! Its closeness was that of which Peter spoke in the verse we just studied: "But the end of all things is at hand: be ye therefore sober, and watch unto prayer" (I Peter 4:7)!

But why would the church look forward to such an awful event? Well, for one thing they would get relief from their Jewish persecutors. It would be Judgment Day, the time for rewards, both good and bad! It would be the time of the separating of the wheat from the tares, the saints from the sinners, because this would be "the end of this world [age]"! And Jesus had said some forty years earlier, "so shall it be in the end of this world [age]" (Matt. 13:40). The Lord would be coming while "some" of those to whom He had spoken forty years earlier were still living! And He would be bringing His rewards for "every

V. End of the World

man according to his works" (Matt. 16:27-28). You will remember that the "wheat" was gathered into His "barn," but the "tares" were "burned in the fire"! The burning of the tares is a picture of the destruction of those who rejected their Messiah. You know that happened by AD 70! This is the same "fire" of II Peter 3:10! Can the picture get any clearer? Yes, always it can. But this passage is now very plain to me! I hope you are beginning to understand what was really happening in the early days of the church.

Before we conclude this section on the End of the World, we must look at the parable of the marriage of the king's son in Matthew 22. The king prepared a wedding for his son and sent his servants to tell those who were invited to come to the wedding for everything was ready. The people paid no heed to the servants; in fact they abused them and even killed some of them. In its most basic interpretation, this parable is a picture of the Jews' rejection of Jesus and the Gospel, and their persecution of the servants of God, who extended to them an invitation to participate in the salvation He offered. The result of their refusal to share in what God had prepared for them was nothing short of horrible! In the parable Jesus describes the consequences like this:

> But when the king heard thereof, he was wroth: and he sent forth his armies, and destroyed those murderers, and burned up their city. (Matt. 22:7)

This is incredible! How plain and powerful is this verse! If we can see what Jesus was talking about here in this parable, **then we will be in a much better position to understand the whole New Testament,** for much of it is about this very matter! Look at verse 7:

1. The "king" was God.

2. God was "wroth" with His people, the Jews, for rejecting His prophets and His Son.

3. He sent "His armies," the Roman legions, "to destroy those murderers," the unbelievers among the Jews.

4. The Romans not only destroyed the people, but they "burned up" their "city," which was Jerusalem!

How much better can any parable fit the actual historical events? We know this is exactly what happened to the Jews, Judea, and Jerusalem! Utter destruction came to the people and the land by AD 70. As I said earlier, if we can get a clear grasp of this parable and verse 7, then it will be much easier to understand all of the New Testament. The New Testament is very much about:

God sending His Son, Jesus
Jesus being rejected by His people
The Judgment of God coming as a result
That old age and world coming to its end
A new world and age beginning through the atoning work of Christ

Verse 7 in the parable of The Marriage of the King's Son was the time when many prophecies in both the Old and New Testaments came to pass:

THIS was when "the heavens" passed away, when "the elements" melted, and when "the earth" "burned up" (II Peter 3:10)!

THIS was when the tares in Matthew 13:40 were "gathered and burned in the fire"!

THIS was the time of which Jesus was speaking in Matthew 13:40 when He said: "So shall it be at the end of this world [age]."

THIS was when the last day of the Last Days arrived!

THIS was when Malachi 4:1 was fulfilled: "For behold the day cometh, that shall burn as an oven; and all the proud, yea, and all that do wickedly, shall be stubble: and the day that cometh shall burn them up, saith the Lord of hosts, that it shall leave neither root nor branch"!

V. End of the World

THIS was "the coming of the great and dreadful day of the Lord" (Mal. 4:5)!

THIS was "the end" of which Jesus spoke when He said: "Then shall the end come," and the time of which He said: "Let them which be in Judea, flee into the mountains" (Matt. 24:14 and 16)!

THIS was the calamity of which Paul was warning when he said: "Brethren, the time is short" (I Cor. 7:29)!

THIS was "the end" of which Peter warned when he said: "But the end of all things is at hand" (I Peter 4:7)!

THIS was when "the former things [the age of the Old Covenant and all that pertained to it] . . . passed away" (Rev. 21:4)!

THIS was the Judgment of which Jesus spoke when He said: "Ye serpents, ye generation of vipers, how can ye escape the damnation of hell [Gehenna]" (Matt. 23:33)?

The list could go on and on and on! I would venture to say that nearly every time "the end" is mentioned in the New Testament it refers to this same end—the end of the world of old Israel, the Jews, and all that pertained to them. **What a personal revelation this was for me, when I came to see that this was the biblical End of the World!** I hope it will be the same for you! The Bible makes more sense now! It all fits and comes together much better! But, I am still studying and learning. I hope my book will inspire you to do the same!

So, II Peter 3:10 is all about the Judgment and wrath of God upon His Old Covenant people for having forsaken Him! The "heavens and earth" that were "burned up" were the world of those Old Covenant people. It is not about our day and time at all! The Bible never mentions the end of time! It never teaches the end of our planet Earth and the beautiful, glorious, and awesome natural heavens that surround us!

With the spread of nuclear weapons today, who knows what some foolish person may do in the future to damage our wonderful Earth? Just remember if that should occur, it will not be in fulfillment of any Bible prophecy and it will not be a biblical sign of any event about to happen in our day! In our Good Book neither prophecies nor signs are waiting to be fulfilled today! Like the Last Days and like the End of the World, they are all yesterday's news—they are all history!

In this book we are searching for the answer to the question, **"When does the Bible say Jesus would come again?"** We have our answer:

1. The Bible plainly teaches and virtually all Christians believe Jesus was going to return at the End of the World.
2. But we have learned that this biblical End of the World has already occurred! It came in the first century, in the days and times of the early church.
3. So in order for Jesus to come at the End of the World, He had to return in that first century AD.

Does this surprise you? You should not be shocked! The first century is exactly the time Jesus said He was coming, both in the Gospels and in Revelation! **THE HARMONY OF THE BIBLE IS AWESOME!** Praise His name! Keep reading! All of this will keep getting clearer and clearer!

VI

THE JUDGMENT

We associate the Last Days and the End of the World with the time of the Second Coming of Jesus. This is a correct association! When we locate the time of these two events, we will find "when" Jesus came back or will come back! In the previous two chapters we learned that these two events occurred in the first century AD. We saw that Jesus had to return at that same time in order to come when He said He would! If He did not return in that time period, then He was a false prophet, and you and I can forget about His being the pure Son of God! But He was not a false prophet and I believe He returned exactly "when" He had promised!

We also associate the Judgment with the time of the coming of the Lord, and I believe this also is a correct association. If we can know when the Judgment was, or is going to be, then we can know "when" Jesus returned or is going to return.

The church teaches that at some point yet in our future, Jesus will finally make His second appearance. At that time, all people who have ever lived on Earth will stand before God to be judged. Judgment will be based not on what God knows about us, but on what is found written about us in a record book of our lives. The good people will be there and the bad too! Those of us still living at that time will be there. The multiplied billions of people who have lived and died since creation, will be resurrected back to life and they will be there as well. Somewhere I have read that if everyone who ever lived was alive at one time, we would all be standing seven persons deep, one on top of the other and covering the whole planet. I cannot say whether that is a true assessment of the situation. However, the number of people who have lived on Earth staggers my wildest imagination.

How many thousands of years do you suppose it would take to read from the record book all the deeds everybody has ever done? And can you even imagine how huge such a record book would be? How long would it take to make individual decisions on whether each person is innocent or guilty? But the Christian church teaches that this is what will happen at the Judgment and we are all going to be there to hear our fate! God will decide whether we are saved or lost. The lost He will send into eternal, never-ending torture in a place called hell. The saved He will welcome to heaven for eternity. This is all very bizarre! It is a wonder we can get any thinking person to believe and convert to Christianity!

But that is not all! The church teaches that when we die, immediately our "immortal soul" (a term not found in the Bible) goes to heaven if we have believed in Jesus. It goes to hell if we did not believe in Him. Then, in the future at Jesus' Second Coming, our long decayed natural bodies will be resurrected. Our "immortal souls" will leave heaven and hell, and enter our bodies again. Then the judging described in the preceding paragraph begins. How can Christians believe such a scenario? Our God is a reasonable God, and this totally lacks sanity! Think about this! A person who died and went to heaven 500 years before Christ returns, has now got to come back from heaven, stand before God and be judged. Why? Was he sent to heaven in error? Could he end up in the other place? This makes absolutely no sense at all! It appears that a person who has been in hell for 1,000 years will get a break! He will come back to stand and be judged. Why? Was some mistake made when he died? Should he not have been sent to hell? Might he now get to go to heaven, instead of being sent back to hell? What a dilemma Christianity has created for itself!

I have readily admitted to being wrong about many things, but thank God I never did believe these totally unreasonable and unbiblical Judgment Day doctrines taught by the Christian church! How can anyone believe such? It is probably because most Christians have never stopped and really thought about it. Any reasonable, thinking person can easily see real problems here! Let us see if we can find some plausible answers.

VI. The Judgment

When we read the word "judgment" and the words "the judgment" in the New Testament, of what is the writer speaking? As I have already revealed in our studies of the Last Days and the End of the World, I believe the final destruction of Jerusalem in AD 70 was the time of the Judgment of which Christ and His apostles spoke so often. Quite honestly, I never quite understood these references to the Judgment in the New Testament until I came to realize that most of these Scriptures were speaking of the impending, catastrophic Judgment soon to come upon the Jewish nation. Then, and only then, did the Judgment passages begin to come together and make sense to me. Judgment Day was coming in the Last Days at the End of the World. We have seen that the Last Days and the End of the World are both history. Therefore, the Judgment must be history too, and it is! Let us begin our study!

After what you have already read so far, I hope you are beginning to understand what was happening in the days of the New Testament. The old age of Moses was ending and the new age of Christ was beginning. Jesus came in final and complete fulfillment of all of the types and shadows of the Law. He died for the sins of man, perfectly fulfilling the type of all the animal sacrifices under the old Law. Jesus brought that Law to its end, not by destroying it but by fulfilling it.

Jesus came as a Savior to those who would believe and become His followers. But in stark contrast to that, He came as a Judge to those who would not believe in and accept Him as their Messiah. Like the role of being their Savior, His role of being their Judge had been prophesied many times in the Old Testament. While He was the Savior of some, He was the Judge who executed the wrath and fury of God upon others.

You know of the utter frustration that God experienced with His chosen people, Israel. They were continually disobeying His Law, forsaking Him, and going after other gods. He sent them prophets, whom they ignored, mistreated, and even killed. Because of this, hundreds of years before Christ, God sent most of His people (the ten tribes) away into Assyrian captivity, from which they never returned as a nation. The balance of His people, called Judah, lived under almost constant captivity or occupation by foreign powers. Even when Christ was born, Judea was under the dominion of the Caesars and their Roman Empire. But God kept and maintained Judah in Jerusalem and Judea, until the prophesied Messiah was born of the tribe of Judah, as the Old Testament had predicted. Once Judah rejected His Son, as they had His prophets, God's patience and longsuffering were exhausted. This resulted in the Judgment, when the wrath of God was poured out on the land of Judea in the mid-60s to AD 70. Judah, the only remaining portion of the old nation of Israel, was utterly destroyed.

This destruction of the nation of Judah was the coming Judgment of which both the Old and New Testaments speak. It was the coming wrath of God so often mentioned. It was the coming "great and dreadful day of the Lord" of which Malachi prophesied (4:5).

Some 400 years before Christ, Malachi was a prophet of doom. His book is a record of God's accusations against His people for all their sins and wrongs. They questioned and rejected His charges, saying things like, "Wherein have we wearied Him?" and "Wherein have we robbed Thee?" (2:17, 3:8). Malachi ended his book by prophesying the coming Judgment:

> For, behold the day cometh, that shall burn as an oven; and all the proud, yea, and all that do wickedly, shall be stubble: and the day that cometh shall burn them up, saith the Lord of hosts, that it shall leave them neither root nor branch. (Mal. 4:1)

As we shall come to see, this verse is a prophecy of the coming destruction of Judah. But our God, always a God of mercy, said in the next verse, Malachi 4:2, "But unto you that fear My name shall the Sun of Righteousness arise with healing in His wings." This latter verse is a prophecy of Jesus' coming and providing escape for those who would believe. In 4:4 God continued to offer a way out: "Remember ye the law of Moses." In 4:5 He promised, before this awful day, to send them one more prophet, Elijah, in hope of turning their hearts back to Him:

> Behold, I will send you Elijah the prophet before the coming of the great and dreadful day of the Lord. (Mal. 4:5)

VI. The Judgment

This "great and dreadful day of the Lord" is the same day as described in verse 1: "The day that cometh shall burn them up . . . that it shall leave them neither root nor branch." What an awful way for the Old Testament to end, with God fed up with the sins of His chosen people, and promising a horrible, coming Judgment Day.

Although about 400 years elapsed from Malachi to Matthew, the story picks up in the New Testament exactly where it left off in the Old. John the Baptist came preaching repentance and Jesus said of him: "He is Elijah who is to come" (Matt. 11:14 NKJV), fulfilling Malachi's prophecy in Malachi 4:5, above. As did Malachi, John the Baptist offered hope through repentance. Otherwise, he preached the same Judgment message as Malachi:

> But when he saw many of the Pharisees and Sadducees come to his baptism, he said unto them, "O generation of vipers, who hath warned you to flee the wrath to come? (*mello*, about to come, Matt. 3:7)

This was the same "wrath" Malachi had prophesied. It was more than 400 years in the future when Malachi predicted it; but by the time John came on the scene it was only forty or so years away, and "about to come" (*mello*). John continued using some of Malachi's same words: "The axe is laid unto the root of the trees," and "he will burn up the chaff with unquenchable fire" (Matt. 3:10, 12; Mal. 4:1). All of these words are prophecies of the coming Judgment of God upon the land of Judah, that "great and dreadful day of the Lord."

God had promised through Malachi (4:5) that He would send one more prophet **BEFORE** this "dreadful" Day of Judgment. As we saw in Matthew 11:14, Jesus identified John the Baptist as that prophet (Elijah). So if the coming of this prophet (John the Baptist) was to be before Judgment Day, once he came that day must not have been very far away! And it was not, as we have already learned. That is why John spoke of it, in verse 3 above, as "the wrath about to come." Within about forty years, "the great and dreadful day of the Lord" came upon the land. God cut down the mighty "trees" of Judah (Matt. 3:10)! He burned them up like "stubble" (Mal. 4:1) and like "chaff" (Matt.

3:12)! This is the same imagery Jesus used in the parable of the wheat and the tares in Matthew 13:40! Remember the tares were "gathered and burned in the fire." It is the same imagery Peter used in II Peter 3:10-12! Again, remember Peter said the heavens would dissolve and the earth would be "burned up." **All these verses are about Judgment Day, the coming desolation of Judah and the land of Judea!**

For many years I preached that this Day of the Lord had not yet come. I declared it could come any day! How mistaken I was! Think about this. John the Baptist (Elijah) was coming **BEFORE** this terrible day. If 2,000 years later this Judgment Day has not come, then John's coming was totally unrelated to the coming of the great day! What kind of sign is that to give as a warning to the people? It is no sign at all if 2,000 years later Judgment Day has not come! But as we have learned, the day did come in a matter of a few decades. So it can be truthfully said that John did come before the Judgment Day. And he appeared on the scene near enough to that day for his appearance to be relevant.

Another event was also prophesied to occur before this horrible Judgment Day arrived. The prophecy is in Joel 2:28-32, which we looked at in our study of the Last Days. Among other things, Joel quoted God as saying:

> I will pour out my spirit upon all flesh. (Joel 2:28)
> Before the great and terrible day of the Lord come. (2:31)

On the day of Pentecost, as we have seen, Peter used this text from Joel in his preaching (Acts 2:14-21). Peter said to the people, regarding the strange things they were seeing and hearing:

> But this is that which was spoken by the prophet Joel. (Acts 2:16)

Thus Peter plainly stated that Joel's prophecy of the outpouring of God's spirit was being fulfilled on that Pentecost day. Peter quoted Joel and said: "This is that!" Peter stated emphatically that Joel's prophecies were being fulfilled! This coming of the Spirit, along with the other wonders about which Joel prophesied, was to occur **before** "that great and notable day of the Lord come" (Acts 2:20).

VI. The Judgment

First we had God's promise to send "Elijah," John the Baptist, **BEFORE** that great day. Now we have another promise by God to "pour out my Spirit," "Before the great and terrible day of the Lord come." And Peter declared to the mockers that what happened at Pentecost was indeed the pouring out of the Spirit of which Joel prophesied. So, if this outpouring of the Spirit was coming **BEFORE** "the great day," then that great Day of Judgment could not be very far away from Pentecost. And it was not! Within forty years of Pentecost Judea and Jerusalem lay in ruins!

Many times I have preached about Pentecost and the outpouring of the Spirit. I talked about how this was all to happen before the Lord would come back and judge the world. I said this "great and terrible day of the Lord" could happen any day. How wrong I was, at least with my timing! The Spirit was indeed to come **BEFORE** "the great and terrible day of the Lord." But if 2,000 years later that great Judgment Day has not yet come, what kind of sign is that? It is no sign at all! The coming of the Spirit at Pentecost becomes totally irrelevant to the coming of that great day.

But (1) the coming of John the Baptist and (2) the coming of the Holy Spirit on the day of Pentecost **were each relevant** to the coming of the great Judgment Day. These two events, prophesied hundreds of years earlier, both came to pass within a few years of each other, and they came to pass in the days of Jesus and His apostles. These two events were to precede the coming of that Judgment Day, and they did! Within forty-some years of both events, the Roman armies killed or captured the people of Judah, destroyed the land of Judea, and burned down Jerusalem and the temple.

This utter annihilation of the land and nation of Judah, suffering the great wrath of its God, was the biblical Judgment Day! It is that to which a multitude of Scriptures refer:

> It was when Malachi's prophecy came to pass, "the day cometh that shall burn as an oven," when the wicked were as "stubble" and God would "burn them up," and "leave them neither root nor branch" (Mal. 4:1).

It was "the great and dreadful day of the Lord" (Mal.4:5).

It was "the great and terrible day of the Lord" (Joel 2:31).

It was "that great and notable day of the Lord" (Acts 2:20).

It was when the tares were "gathered and burned in the fire" (Matt. 13:40).

It was when these words of Jesus were fulfilled: "All these things shall come upon this generation," "Behold your house is left unto you desolate," and when "all the righteous blood shed upon the earth" was avenged by the Almighty (Matt. 23:33-38)!

It was when "the elements" melted, when "heaven and earth" passed away and all the works therein "burned up" (Matt. 24:35, II Peter 3:10).

These were "the days of vengeance, that all things written [ALL THE OLD TESTAMENT PROPHECIES] may be fulfilled" (Luke 21:22).

This was "when the Lord Jesus" was "revealed from heaven with His mighty angels in flaming fire taking vengeance on them that know not God and obey not the gospel of our Lord Jesus Christ" (II Thess. 3:7-8).

These were the days to which Jesus referred, when He spoke to the weeping women following Him to Calvary: "Daughters of Jerusalem, weep not for me, but weep for yourselves, and for your children. For behold the days are coming, in which they shall say, Blessed are the barren . . . and the paps which never gave suck" (Luke 23:28-29).

VI. The Judgment

Then was fulfilled another prophecy of Jesus: "For the days shall come upon thee, that thine enemies shall cast a trench about thee, and compass thee round, and keep thee in on every side, and shall lay thee even with the ground, and thy children within thee; and they shall not leave in thee one stone upon another" (Luke 19:43-44).

This was the time of which Jesus prophesied: "Then shall they begin to say to the mountains, Fall on us; and to the hills, Cover us" (Luke 23:30).

Corresponding to Luke 23:30 above is the passage from Revelation 6:15-16: "And every free man, hid themselves in the dens and in the rocks of the mountains; and said to the mountains and rocks, Fall on us, and hide us."

This was also the time of Revelation 6:17: "For the great day of His wrath is come; and who shall be able to stand?"

And it was the time of Revelation 10:6 and 22:11, when it was **TOO LATE TO REPENT!** The Jewish nation had "time no longer" to accept their Messiah! He that was "unjust" and he that was "filthy" had to remain "unjust still" and "filthy still." God would "delay no longer" (NASB) in executing Judgment!

This list could go on for page after page! Even though we constantly hear some of these verses applied to us today, they all applied to the Jewish people of Jesus' day and to the soon coming "wrath of God" on them! These verses are not talking about us or anything in our future. **NOT ANY OF THEM!** This will become clearer as we continue our study.

What an emotional experience it was for me to see all these Scriptures come together. They speak of events, terrible beyond description, and I do not rejoice in the least that the people of Judea had to experience this wrath of God. However, it was wonderful to get a better understanding of where these passages fit in time and what they mean. It was a relief to know that these prophecies are all in the past and not events about to come in the future. I am very grateful to my Lord and to others who helped me! I pray that this picture is coming together for you too, and that the Scriptures are getting clearer and clearer.

But let us move on to other passages about the Judgment. Let us see if the apostles and other Bible writers believed the Judgment was nearby and about to occur in their day in that first century AD.

Earlier in our studies, we encountered the Greek word *mello,* and we are about to do so again. So before we go any further, I briefly interrupt our study of the Judgment. We must again take a quick look at this word *mello,* and try to get a basic understanding of it. This word, and its other forms, is used about 109 times by the New Testament writers. As we have already seen, the KJV translators often did not properly translate the word *mello* into English. This "error" happened so often that I am made to wonder if it was intentional, perhaps caused by the translators' own biases. When properly translated, *mello* changes the understanding and the sense of the timing of many passages.

Strong's Exhaustive Concordance of the Bible shows *mello* as word number 3195 in its Greek dictionary. *Mello* is defined as meaning "to be about to be, or to be about to do" something. It means "about to happen," "on the verge of," and "at the point of." In the following verses from the KJV, you can see how *mello* was used and what it means, when the translators **properly** translated it into English:

> And a certain centurion's servant, who was dear unto him, was sick, and ready to *[mello]* die. (Luke 7:2)

> When he heard that Jesus was come out of Judaea into Galilee, he went unto Him and besought Him that He would come down, and heal his son, for he was at the point of *[mello]* death. (John 4:47)

> Who seeing Peter and John about to *[mello]* go into the temple asked an alm. (Acts 3:3)

VI. The Judgment

And when Paul was now about to *[mello]* open his mouth, Gallio said unto the Jews. (Acts 18:14)

And as the Jews laid wait for him, as he was about to *[mello]* sail into Syria, he purposed to return through Macedonia. (Acts 20:3)

And upon the first day of the week, when the disciples came together to break bread, Paul preached unto them, ready to *[mello]* depart on the morrow. (Acts 20:7)

And when the seven days were almost *[mello]* ended, the Jews which were of Asia, when they saw him in the temple, stirred up all the people, and laid hands on him. (Acts 21:27)

As Moses was admonished of God when he was about to *[mello]* make the tabernacle: See, saith He, that thou make all things according to the pattern. (Heb. 8:5)

In all these verses where *mello* was used, it is easy to see that whatever was going to happen was on the verge of happening. We find no indication of much further delay. Whatever was to occur was near to occurring. The "servant" and the "son" were both near death! Go back and read each verse again. In every case, the event was "about to" happen!

This little study of *mello* is important to our search for "when" Jesus would return. We have already come across verses in the KJV that simply said some event "should" happen, but gave no indication as to when it should happen. A deeper look at these verses revealed that what the Bible really said was not simply that something "shall" happen; but, because *mello* was used, the Bible was saying that something was "about to" happen. This gives a whole different sense to the event. No longer do we understand that the event would occur sometime by and by; now we see that it was on the verge of occurring.

But it seems when *mello* was used by the Bible writers in regard to the nearness of end time events, the King James translators consistently did not include the proper sense of timing in their translation. As you have read in the examples above, when *mello* was used to indicate the nearness of other things, it was usually properly translated into English. Therefore, in the above verses we get the full meaning of what the writers wrote. We know the events were "ready," "almost," and "at the point of" happening.

So now let us get back to the Judgment. I have taken the position that "the great and terrible day of the Lord," the Judgment Day, was a first-century event. It was the time of Rome's war with Judah in the late 60s and ending in AD 70 with the destruction of Jerusalem. The Judgment, that "great and terrible day," was a matter between God and His chosen people. It has nothing to do with us today. It was all about "the wrath," "the vengeance," and "the justice" of God on Israel and Judah for having killed His prophets and crucified His Son. Upon THAT GENERATION came the wrath of God for "all the righteous blood shed upon the earth" (Matt. 23:31-36). It was indeed a great and terrible day! But it is not a day coming in our future; it is history, over and done!

As we have seen, (1) John the Baptist and (2) the outpouring of the Spirit on Pentecost were both to come **before** the "great and dreadful day of the Lord." This is exactly what happened. Within a few decades of these two events, the Lord came in harsh and everlasting vengeance on His people. We can find many more verses showing this same time frame for the Judgment. These passages portray the Judgment Day as being close by, near, and on the verge of coming in the days of the apostles. Let us look at a few. The following verses contain the word *mello* too. However, the word is **not properly** translated in the KJV. So to help us get the correct sense of timing in these verses, I have shown two versions of each verse. The **first** presentation of each verse is the KJV rendering. The **second** is the English translation opposite the original Greek in *The Emphatic Diaglott*. This English version gives us the true sense of each verse. We can easily see that the Judgment was "ready" and "at the point of" occurring! In each of the second verses, the bold letters are my own emphasis to help us see the true sense of timing:

> He said unto them, O generation of vipers, who hath warned you to flee from the wrath to come? (Matt. 3:7).
> "Who has admonished you to fly from the **approaching vengeance**?"

VI. The Judgment

Because He hath appointed a day, in the which He will judge the world in righteousness by that Man whom He hath ordained. (Acts 17:31)
Because He has established a day in which He is **about to judge** the habitable in Righteousness, by a Man whom He has appointed.

Then said Paul unto him [the high priest], God shall smite thee, thou whited wall. (Acts 23:3)
Then Paul said to him, God **is about to strike** thee.

And as he reasoned of righteousness, temperance, and judgment to come, Felix trembled, and answered, Go thy way for this time. (Acts 24:25)
And as he was discoursing concerning Justice, Self-government, and that judgment **about to come**, Felix being terrified answered.

I charge thee therefore before God, and the Lord Jesus Christ, who shall judge the quick and the dead at His appearing and in His kingdom. (II Tim. 4:1)
I adjure thee before that God and Christ Jesus who is **about to judge** the living and the dead, and by His appearing and by His kingdom.

But a certain fearful looking for of judgment and fiery indignation, which shall devour the adversaries. (Heb. 10:27)
But some terrible expectation of judgment, even of a fiery indignation which is **about to consume** the opponents.

What more biblical proof do we need? Can you see that the Judgment was close in the days of the apostles? **Every one of these verses tells us that Judgment Day was near and on the verge of beginning.**

But other verses do not involve *mello* and they, too, declare that Judgment Day was nearby! Here is what James said:

Behold, the Judge standeth before the door. (James 5:9)

What a statement! The Judgment was about to begin! Jesus was standing before the door, ready to start judging! If the Judgment is still in the future, He has been standing there nearly 2,000 years! But Jesus was about to come and execute Judgment THEN! In the verse before this one (5:8), James said: "for the coming of the Lord draweth nigh." How very clear this is! Can you see it? James answered our question, "When was Jesus coming?" James said His coming was drawing "nigh," and that was 2,000 years ago! As the Judge, He was standing at "the door," ready to go! What a revelation? How many times I have misused these verses. Thank God for this second chance for me to get them right!

Listen to Peter:

> Who shall give account to Him that is ready to judge the quick and the dead. (I Peter 4:5)
> But the end of all things is at hand. (I Peter 4:7)
> For the time has come for judgment to begin at the house of God. (I Peter 4:17 NKJV)

What more needs to be said? The Judge was "ready"! "The end" was "at hand"! The time had come FOR JUDGMENT TO BEGIN at the house of God, which was the temple in Jerusalem! It was time for the start of the catastrophe that was the "wrath" of God! It was time for the beginning of "the great and terrible day of the Lord"! Do you see this? Is it getting plainer to you? I do pray so!

In II Peter 3:3, Peter talks about the "scoffers" and mockers who belittled this coming Judgment Day. They said, in effect, that it had been prophesied a long, long time ago and still had not come to pass. But as we have seen, it was now "about to" come! This is that to which Peter was referring when he said in the previous chapter: "for a long time their judgment has not been idle, and their destruction does not slumber" (II Peter 2:3 NKJV). Yes, the Judgment had been prophesied hundreds of years earlier, and for centuries it had lain dormant. But now that the Last Days had arrived, now that "Elijah" had come, and now that the "Spirit" had been poured out, "their judgment" was no longer "idle." Their prophesied destruction was no longer sleeping. Now it was

VI. The Judgment

awakening like a tremendous giant, and soon the wrath of God would fall upon the land of Judah and the nation of the Jews. What a sad and awful time it was, not only in the history of Israel but also in the history of the whole world.

The author of the letter to these Hebrews described well the terrifying circumstance that was about to befall their land!

> For we know Him that hath said, Vengeance belongeth unto me, I will recompense, saith the Lord. And again, The Lord shall judge His people. It is a fearful thing to fall into the hands of the living God. (Heb. 10:30-31)

This was about to happen to Judah! They were about "to fall into the hands" of a God whose "longsuffering" and patience were exhausted! They had filled up "the measure" of their fathers' sins (Matt. 23:32)! Their God could take no more! It was near the time of Revelation 10:6: "that there should be time [delay] no longer." The fulfilling of Revelation 22:11 was at hand: "He that is unjust, let him be unjust still." God had almost given up on His people, and soon would do so. Please note that these two verses above, Hebrews 10:30-31, follow right behind a verse we saw earlier, verse 27, which said that all of this was **about to occur!** The Judge was standing at "the door." "The end of all things" pertaining to the house of Judah was "at hand." What a horrible, dreadful time it was for the Jewish people! "It is a fearful thing to fall into the hands of the living God" (Heb. 10:31).

Most of our knowledge about the sufferings of the Jews during the siege and fall of Jerusalem comes from the writings of **Flavius Josephus,** who was a Jewish general who fought against the Romans but was captured in July of AD 67. He made a most unlikely prophecy that his captor, the Roman general, Vespasian, would one day become the Emperor of the Roman Empire. The prophecy seemed most unlikely because Vespasian lacked a proper Roman nobility pedigree. Nevertheless, about two years after the Emperor Nero's suicide, Vespasian did become the Emperor. Impressed, Vespasian freed Josephus, granted him Roman citizenship, adopted him into his family (the Flavians), and commissioned him to write a history of the Jewish people.[iii]

Josephus' first work was ***The Wars of the Jews.*** When Vespasian's son, Titus, led the Roman legions back to Jerusalem for the final campaign, Josephus went with him. This enabled Josephus to have firsthand knowledge of the last years of the war, the burning of the city, and the destruction of the temple.[iv] Josephus went around the city wall, trying to persuade his people to surrender. They would not, so he personally witnessed and chronicled what it was like "to fall into the hands of the living God" (Heb. 10:31).

Josephus tells us of the starvation of the people. The Jews had sufficient corn for many years, but they fought among themselves and ended up burning their own corn supply.[v] They robbed and killed one another by the most brutal means. They did as much harm to themselves as did the Romans.[vi] Dead bodies were everywhere in the city, so that people could not walk without stepping on them. At first they buried the dead, then they piled them in houses and shut the doors, and then they threw thousands upon thousands of them over the wall of the city into the valleys below.[vii] Josephus gave the following account of Titus:

> However, when Titus, in going his rounds along those valleys saw them full of dead bodies, and the thick putrefaction running about them, he gave a groan; and spreading out his hands to heaven, called God to witness that this was not his doing: and such was the sad case of the city itself.[viii]

These valleys full of dead bodies, and the Judgment they represented, are what Jesus was referring to in Matthew 23:33 when He said: "Ye serpents, ye generation of vipers, how can ye escape the damnation of hell?" The word "hell" is an improper KJV translation! Jesus DID NOT use a Greek word that means what our English word "hell" means today. He said, *"Gehenna,"* which in English means "the valley of Hinnom," NOT HELL! Hinnom was one of the valleys surrounding Jerusalem, and that valley became full of dead bodies. Jesus was saying that this "generation of vipers" would not escape "the damnation of the valley of Hinnom." **The original Greek text reads,** "how can you flee from the judgment of Gehenna?" *Gehenna*, like Jerusalem or Bethel, is a proper name; and like other proper names in the Bible, it should never have been translated. These words in Matthew 23:33 were spoken in connection with the other verses in Matthew 23 and 24 regarding the coming destruction of

VI. The Judgment

Jerusalem. They have nothing at all to do with "hell" as it is taught by the Christian church! The topic of "hell" would require another book. But let me just say, Jesus was not teaching eternal torture, but was prophesying the horrible Judgment coming upon that "generation" (Matt. 23:36). And it came to pass just as Jesus had said! They did not escape the horrors of the valley of Hinnom and the Judgment of which He spoke!

Josephus told of a mother "snatching up her son, who was a child sucking at her breast." She then "slew her son," and "roasted him, and ate the one half of him" and hid the rest for later. He said, "Those distressed by the famine were very desirous to die; and those already dead were esteemed happy." In their "terrible distress," they searched "the common sewers and old dung-hills of cattle," and ate "the dung which they got there; and what they of old could not so much as endure to see, they now used for food."[ix]

Meanwhile, outside the city, the soldiers caught more than 500 people every day, trying to escape. These were crucified in huge numbers. According to Josephus, "their multitude was so great, that room was wanting for the crosses, and crosses wanting for the bodies."[x] We can hardly fathom such horrors!

Josephus concluded, "That neither did any other city ever suffer such miseries, nor did any age ever breed a generation [Jesus' generation] more fruitful in wickedness than this was, from the beginning of the world."[xi] He said, "Those carried away captive" numbered 97,000 and "those that perished" were 1,100,000![xii] The number of people in Jerusalem was much greater than normal because multitudes of Jews had come to the city for the Passover, just in time to be entrapped when the Romans began their siege.

We have looked briefly at "the wrath of God" that befell the Jewish people. Whole books have been written on this subject. We wanted to give you a little idea about what the Judgment on Judah, Judea, and Jerusalem was like.

This was the "great tribulation" that Jesus predicted in Matthew 24:16-21, Mark 13:19 and Luke 21:21-24. This tribulation prophecy followed immediately after this verse: "And when ye shall see Jerusalem compassed with armies, then know that the desolation thereof is nigh" (Luke 21:20). The very next words Jesus spoke were, "Then," **not thousands of years later—but THEN,** the people would endure "great distress in the land." These great tribulations were going to come in those days, on that "land," during the time of the Jews' war with Rome. I repeat, Jesus said, "Then," not today, would come "great tribulation." As you have read briefly from Josephus' accounts, great tribulations did come: "neither did any city ever suffer such miseries." This horrible time of suffering by the Jewish people was the period of the "great tribulation," and part of the Judgment of God on Judah.

This, of course, is opposite from everything you and I hear preached today. We often hear prophecies of the soon coming "great tribulation" in our day. Jesus plainly said that the "great tribulation" would occur when Jerusalem was "compassed with armies" (Matt. 24:15-21, Mark 13:14-19, Luke 21:20-24). That happened nearly 2,000 years ago! So we can stop worrying—the "great tribulation" is history! It was all about the wrath and Judgment of God on His people and it has nothing to do with us today. **NOTHING!** Jesus made that perfectly clear. After He had made the prophecy of the "great tribulation," He said: "Verily I say unto you, This generation shall not pass, till all these things be fulfilled" (Matt. 24:34). Mark 13:30 and Luke 21:30 say the same thing! Do not be misled! **The "great tribulation" of the Bible is over and done!** It is history! It is neither about to occur in our day and time, NOR ANY DAY IN THE FUTURE!

When Jesus predicted this calamity in Matthew 23 and 24 and elsewhere, He also spoke of those faithful to Him, who would "flee into the mountains" (24:16) and thus be able to endure to "the end" and be saved. He said:

But he that shall endure unto the end shall be saved. (Matt. 24:13)

We must not forget that the Judgment Day was a time when both the good and the bad would be judged. It was the same day for both! This verse 13 declares that those followers of Jesus who were faithful during these years of persecution would be saved from all this "wrath" of God. He had also promised, in Matthew 16:27-28, that He would come again while some of the original

VI. The Judgment

disciples were still living. He promised that upon His return He would "reward every man according to his works." Remember, this Day of the Lord was not only "terrible," it was also "great." For those suffering saints of God, who had been faithful and true to Jesus, Judgment Day was a "great" day!

The saints had already done their suffering at the hands of their persecutors, who were mainly the Jews but for a while the Romans too. They welcomed Judgment Day! They would get relief from their adversaries, as the following verses promised:

> And the God of peace will crush Satan [the Jews, who were the Christians' adversaries] under your feet shortly [at the Judgment, AD 70]. (Rom. 16:20 NKJV)

> Judgment and fiery indignation which shall [*mello,* "is about to"] devour the adversaries [the Jews]. (Heb. 10:27)

> God is just: He will pay back trouble to those [their persecutors, the Jews] who trouble you and give relief to you [the church] who are troubled, and to us [the apostle Paul] as well. This will happen when the Lord Jesus is revealed from heaven . . . on the day [by AD 70] He comes to be glorified. (II Thess. 1:6-10 NIV)

The nation of Judah had rejected their Messiah. Yet they were still looking for their God to come and deliver them from their enemies, the Romans. He had indeed delivered them many times before, but He would not do so this time! His patience and longsuffering had been exhausted. Their time was up! The time for their final Judgment had come. I repeat—it was the time of Revelation 10:6, "that there should be time [delay] no longer." For the nation as a whole, the Day of the Lord came "as a thief in the night." While the "scoffers" were saying "Peace and safety; then sudden destruction" came upon the land (I Thess. 5:2-3). On the other hand, the coming destruction did not catch the church unaware or unprepared, as the Scriptures attest:

> But ye, brethren, are not in darkness, that that day should overtake you as a thief. (I Thess. 5:4)

The church would not have to endure the wrath of God on Judgment Day. They had been faithful to the end and were promised salvation, not wrath. The believers that followed Jesus' advice (Matt. 24:16-20) would have fled Jerusalem and Judea while it was still possible to get out. These faithful believers would miss this "wrath of God," as these verses say:

> And to wait for His Son from heaven, whom He raised from the dead, even Jesus, which delivered us from the wrath to come. (I Thess.1:10)

> For God has not appointed us to wrath, but to obtain salvation by our Lord Jesus Christ. (I Thess. 5:9)

The church was: "Looking for and hasting unto the coming of the day of God" (II Peter 3:12). They had been promised good rewards. They were ardently anticipating what that day would hold for them. Here is a partial list of what they were expecting:

> The old "heaven and earth," the age of Moses and the Law, would pass away (Heb. 8:13), and in its place they were looking for "a new heavens and a new earth," the age of Christ and His grace (Isa. 65:17, II Peter 3:13).

> The faithful would be "receiving a kingdom which cannot be moved" (Heb. 12:28).

> The saints were looking for full and complete redemption, for their "salvation was nearer than when" they had first believed on Jesus, and their salvation was "ready to be revealed in the last time" (Rom. 13:11, I Peter 1:5).

> They were expecting to "be changed" (I Cor. 15:51-52).

VI. The Judgment

The church had been engaged to marry, and they were eagerly anticipating being presented "as a chaste virgin to Christ" (II Cor. 11:2).

They were looking to receive a "crown of righteousness" (II Tim. 4:8).

They were looking to receive "eternal life" (I John 2:25).

They were looking to "be like Him" (I John 3:2).

The saints were expecting to "ever be with the Lord" (I Thess. 4:17)!

In the following passages, consider the "glory" the saints were expecting, and how near they were to receiving it:

> For I reckon that the sufferings of this present time are not worthy to be compared with the glory which shall be revealed in us [*mello*, "about to be revealed in us"]. (Rom. 8:18)

> The elders which are among you I exhort, who am also an elder, and a witness of the sufferings of Christ, and also a partaker of the glory that shall be revealed [*mello*, "about to be revealed"]. (I Peter 5:1)

> And when the Chief Shepherd shall appear, ye shall receive a crown of glory that fadeth not away. (I Peter 5:4)

> When Christ, who is our life, shall appear, then shall ye also appear with Him in glory. (Col. 3:4)

The list could go on and on! A full understanding of the nature of these rewards is a subject for another time, but it is no wonder that those early saints were "Looking for and hasting unto the coming of the day of God" (II Peter 3:12). We find much in the New Testament about what the church was anticipating when Jesus returned on that "great and terrible day of the Lord," Judgment Day! Jesus certainly had promised to return with rewards for His people while some of those first believers were still living (Matt. 16:27-28). I believe He did! I hope you, too, are coming to believe that He did! **Otherwise, we can forget about putting any trust in any of His promises!**

I have not begun to exhaust the Scriptures about the Judgment, or come to thoroughly understand them all. But I have spent more time on the subject than I had anticipated. I did so because understanding "when" the Judgment came is vital to our understanding "when Jesus would come again." As I said in the second paragraph of this chapter, we all believe Jesus was coming on Judgment Day. Well, we have just learned that Judgment Day came in the first century AD, so Jesus came then too! Again, this agrees with **everything** else we have seen so far. THE HARMONY OF THE SCRIPTURES IS A BEAUTIFUL THING!

I hope that you have, at the least, a good overview of what the Judgment was all about and "when" it occurred! It is very important that we understand that the New Testament was a time of the fulfilling of the Old Testament. It was a time when **ALL** of the yet unfulfilled Old Testament prophecies came to pass! Jesus had said: "For these be the days of vengeance, that all things which are written may be fulfilled" (Luke 21:22). These "days of vengeance" were the times about which we have been studying, the mid-60s to AD 70. This was the time of the "great tribulation." The Jews suffered horrible troubles, first from one another and then finally from the Romans. But it had all been prophesied by God's prophets and His Son. The coming of the Judgment, that "great and terrible day of the Lord" (Joel 2:31), was among those prophecies. It too was fulfilled! The Judgment has nothing to do with us today in the twenty-first century! That "great and dreadful day of the Lord" (Mal. 4:5) has come and gone, centuries and centuries ago! **Like the Last Days and the End of the World, the Judgment is also history!**

But do not forget that Judgment Day had a brighter side. Remember that along with the terrible prophecies came the wonderful promise of Malachi 4:2: "But unto you that fear My name shall the Sun of Righteousness arise with healing in His wings." Also remember Joel's marvelous promise: "And it shall come to pass, that whosoever shall call on the name of the Lord shall be

VI. The Judgment

delivered" (2:32). And then recall the promises of the Savior recorded by Luke in the same chapter where we saw the "vengeance" and "wrath":

> And when these things begin to come to pass, then look up, and lift up your heads; for your redemption draweth nigh. (Luke 21:28)

> So likewise ye, when ye see these things come to pass, know ye that the kingdom of God is nigh at hand. (Luke 21:31)

In the midst of all the horrors and turmoil, the Sun of Righteousness, Jesus the Son, came the second time, and whosoever believed in Him was delivered from the terrors of that day and given eternal redemption! **PRAISE HIS NAME!**

After spending most of my life not understanding the Judgment, and always expecting at any moment the coming of "the great and notable day of the Lord" (Acts 2:20), what a miraculous and amazing revelation it has been for me to see this light! I hope and trust that it will be the same for you! As I indicated earlier, I do not understand or grasp it all. I am still studying and praying. I invite you, I beg you, to please join me!

SUMMARY OF CHAPTERS IV, V, and VI

What you have read as we have looked at the subjects of study in the last three chapters may have been surprising to you. Almost everything was different from what we hear preached regularly in our world today. I am made to wonder how Christian doctrine could get so far off the true path. But, then I realized that I preached wrong doctrines for nearly all my life too! As I reflect on my own experiences, these reasons come to mind:

1. We all tend to accept the traditions we inherit.
2. We all tend to completely trust the good, honest, and faithful Christians who teach us.
3. We all hesitate to question the well-educated leaders in our lives.
4. We never give any thoughts to the possibility that what we believe may be wrong.
5. We all do not study our Bibles for ourselves as we should.
6. When we do study, usually we are trying to prove that what we believe is the truth, instead of trying to listen to what the Scriptures actually say!

This results in doctrinal errors, which get perpetuated and handed down from one generation to the next. But today we are seeing many eyes opened to the truth in this book. Hopefully, a revolution in biblical understanding of eschatology is presently underway! Eschatology, again, is the study of last things, the things we are considering in this book.

The **Last Days,** as we have learned, were in the days of Jesus and His apostles. Peter and the author of Hebrews specifically and plainly said so! The Last Days began and ended in the first century AD. When the end was very near the apostle John stopped referring to the time they were in as the Last Days and instead spoke of it as being "the last hour."

We learned that the Last Days referred to things that were in their last days of existence and in the process of passing away. Those things, we saw, had to do with the old nation of Israel. **All of their physical things** were in their

VI. The Judgment

final days of existence: their holy city, their holy temple, their nation, their government, and their way of life. **All of their spiritual things** were likewise in their final days and dying: their Old Covenant, their Law of Moses with all of its rules and rituals, their priesthood with all of its ceremonies, and their being the true Israel of God because they were the natural children of Abraham.

We learned that the ending of old Israel was what the Last Days were all about! Nowhere did we find any grounds for believing that we, today in the twenty-first century, are living in the Last Days. **Nowhere!** The Last Days are over and done! They ended with old Israel's natural and religious destruction in AD 70.

In our look at "The End of the World," we learned that with proper translation, this phrase is not even in the Bible. When we do read it in the KJV, it means the end of the age, not the end of the natural earth and world. The time of the End of the World [Age] was specifically identified for us as the time of Jesus and His apostles. Hebrews 9:26 revealed to us that when Jesus died, He did so in the time of "the end of the world [age]." We saw that the Bible does not teach the end of our natural, physical world and Earth. Instead the Scripture teaches that our Earth abides forever. We further learned that the term "the end of time" is not in our KJV Bible and that the Bible never teaches us that time, as we know it, will end.

We found that the world of Judaism was in its closing days, and that this was the world, or age, that was coming to its end. That world of Moses and the prophets, known as "this age," was about to end. In the days of the New Testament that Old Covenant age was in its final days and "ready to vanish away" (Heb. 8:13). This world of the Old Covenant people was the "heaven and earth" that would pass away.

Finally, we looked at the **Judgment,** that "great and terrible day of the Lord." We saw that the arrival of John the Baptist and the coming of the Holy Spirit on Pentecost were both signs that the great day was near. The apostles declared its closeness and that it was "about to" occur. They further declared it was time for the Judgment to begin and that the Judge was standing at the door and ready to judge. We saw that by AD 70, God had executed Judgment upon the land of Judea. What remained of old Israel, the nation of Judah, was utterly destroyed. On the other hand, the faithful were "receiving a kingdom which cannot be moved" (Heb. 12:28). The coming of the Judgment brought to pass the last day of the Last Days and the End of the World [Age] of the Old Covenant, the Old Testament people, and the old nation of Israel! **The Judgment Day, the Last Days, and the End of the World are all history! They were all a part of the first century AD!**

All three of these subjects are inseparably linked together! I have spent a lot of time on them because understanding them is very important to properly understanding the Bible. As a result, I hope the New Testament will come alive with new meaning for you, as it did for me once I better understood what was going on in that first age of the church. We have learned that it was the time of the **Last Days**, a time of transition, when "this age," the age of Moses, was ending and "the age to come," the age of Messiah, was beginning. God's people did not accept their Messiah or His new age. Therefore, they incurred the **Judgment** of their God and His wrath fell upon them, bringing **their world to an end.** "But as many as received Him, to them gave He power to become the sons of God" (John 1:12). **This is the story of the New Testament!** I believe it would be safe to say that at least half of the New Testament is about these things! That is why this is very important!

I hope that reading my book is proving to be helpful to you and that it will move you to earnestly study these matters. Personally, I am still looking for a better understanding of all of these subjects. Again, I beg you to join me as I continue to search the Scriptures!

VII

WHEN DID THE APOSTLES SAY JESUS WAS COMING?

Christianity's Great Dilemma is about the conflict between what the church teaches about the Second Coming of Jesus and what the Bible actually says. We have seen quite a huge difference between the church and the Bible on this subject. This is the dilemma! The Bible is Christianity's Holy Book and the teachings of the church are supposed to come from its pages. It is disturbing to learn that the church's doctrines about the Second Coming of Jesus are totally opposed to what the Bible teaches. It is indeed a great dilemma! It is a dilemma desperately needing the attention of Christians everywhere so that it might be dealt with by our leaders and churches and quickly corrected.

The church teaches today, in the twenty-first century, that Jesus is coming back and He is coming back soon. It further declares that we are living in the Last Days and the End of the World is near! Thus far in our study, we have found **NOTHING** to support these teachings. We found that Jesus did promise on numerous occasions to return, but whenever He identified "when" He was coming, it was **ALWAYS** limited to the first century. **He never even hinted** that His coming might be 2,000 years or more in the future. What Jesus said when He talked about the timing of His return was:

> He would return during the time frame of God's judgments on the nation of Judah, which reached their climax in AD 70.

He would return during the generation of people to whom He preached while He was on Earth.

He would return while some of the people to whom He spoke were still living.

He would return while some of His apostles were still preaching and still fleeing from city to city because of persecution.

And in His words to the seven churches in Asia, He exhorted His followers to hold on a little longer and then, again and again, assured them that He would certainly be coming quickly!

How then can the church today say Jesus has not yet come, but He is coming very soon? Either Jesus lied to His followers and deceived them, or He came back over 1,900 years ago as He promised. **Again, this is the dilemma facing Christianity today!**

So now it is time for us to look at the men Jesus chose to be the founding fathers upon whose preaching, labor, and sacrifice He would build His church. He fully trusted them and left them in charge of His work on Earth. Did they preach what their Master taught them about His coming? Or, did they receive new revelations and conclude, as many have done today, that Jesus did not know what He was talking about and was simply wrong? Did they say anything that would justify the church's doctrine today that "Jesus is coming soon" in our day?

The only sources we have for trying to learn "when" the apostles believed and taught Jesus was coming are twenty-two books of the New Testament, Acts through the Epistles. The four Gospels and Revelation, which we have already studied, complete the total of twenty-seven books in the New Testament. In the previous three chapters about the Last Days, the End of the World, and the Judgment, I quoted many passages from Acts and from the Epistles. But in this chapter I want us to look at the writings of the apostles more closely, to see if we can find an answer to our question, **"When did the apostles say Jesus was coming?"**

VII. The Apostles

Even before we begin our search, we already know Bible scholars generally agree that the apostles and the early Christians were looking for Jesus to return during their lifetime. We find little disagreement among these scholars that the writings in the New Testament portray a sense of imminence in the church regarding the Lord's return. Even Christians who strongly oppose my position in this book, that Jesus has already come, still agree that the early church believed His return was imminent. I am made to wonder, if the imminent return of Jesus is this plainly revealed in the New Testament, why do not all Christians just believe and accept what the Scriptures say? Christians profess to believe the Bible! Where is everyone's faith and trust in Jesus on this issue?

This imminent expectation of Jesus' coming creates lots of other questions and problems for Christianity. Again, this is a great dilemma. **If the return of Jesus was imminent in the first century, it cannot also be imminent today in the twenty-first century.** Yet this is what is preached today by most of the ministry of His church. We are constantly told, "Jesus could come at any moment." If words are to have any meaning at all, then this just cannot be right. Nevertheless, the same preachers who say the Lord's coming is imminent today also say His coming was imminent nearly 2,000 years ago. Obviously something is wrong; we cannot have it both ways! I address this problem in the last chapter of this book.

I ask a question: "Where did the early church get the belief that Jesus would return soon?" Well, some of His first followers, who knew Jesus personally, could certainly have received the idea from Him. We know this is true from our study so far. The apostle Paul received it by direct revelation from God. Others who became a part of the church through those early years would have received this sense of imminence from the preaching and teaching of the apostles. Yet today, the church says Jesus did not come then, and still has not come nearly 2,000 years later. What does that make the apostles? The only answer is: they were just a bunch of false prophets. What a dilemma this presents, but what other conclusion can we honestly reach?

We could harshly condemn the Lord's chosen twelve men if, indeed, they misled the people. They would have been hypocrites and deceivers of the worst kind! Jesus had given these men the Holy Ghost and had promised that: "He will guide you into all truth" (John 16:13). But if the Lord did not come soon, as they declared He would, they were preaching lies instead of "truth." Jesus had further promised of the Holy Ghost: "And He will shew you things to come" (John 16:13). Well, they were preaching "things to come" all right, like the soon return of Jesus. The only problem is, their predictions did not come to pass if indeed Jesus failed to come back!

What a problem all of this is for Christianity! What a problem it is for Christians who honestly and sincerely love Jesus, who believe in Him, who believe His Word, and who are trying their best to be good followers. If the founding fathers of our Lord's church did not know what they were talking about, then all of Christianity is in big trouble. If the apostles were wrong about the imminent return of their Lord, what does that say about Jesus' own wisdom? He chose and commissioned them! What does it say about the Holy Ghost who was to guide, teach, and show these men the future? As we have said before, if they were wrong about this great and important doctrine, about what else might they be wrong? Can we trust anything they said? No, we cannot! We may as well discard our Bibles. God help us as we continue to search for the right answer to this grave dilemma.

Let us move on in our study as we search for an answer to our question about "when" the Bible says that Jesus would come again. We have considered the words of Jesus; we now turn to the words of His apostles, beginning with their leader, the man to whom Jesus gave the keys to the kingdom, the apostle Peter.

THE APOSTLE PETER

When did the apostle Peter say Jesus was coming? Let us look at his words preserved in the Bible and see if we can get any sense of what Peter believed and taught about "when" His Master would be returning.

I Peter 5:4

> And when the chief Shepherd shall appear, ye shall receive a crown of glory that fadeth not away.

This verse is not specific, but we can understand how the people would believe that they would still be alive when Jesus came back. The Bible often speaks of the "glory" awaiting the saints, when Jesus returned. Here it is called "a crown of glory." Note Peter did not tell them that Jesus would appear, they would be resurrected, and then they would receive their crown. The sense of his promise was that they would be alive when He appeared.

I Peter 5:1

> The elders which are among you I exhort, who am also an elder, and a witness of the sufferings of Christ, and also a partaker of the glory that shall be revealed.

This passage in the original Greek contains the Greek word *mello,* which means "about to," or "on the verge of." Properly translated it would read, "a partaker of the glory about to be revealed." The Greek text says, "the being about to be revealed glory." No wonder the saints to whom Peter wrote were expecting to be alive when Jesus came. If the "glory" they expected to receive when He appeared was "about to be revealed," **then His coming could not be too far away.**

Peter wrote this first Epistle in about AD 64-65. As we have learned from our studies, Jesus came in judgment by AD 70. That was just a few years away. It was Judgment Day and Jesus brought destruction and death to His enemies. But to His saints, He brought glory, "a crown of glory that fadeth not away." Peter promised the saints it was all "about to be revealed." We can understand why the church lived with such high expectations of His imminent return.

I Peter 4:5

Who shall give account to Him that is ready to judge the quick and the dead.

This verse was written at the same time as those above. Peter knew from the signs around him that Judgment Day was drawing near and that the Lord was "ready to judge." Thus the coming of Jesus, the Judge, could not be very far away.

I Peter 4:7

But the end of all things is at hand: be ye therefore sober, and watch unto prayer.

We have seen this verse before. We learned that Peter was not speaking of "all things" in our natural world. They are all still here after nearly 2,000 years. Peter spoke of the end of "all things" that made up the world of Judaism—an end that Peter knew was "at hand," and nearby. Jesus said He would come at "the end," so if "the end" was "at hand," **then His coming was at hand too.** In Matthew 24:14 Jesus said, "then shall the end come." Continuing in the same discourse in verse 30 He says, "Then [meaning when the end came] . . . they shall see the Son of Man coming in the clouds of heaven

VII. The Apostle Peter

with power and great glory." So the end of the age, which Peter said was "at hand," was also going to bring the "glorious appearing" of Jesus. **So Peter believed and taught, at this time in his life,** that "the end" was "at hand," and this meant His Master's return was "at hand" too.

Would you be surprised to learn that at one time in Peter's life he DID NOT preach "the end of all things is at hand," a time when he DID NOT preach "Jesus is coming soon"? It is true! One such instance happened just after Pentecost in AD 30, in Peter's second sermon (Acts 3:21), which we shall study next. Why would Peter have told the people the coming of the Lord was not near? It was because Peter knew many events had to occur first, before the Lord returned. Jesus had told him and the other apostles about these things (signs) in Matthew 24, Mark 13, and Luke 21. So Peter knew "the end" and "the coming of the Lord" were not nearby or at hand at that time (AD 30). So while he gave the people the promise, that the just-departed Jesus would return, he wanted them to understand that it would not be happening immediately.

In contrast, Peter's statement that we are considering now in I Peter 4:7 was made about thirty-five years later, around AD 65. By that time, Peter had seen many things happen, things Jesus had said must occur before He returned. And no doubt, he was watching other predicted events unfold right before his eyes. These "signs" being fulfilled, as Jesus had said they would be, made Peter know that Jesus' coming was drawing near. So thirty-five years after Jesus ascended, Peter wrote to the saints, "The end of all things is at hand." I hope you understand this! These are the same "signs" that today's prophets read about and then predict the soon coming of Jesus. But these "signs" have nothing to do with us today. They have already come and gone! **The Lord told Peter that ALL the signs would come to pass in Peter's own generation (Matt. 24:34).**

Acts 3: 19-21

Peter's second sermon is found in Acts 3. Peter and John had healed the lame man at the gate called Beautiful. An amazed and curious crowd gathered. Peter recognized a great opportunity to preach the Gospel, and did so. Here is a portion of his sermon:

19 Repent ye therefore, and be converted, that your sins may be blotted out, when the times of refreshing shall come from the presence of the Lord,
20 And He shall send Jesus Christ, which before was preached unto you,
21 Whom the heaven must receive until the times of restitution of all things, which God hath spoken by the mouth of all his holy prophets since the world began.

You see in verse 19, Peter called on the people to repent for having "killed the Prince of life" (verse 15). They had missed their Messiah the first time, but Peter said in verse 20 that God would "send" Him again. In verse 21 is where he told the people that Jesus was not coming back right then because something else must happen first. Just a few days earlier, Jesus had ascended into the heavens and a cloud had hidden Him from the sight of the apostles. Already Peter was promising that Jesus would come back, but he said, "the heaven must receive Him until the times of restitution of all things." Did you get that? Read verse 21 again! Peter has just told us when Jesus would be returning—**the heavens would keep Jesus UNTIL the times of restitution of all things arrived.** This is amazing information! If we could know when the "times of restitution" came, or will come, then we could know exactly when Jesus came, or will come.

I believe "the times of restitution," or "restoration" as it is translated in many versions, has to do with the ending of the Jewish age, the age of Moses, and the establishment of the age of the Messiah and His kingdom. As we have learned, this was accomplished by AD 70. This means sometime about AD 70 would have been the time that the "heaven' would have released Jesus to come again, as Peter had said.

"Restitution" has to do with making things right and restoring things to the way they should be. In the ending of the Mosaic age and the beginning of the Messianic age, making things right and restoring things to the way they should have been was what God was doing. "Restitution" has to do with justice. The Judgment leading up to and including AD 70, I believe, was the "times of

VII. The Apostle Peter

restitution." Jesus was making things right, administering justice: death and destruction for the guilty nation, and "a crown of glory that fadeth not away" (I Peter 5:4) for those who believed and followed Him. Jesus had promised that before all of His followers would die, He would "come in the glory of His Father with His angels" and "reward every man according to His works" (Matt. 16:27-28). This sounds like "restitution"! Indeed it was! It all happened in that "generation." At sometime around AD 70, "the heaven" that would "receive" Jesus "until the times of restitution" released Him and He returned, as He had promised.

While it may be difficult to satisfactorily show the exact time frame for "the times of restitution," it is easier to show that it is in the past and not in the future. Since Peter said the arrival of "the times of restitution" would signal the return of Jesus, if "the times of restitution" are in the past, then the Second Coming of Jesus is in the past too.

Peter said in verse 21, above, that the "times of restitution" had been foretold by "all His holy prophets." The ministers and churches with whom I have been privileged to have fellowship, have always believed that all the prophecies of the Old Testament prophets have already been fulfilled. I believed that too! Thus:

1. Since "the times of restitution" were prophesied by the prophets, and
2. Since their prophecies have all been fulfilled,
3. Then the prophesied "times of restitution" have been fulfilled too.
4. Since Jesus would return when "the times of restitution" arrived,
5. Then Jesus has come again too!

How did I ever miss this for so many decades? But in all those years of my believing that Jesus had not returned, the obvious truth in this verse evaded my attention and detection! The truth was, Jesus had already come!

But you may not believe that all of the prophecies have been fulfilled. We hear preachers today preaching from the Old Testament and telling us things that are about to happen. But consider what Jesus said about the words of the Old Covenant prophets when He was talking about the destruction of Jerusalem and the related suffering:

> For these be the days of vengeance, that all things which are written may be fulfilled. (Luke 21:22)

Jesus was saying that during these difficult times of the coming Judgment, climaxing in AD 70, **ALL the writings of the prophets would be fulfilled.** In reality, many of their prophecies had already been fulfilled with the arrival of the Babe in a manger. More of them would shortly be fulfilled with His death, burial, resurrection, ascension, and the coming of the Spirit at Pentecost. Jesus was saying in this verse 21 that whatever had been written by the prophets and not yet fulfilled, would "all" be fulfilled in the "days of vengeance," which ended in AD 70. This would mean the prophesied "times of restitution" would be fulfilled by that time too. Since Jesus was coming when "the times of restitution" arrived, then Jesus came again at that time also! In summary:

1. Since the Old Testament prophets prophesied "the times of restitution," and
2. Since Jesus said that everything the prophets had written was going to be fulfilled during the "days of vengeance," which ended with the destruction of Jerusalem and the temple (Luke 21:22),
3. Then the prophecy of "the times of restitution of all things" would have been fulfilled too.
4. Since "the heaven must receive" Jesus "until the times of restitution," the arrival of these "times" by the AD 70 destruction of Jerusalem
5. Means Jesus returned by AD 70 too!

Again, how did I miss this obvious truth for so many decades of my life? These "days of vengeance" were "the times of restitution" of which Peter prophesied. **So somewhere during these days of suffering and war ending in AD 70, Jesus came back for His people.** The Advent of Jesus in the first century is exactly the same time that we have found **everywhere** else in our studies.

VII. The Apostle Peter

This concludes our study about **"When did the apostle Peter say Jesus was coming?"** In AD 30 he believed that it was going to be a while before his Master's return. By AD 65 he believed Jesus' coming was "at hand" and warned his followers to be "sober and watch" (I Peter 4:7). He believed the coming of the Lord was near because "the glory" that would accompany His coming was "about to be revealed" (I Peter 5:1). This fits perfectly with "when" Jesus said He was coming. This should come as no shock to us. Peter preached what Jesus had taught him! **The harmony in their messages is beautiful!**

ONE DAY AS A THOUSAND YEARS

Before we leave the writings and words of the apostle Peter, we must consider the following passage in II Peter 3:3-10. These verses are about the Second Coming of Jesus and His Judgment on the Jewish nation. Like many other passages about Jesus' coming, no clear and plain statements here tell us "when" Jesus was coming. So, as with the others, we could just skip these Scriptures, except for one verse. We are here because verse 8 is often used as an explanation as to why Jesus has not yet come. Even though the New Testament declares His coming was imminent in the first century, we are told this verse explains why it did not happen, as Jesus and His apostles had said it would. For this reason we must study this passage.

II Peter 3:3-10

3. Knowing this first, that there shall come in the last days scoffers, walking after their own lusts,
4. And saying, Where is the promise of His coming? for since the fathers fell asleep, all things continue as they were from the beginning of creation.
5. For this they willingly are ignorant of, that by the word of God the heavens were of old, and the earth standing out of the water and in the water:
6. Whereby the world that then was, being overflowed with water, perished:

7. But the heavens and the earth, which are now, by the same word are kept in store, reserved unto fire against the day of judgment and perdition of ungodly men.

8. But, beloved, be not ignorant of this one thing, that one day is with the Lord as a thousand years, and a thousand years as one day.

9. The Lord is not slack concerning His promise, as some men count slackness; but is longsuffering to us-ward, not willing that any should perish, but that all should come to repentance.

10. But the day of the Lord will come as a thief in the night.

II Peter 3:8 is used today as the major explanation and reason why Jesus has not yet returned. Here is how the verse 8 reasoning goes, and this is the camp I was in too! I said that since one day and a thousand years were the same to God, and since it has been about 2,000 years since the apostles taught that Jesus was coming soon, then in God's world and on His calendar it has been only a couple of days. So Jesus can come anytime now and, as He sees time, He will still have come soon. What a stretch this was! What a wrong application of Scripture it was! Yet in all my many years of preaching that Jesus was coming soon, this verse was the only possible explanation I could find for Jesus' non-appearance. I could find no other reason as to why my Jesus, whose coming was "near" and "at hand" 2,000 years ago, still had not come. I would tell anyone who questioned me about why the Lord had not come after all these years, that "one day is with the Lord as a thousand years." It was the only excuse I could find for the Lord's delay! It was the only crutch I had to lean on as I tried to encourage weary Christians to be faithful, to keep waiting, and not to lose hope. I now know that I terribly abused this verse! The truth was that I never had seriously studied the origin of verse 8 or explored what the phrase really meant.

While Peter does not give us a definite answer in chapter 3 to our "when" question, we know our question was the subject here. Peter states in verses 3 and 4 that in the Last Days, "scoffers" would come and they would ask, "Where is the promise of His coming?"

Peter said these "scoffers" would come in the Last Days. I used to preach from this passage and I would apply it to my day. I would say that multitudes are denying Jesus is coming again, so surely we must be in the Last

VII. The Apostle Peter

Days. I now know from my studies that I do not live in the Last Days! That was Peter! He lived in the Last Days when the "scoffers" would come. I hope you have learned this too!

As for these scoffers, they were indeed already present. Peter refers to them in the present tense in verse 5 saying, "For this they willingly are ignorant of." Jude was written around AD 68-70, shortly after II Peter. In verses 4, 17, 18, and 19 Jude refers to the scoffers as being present. So the scoffers that were coming in the Last Days were present at the time II Peter was written, which was around AD 67-68. The "scoffers" were mocking the Gospel **THEN** and Peter was answering them!

The scoffers and the mockers were asking our question in the present tense. If I may paraphrase, they asked, "When is Jesus coming back? He promised to return a long time ago, but He has not done so"! Apparently their questioning was not to learn, but rather to mock and belittle the believers. The apostles had also been preaching for about thirty-eight years that Jesus was coming back and He was going to bring Judgment on the nation. The scoffers were saying He had not come back and nothing had changed, and we can be sure they were confident nothing was going to change.

Peter told them in verse 9 the reason for the delay was not Jesus' "slackness concerning His promise," but His "longsuffering." He said Jesus did not want anyone to "perish" but for all to "come to repentance." As I mentioned before, Jesus waited as long as He could possibly wait and still remain faithful to His own words and prophecy. In Matthew 24, Mark 13, and Luke 21 He prophesied (1) His return and (2) the awful Judgment coming on the Jewish nation. **In all three Gospels He said these things would happen in "this generation."** Jesus made His prophecies in AD 30, so He had until AD 70 (a generation, forty years) to come again and still return within "this generation." The same time limitations applied to His prophecies of the destruction of the nation, the temple, and Jerusalem. So Peter was saying, in verse 9, that Jesus was waiting and being patient as long as he could, because He wanted no one to "perish" in the coming disaster. The way to avoid this disaster was to "come to repentance" and have faith in their Messiah, Jesus Christ. Peter wrote these words around AD 68. In about two years, the nation of the Jews and those who rejected their Lord were destroyed. Jesus, the Judge, came as He had promised and executed a horrible Judgment upon the guilty ones, but gathered "together His elect" to "ever be with" Him. Jesus waited as long as He could (a generation, forty years) and still return within the time He promised. Time ran out as Revelation 10:6 said it would: "that there should be time [delay] no longer."

Christians who believe that Jesus' coming is in our future, call my attention back to verse 8. They tell me, as I used to tell others: "The reason Jesus has not come back yet is because one day is with the Lord as a thousand years. Jesus and His apostles may have preached He was coming back soon. But we are on God's time and while 'soon' could be one day to man, it could be a thousand years to God. So whenever Jesus does decide to come again, He will still be coming 'soon,' as He thinks of time. You have to realize time in God's world is different from time in our world."

Obviously, I now believe this is a wrong application of verse 8. The verse does not say one day "equals" a thousand years but it is "as" a thousand years. Peter was not saying it might be thousands of years before Jesus returned because God looks at time differently than we do. **That would directly contradict everything else that Peter, his fellow apostles, and his Master had said.** Whatever Peter's purpose was in quoting this Old Testament Scripture, he surely did not intend to negate or discredit the multitude of passages that declare the Lord's coming was at hand in that first century.

It is noteworthy that whenever Jesus and His apostles spoke about "when" Jesus was coming back, they never spoke of a number of days or years. They always used some other measurement of time. Jesus said He would come in "this generation," while some of His apostles were still being persecuted and fleeing from one "city" to another, and before all of His followers would "taste of death"(Matt. 24:34, 10:23, 16:28). **One day being as a thousand years with the Lord has no relevance at all to these time statements of Jesus about when He would return!** We find no mention of any number of days. The same is true of the apostles. They spoke of the Lord's coming as being "near," "at hand," and "drawing nigh." We cannot relate "one day is with the Lord as a thousand years" to these words and make any sense of them.

VII. The Apostle Peter

In verse 8 we see two comparisons, but the second one gets no attention. First, a day in God's eternal realm is as a thousand years in man's world. Second, a thousand years in God's world is as a day in man's world. We cannot use these statements as formulas to calculate time. They do not even agree with each other! The verse is not meant to be used to calculate time. It simply intends to show that man's time is very limited, but God is eternal and therefore has no limitations on His time.

If we insist on taking the phrases in verse 8 as literal measurements of time, consider what this does to the popular (but wrong) theology about the literal 1,000-year reign of Christ in Revelation 20:4. First, "one day . . . as a thousand years" could make the reign of Christ last 365 million years (1 day = 1,000 years, so 1,000 years x 365 days per year = 365,000 days x 1,000 years for each day = 365,000,000 years). But second, and usually ignored, verse 8 also says, "A thousand years as one day." Thus, the coming millennium everyone is anticipating could possibly last for only one day (1,000 years = 1 day). This demonstrates the impossibility and unreasonableness of trying to use verse 8 as a measurement of time. We just cannot rightly use this verse as a literal means to calculate time! The 1,000-year periods in Revelation are neither "365 million years" nor "one day." Nor are they a literal one thousand years! How can I know this? Because in our study of Revelation, we learned that all the prophecies had to be fulfilled within the time limitations specifically defined in the opening and closing verses of the book. You remember them: everything "must shortly come to pass" (1:1) and "must shortly be done" (22:6). It is impossible to fit a literal thousand years within these time restrictions!

So what does verse 8 imply, what does it mean, and why did Peter use it? Peter's Old Testament reference that he partly quoted is found in Psalm 90:4:

> For a thousand years in thy sight are but as yesterday when it is past,
> and as a watch in the night.

The psalmist is comparing God's existence to man's. In verse 2 he says God is "from everlasting to everlasting." In verse 4 he teaches God has unlimited time. "A thousand years," "yesterday," or "a watch in the night," it does not matter to Him. He has all eternity! In contrast, in verses 5 and 6 man is like "grass." He may grow up in the morning, but in the evening he is "cut down and withereth."

Psalm 90:4 and II Peter 3:8 are about God's eternal, unlimited time compared to man's short, limited time. These passages cannot be used to calculate any time period in man's world. Just as we saw in II Peter 3:8, Psalm 90:4 gives two formulas that do not even agree with each other. First the psalmist says a thousand years in God's world is like "yesterday" in man's world. But then he says a thousand years in God's sight is like a "watch in the night" in man's life. What does this mean?

A "watch in the night" is the portion of time during which one watches or remains awake. For military and security purposes the twelve hours of the night were divided into equal "watches" or shifts. "Before the Captivity, there were three night-watches, whereas in Matthew 14:25 a fourth watch is mentioned, having been introduced among the Jews by the Romans."[xiii] So in the New Testament the twelve hours of the night were divided into four watches of three hours each. But in the days of the psalmist, there were three watches of four hours each. A soldier who was on duty for a "watch" in the night in the days of the Old Testament would have stood guard for four hours. So the psalmist says first, in God's sight "a thousand years" are as "yesterday" (twenty-four hours). Then he says "a thousand years" are as "a watch in the night" (four hours). Which is correct? They both are correct! Again, the writer is not giving a formula for the calculating of time. He is just saying that man is mortal and finite, that his time is limited, and that he soon dies.

In contrast to man, God is everlasting and His time is endless. Psalm 90:4 and II Peter 3:8 are like figures of speech denoting God's eternality, His state of being everlasting, never ending, and without any time limitations. Each of these verses teaches us that in God's realm, time cannot be measured. A day is not only the same as 1,000 years to God. It is also the same as 500 years, 5,000 years, 10,000 years, or "as a watch in the night" (four hours)! In His eternal realm time is of no concern—it will never run out!

VII. The Apostle Peter

However, when God deals with man about time, He does so in terms of man's world and man's understanding of time. Otherwise we could never understand any time statements from God. He may as well not tell us anything if He is not going to speak to us in terms we can understand. Besides, how deceptive it would be of God to tell us He is going to do something in five days, when He knows He is not going to do it for 5,000 years! Our God is not interested in deceiving or tricking us; He wants to communicate with us in a manner we can understand. He wants us to know what His will is, so we can walk in His ways.

When God told Noah, "For yet seven days, and I will cause it to rain upon the earth for forty days and forty nights," He meant seven days and forty days, as Noah understood time (Gen. 7:4). But if we apply II Peter 3:8 as it is popularly used today, then God could have meant that in 7,000 years He would send rain, and that it would rain for 40,000 years! It is easy to see what an improper use of verse 8 this would be! When Jeremiah prophesied that the Babylonian captivity would last for seventy years, God meant seventy years in man's world, not some other astronomical number (Jer. 29:10). When Jesus predicted He would spend "three days and three nights in the heart of the earth" (Matt. 12:40), He meant three days and three nights in man's understanding of time, not 3,000 years! To my knowledge, the Bible contains **NO EXAMPLE** of God's telling man that He was going to act in one day, ten days, or fifteen days but He really meant that it would be 1,000, 10,000, or 15,000 years before He would actually do what He said.

In the Bible, when it is not speaking literally of an actual count of 1,000, as 1,000 horses, the word "thousand" is often used to symbolize "completeness," indicating "all of something." No number—no certain amount or quantity—is implied, just ALL of whatever is being referenced. Any other number, ten thousand, a million, etc., could have been used, but apparently in the culture of the Bible writers it was the number "thousand" that seems to have been used to represent ALL of whatever they were addressing.

In Psalm 90:4, above, "a thousand years" meant **ALL THE YEARS**. All the years to God "are but as yesterday." Peter used this verse from Psalm 90:4, and it meant the same thing in II Peter 3:8. The Lord having "a thousand years" meant He had **ALL THE YEARS.** No number is implied by the use of "thousand." As we are considering the word here, "thousand" cannot be truthfully used to calculate any amount of time in man's world!

Consider Psalm 50:10:

For every beast of the forest is mine, and the cattle upon a thousand hills.

Does this mean the cattle on hill number 1,001 do not belong to God? Of course not! The verse is plainly portraying that God owns "the cattle upon" **ALL THE HILLS.** Just as "every beast of the forest" is His, ALL the cattle on ALL the hills are His too. No number is implied or intended by the use of "thousand." An exact count of hills and cattle is of no importance; they are wholly and completely His. He owns them ALL! Continuing the same thought, God says just two verses later (v. 12), "for the world is mine, and the fullness thereof." This further supports my point. Saying God owned the cattle on a "thousand hills" was just another way of saying He owned ALL the cattle on ALL the hills. This must be true since ALL "the world" and "the fullness thereof" were His.

Consider Psalm 84:10:

For a day in thy courts is better than a thousand. I had rather be a doorkeeper in the house of my God, than to dwell in the tents of wickedness.

Here again, the obvious meaning is that the psalmist would not give up his one day in the Lord's "courts" for **ALL THE DAYS** somewhere else. He is not implying that if he were offered a better deal, say 5,000 days, then he would trade his "day" in the Lord's courts. An exact count of days is not necessary. "A thousand" meant that for ALL the days available he would not give up his one day in the Lord's house. ALL the days—"a thousand"—outside of God's courts were not as good as just one day in His courts.

Look at one more example in Psalm 105:8:

VII. The Apostle Peter

He hath remembered His covenant forever, the word which he commanded to a thousand generations.

Again, "a thousand generations" means **ALL THE GENERATIONS** (completeness). Literally, when the psalmist wrote this verse, a thousand generations had not yet lived upon Earth. But the psalmist is not counting! An exact number is not the point. As with the previous passages this verse shows, "a thousand" is not about any certain number. "A thousand" just means ALL of the generations. "A thousand" may be more than a literal 1,000, or, as in this verse, much less than a literal 1,000. Again, no number is implied, just ALL of whatever is being discussed.

So likewise, in Psalm 90:4 and in II Peter 3:8, the use of the number "thousand" just indicates God has **ALL THE TIME** in the world. Man may have a "day," but God has a "thousand," and this means that while man's time is limited, God has ALL the days and ALL the time He desires. You cannot put a literal number on how much time God has! **But, when the Bible writers wanted a number to describe something about their God, "a thousand" satisfied their need.**

Looking back at II Peter 3:8, I hope it is obvious that:

1. We cannot use this verse to calculate any earthly time.
2. It would be very deceptive of God to use "double talk," speaking of time as man sees time, but really meaning time as He views time in His eternal world.
3. The word "thousand," when not obviously meaning the literal number, often means ALL of whatever is being considered. "Thousand" symbolizes COMPLETENESS!

The question remains as to why Peter told the scoffers "one day is with the Lord as a thousand years." I am sure Peter did not intend to imply that Jesus would be coming back hundreds or thousands of years later. This would have contradicted what he, the other apostles, and Jesus had said. **<u>I believe Peter quoted Psalm 90:4 to remind the scoffers that God still had plenty of time</u>**

in which to keep His promise. I believe they got Peter's message! They were familiar with the ninetieth Psalm; they knew what "a thousand" meant in the Hebrew Scriptures!

Peter was responding to the scoffers and the mockers who were saying Jesus had not kept His promise. It had been about thirty-eight years since Jesus had promised He would come again in that present generation. The scoffers knew this, and they were saying Jesus' promises to return were just false prophecies and empty promises. After nearly four decades they were sure Jesus was not coming again.

Think about this. Today, Christianity teaches it has been nearly 2,000 years and Jesus still has not kept His promise to return. Today's preachers are not mocking, but they are saying the same thing the scoffers said: "all things continue as they were." Of course, they add that it will not remain that way much longer because "Jesus is coming soon." **The truth is, if Jesus still has not returned perhaps the scoffers were right after all!** After 2,000 years we can certainly understand why modern-day skeptics are mocking and belittling Jesus' promise to return before all of His first followers died. But as we have learned, in about two years after Peter wrote his second Epistle Jesus did return and did execute the predicted Judgment. We just have to get the word out to the twenty-first century mockers and scoffers. Jesus did keep His promise! As He had prophesied, "Heaven and earth" (the world of Judaism) passed "away," but His words (Jesus' promises) did "not pass away" (Matt. 24:35). They were all fulfilled!

Let us look at the big picture in these verses in II Peter 3. I risk being a little repetitious, but perhaps that will be good. In responding to the scoffers' complaints, Peter made the following points:

First, in verses 5 and 6 Peter reminded them of a similar event in history with which they were familiar, but which they seemed to be ignoring. He said a "heavens" and an "earth" existed, past tense. It was the "world" of Noah's day. And as God had promised, He came in Judgment and destroyed that "world" with water.

Second, in verse 7 Peter told them of another "heavens" and "earth," "which are now," and that world (of Judaism), as had been the case with the world of Noah, was "reserved" for its "day of judgment."

Third, in verse 8 Peter told them the delay in Jesus' return was not because Jesus had run out of time. While it may have been thirty-eight years, Jesus still had plenty of time in which to keep His promise. The Lord had "a thousand years," meaning the Lord had ALL the time He needed. Peter was not, in the least, implying that Jesus would not keep His promise to come, or that He might not return within the time period He had predicted. He was warning the scoffers not to make the mistake of thinking it was too late for Jesus to keep His promise to come again and judge their nation.

Fourth, in verse 9 Peter further warned the scoffers that they should not make the mistake of believing Jesus had forgotten or overlooked His promise to return. Peter assured them the delay in Jesus' coming was not because He was "slack" about keeping His "promise." He had not forgotten "when" He said He would return. Jesus had plenty of time left and He would surely keep His promise to come again within that generation.

Fifth, continuing in verse 9 Peter gave them the reason for this delay. It was the "longsuffering" of Jesus, His patience with His people, and His desire that not "any should perish," that kept Him delaying and kept the Judgment waiting. The Lord did not want anyone, even the scoffers, to "perish" in the fiery Judgment He knew would accompany His coming. So Peter said Jesus was patiently waiting for His people to "come to repentance," accept Him as their Messiah, and be saved. Jesus waited as long as He possibly could—a generation (forty years).

Sixth, in verse 10 Peter assured the scoffers in no uncertain terms that "the day of the Lord" would come and it would come "as a thief in the night." They should not be lulled to sleep by this seemingly long delay!

Here is a brief summary of the points Peter made to the "scoffers" in those "last days" just before the AD 70 coming of Jesus:

1. Remember, God did come in Noah's day and destroyed that world.
2. Their world was reserved for a similar fate.
3. The delay was not because Jesus had run out of time in which to keep His promise.
4. The delay was not because Jesus was just being "slack" about keeping His promise.
5. The delay was because Jesus was being patient with them. He wanted no one to perish, but for everyone to be saved.
6. But make no mistake, Jesus would come back!

You may be agreeing with me or resisting my explanation of this passage, especially verse 8. Either way, one thing is absolutely certain! **Whatever the explanation, verse 8 does not invalidate all the great multitude of other Scriptures which clearly teach the soon coming of Jesus in the days of the apostles.** Verse 8 does not negate everything else Peter, the other apostles, and Jesus Himself said. They ALL declared His coming was to be in their age, in the lifetime of some of those very first Christians. I believe verse 8 is in harmony with all these other passages!

Our study of II Peter 3:8 was longer than I intended. But, because this verse continues to be abused today, I felt it was necessary to cover it well. (I used to abuse it too!) I hope you now realize that verse 8 cannot truthfully be used today as the major explanation and reason for why Jesus has not yet returned!

THE APOSTLE PAUL

When did the apostle Paul say Jesus was coming? Apparently, Paul did a lot more writing than Peter, or perhaps many more of Paul's letters have been preserved for us in the Bible. Paul wrote many things that gave those first-century Christians reasons to believe they would live to see the coming of Jesus. No wonder the church felt such a great sense of imminence regarding the coming of the Lord. Paul continually encouraged such feelings! Was the apostle Paul being deceptive? Absolutely not! As we are constantly learning, the coming of the Lord was, indeed, set to occur in that first generation of Christians. Paul wrote often about the Lord's coming in his letters to the churches. I shall not try to cite all these references, but we shall look at those verses that have the most to contribute to answering our question about "when" Paul believed Jesus was coming back.

ROMANS 8:18

> For I reckon that the sufferings of this present time are not worthy to be compared with the glory which shall be revealed in us.

Here again the KJV does us a disservice. Paul uses the Greek word *mello,* and what He actually said was: "the glory about to be revealed in us." So the coming of the Lord was getting close. You will remember that these are almost the same words Peter used: "and also a partaker of the glory that shall be [*mello*, about to be] revealed" (I Peter 5:1). Peter and Paul agreed—the "glory" was about to come!

ROMANS 13:11-12

11. And that, knowing the time, that now it is high time to awake out of sleep: for now is our salvation nearer than when we believed.
12. The night is far spent, the day is at hand: let us therefore cast off the works of darkness, and let us put on the armour of light.

"The day" used here was a reference to the Day of the Lord, which was the day when the Lord would come again, Judgment Day. This is generally agreed upon by Bible scholars. That being true, Paul says that "the day," or the coming of the Lord, was "at hand." "At hand" means "near" or "close by." Yet the church teaches that Jesus has not yet come and that we are still in the darkness of "the night." But Paul plainly said the night was "far spent," and that was nearly 2,000 years ago. If "the night" was "far spent," then how can we still be in it today? How can the Lord not have come yet if His coming in Paul's time was "at hand"?

We must be honest and let words have their proper meaning! Paul used "at hand" on another occasion when He spoke of the nearness of his death. He said, "For I am now ready to be offered, and the time of my departure is at hand" (II Tim. 4:6). This verse is not confusing! **Paul was saying his death was near! Likewise, above in Romans, he was saying the coming of the Lord was near.** This is not hard to see if we will be honest with the Scriptures.

Paul, like Peter, **knew** the day of the Lord's coming was near because he **knew the signs of the times.** Paul said, "And that, knowing the time." The apostle was not trying to deceive the church. He was not just trying to keep the saints on their toes. He did not know exactly when Jesus was coming, but from the signs of the times he knew the Advent was getting near. When did the apostle Paul say Jesus was coming? **The answer in these verses is "soon," and that was soon in Paul's day, not today!**

I CORINTHIANS 1:7-8

7. So that ye may come behind in no gift; waiting for the coming of our Lord Jesus Christ,
8. Who shall confirm you unto the end, that ye may be blameless in the day of our Lord Jesus Christ.

With "preaching" like this, no wonder the early saints expected to live to see their Lord return! The saints knew Jesus was coming at "the end." Paul said Jesus would confirm them to "the end," and that they would be blameless in "the day" of the Lord. If they were all going to die before Jesus came, then Paul was being rather deceitful! But he was not! Paul knew the Lord had promised to come in their generation, and he always held up that promise to the people of the Lord. The hope of the early church was that Jesus would come back and they would live to see the event. It was a hope Jesus had initiated when He said, "There be some standing here, which shall not taste of death, till they see the Son of Man in His kingdom" (Matt. 16:28).

I CORINTHIANS 16:22

If any man love not the Lord Jesus Christ, let him be Anathema Maranatha.

Over the years I have heard various interpretations of exactly what the word "Maranatha" means. Most of them were present-tense declarations that "The Lord is coming." This does seem to be correct. The original Greek reads, "The Lord comes!" This is a present-tense statement and it shows Paul's belief and teaching that Jesus' coming was expected by Paul in his day.

PHILIPPIANS 4:5

The Lord is at hand.

"The Lord is at hand" is generally accepted as an Advent verse. Paul was saying the coming of the Lord was "at hand." This interpretation comes from the fact that just a few verses earlier he was writing about Jesus' return. In Philippians 3:20-21 Paul says, "For our conversation is in heaven; from whence also we look for the Savior, the Lord Jesus Christ: Who shall change our vile body that it may be fashioned like unto His glorious body." Then five verses later he says, "The Lord is at hand." Here again we can easily see why such a feeling of imminence about the Lord's coming abounded in the early church. Paul told the Corinthians that "we look for the Savior." This "we" meant Paul and the saints at Corinth. If Jesus was not coming for thousands of years, how deceptive and misleading Paul's words were! But, they were encouraged to "look for the Savior" because His coming was "at hand."

I TIMOTHY 4:8

For bodily exercise profiteth little: but godliness is profitable unto all things, having promise of the life that now is, and of that which is to come.

This verse in its proper form continues to show Paul's belief and teaching that the coming of the Lord was getting near. What he actually told Timothy was, "having promise of the life that now is, and of that which is about to come [*mello*]." Expectations were high among the apostles that the Lord would return in their day, and they passed this anticipation along to their followers.

VII. The Apostle Paul

I TIMOTHY 6:13-14

13. I give thee charge in the sight of God.
14. That thou keep this commandment without spot, unrebukeable, until the appearing of our Lord Jesus Christ.

Here again the imminent expectation of the Lord's return in Paul's day is evident in his charge to Timothy, his son in the faith. In the preceding verses Paul gave instructions about how Christians should live and conduct themselves. Then in verse 12, he told Timothy to "Fight the good fight of faith." He followed with the charge to Timothy to "keep this commandment," without any failings, until Jesus appeared. This statement reveals plainly that Paul expected Timothy to live until Jesus returned. And Timothy surely received these words from the apostle Paul as confirmation that, indeed, he could possibly still be alive when his Lord appeared.

Did Paul not know what he was talking about? Was he misleading Timothy? Any answer that discredits the apostle Paul also discredits more than half of the books of the New Testament, which Paul wrote. It was around AD 64 when Paul wrote this letter to Timothy. The signs of "the end" and the Lord's coming were getting more and more evident to Paul. If Paul had not been expecting his Master soon, then he would have probably told Timothy to "keep this commandment" until you die! That would have been the proper exhortation for Timothy. But Paul knew the Lord's return was imminent! He wanted no sin, no slackness, nothing, to mar that glorious day for Timothy and the saints for whom Timothy was caring.

How many, many times I have honestly misused these verses, and the ones in I Thessalonians 5:1-4, which we shall consider later. I warned my people to always be diligent in their watching for Jesus' coming so they would not be caught as by "a thief in the night." I begged them to always live "without spot" in order to always be ready since Jesus could come at any moment. I never attempted to explain why Paul told the Thessalonians "that day" would not overtake **THEM** "as a thief," since **THEY** were not "in darkness," because **THEY** knew "the times and the seasons." I was sincere, but I was wrong. These, and many other verses, now make much more sense to me. I see now that their Lord had promised to come again in their generation and they were expecting Him to keep His promise! I believe He did! If He did not, then our faith and trust in Jesus and His promises are useless!

TITUS 2:13

Looking for that blessed hope, and the glorious appearing of the great God and our Savior Jesus Christ.

This is perhaps the most beautiful and thrilling verse about Jesus' return. No wonder the early church thought Jesus was coming soon, with exhortations like this one to look for Him. I have quoted this verse many times, and it always excited me! My heart was racing and a tingle ran down my spine. **But my hope was misplaced!** "The glorious appearing" was the hope of Paul and Titus nearly 2,000 years ago. Paul wrote Titus about AD 64. If Jesus did not come soon, then Titus' hope and Paul's hope were misplaced! But their hope was not misplaced. Their hope was based on Jesus' own words, and they could have no better foundation for hope than that!

We cannot deny that the coming of Jesus Christ was imminent in the time of the apostles and the early church. The New Testament is full of verses declaring it! The believers' hope was based on Jesus' own promises to return in that "generation" while some of those who knew Him were still living. It was further based on the preaching, teaching, and writing of the apostles, who were constantly reinforcing the words of Jesus and leading the people to believe "that day" would surely come in THEIR day! If the imminent appearing of Jesus did not occur, then we can just lay the Bible aside because we cannot trust what it says!

VII. The Apostle Paul

I CORINTHIANS 15:51-52

51. Behold, I shew you a mystery; We shall not all sleep, but we shall all be changed,
52. In a moment, in the twinkling of an eye, at the last trump: for the trumpet shall sound, and the dead shall be raised incorruptible, and we shall be changed.

These verses are in Paul's famous resurrection chapter. Many different interpretations have been made about this chapter; but, to my knowledge, everyone I know agrees it refers to the Second Coming of Jesus—when the saints who "sleep" will be resurrected to incorruptibility and the saints who are living will be "changed," all "in the twinkling of an eye."

For decades I preached from this passage and looked for Jesus' coming. I did not know when He would come, but I was looking for Him at any moment. I hoped He would come soon, and that I would miss death and be among the living who would be "changed." However, I failed to see that this passage plainly answers my question, "When did the apostle Paul say Jesus was coming?" And His answer, as we are learning, was not sometime in my future.

Paul was writing around AD 56-57 to the Christians at Corinth about the coming of Jesus and the resurrection. He told **them**, "We shall not all sleep." It is universally agreed that the words "sleep" and "asleep" were often used to refer to Christians who had died. So when Paul said, "We shall not all sleep," he literally meant "We shall not all die" before the Lord's return. Think about this for a moment. **Paul was assuring the Corinthians that some of them would still be living when Jesus came!** This "we" also included the apostle himself! Paul knew the Lord was coming in his day and that it was possible that he could be among those still living when that great day arrived. I had never thought about these things! I had read and reread these Scriptures and had applied them to my day, as if they had just recently been written to me! I took Paul's words personally. Knowing he had said, "We shall not all sleep," I had hoped to be in that number of those still alive when Jesus came.

But Paul was writing to the Corinthians, not to me! He was writing nearly 2,000 years ago, not today. He promised **THEM**, not me, that some of **THEM** would not die before the Lord came back. Where did Paul get a message like that? Well, it sounds just like a promise we have heard before, and it is! We ran across it earlier in our search for "When did Jesus say He was coming?" Jesus had said, "There be some standing here, which shall not taste of death, till they see the Son of Man coming in His kingdom" (Matt.16:28). Later in Matthew 24, Jesus predicted many things, including His "coming in the clouds of heaven" (v. 30). Then in verse 34 He promised, "This generation shall not pass, till all these things be fulfilled." When Paul said, "We shall not all sleep," he was promising the Corinthians PRECISELY and EXACTLY the same thing Jesus had promised to His followers! This is amazing!

But we should not be surprised that Paul and the other apostles preached the same message as their Lord and Master. It is amazing that I spent most of my life missing this insight. If some of the Corinthians were going to live to see Jesus come, then He had to come sometime in that first century AD. **Here is the answer to our question! The apostle Paul said Jesus was coming during the lifetime of some of the saints at Corinth!** Today's church says Jesus has not yet come, but is coming soon. What a dilemma! Christianity is supposed to believe and preach what the Bible says. We are finding that in regard to the Second Coming of Jesus, the church has strayed from what the Bible plainly teaches on this subject.

"We shall not all sleep, but we shall all be changed" is in I Corinthians 15:51. **In verse 52, Paul repeats this promise.** After the dead are raised incorruptible, he says again, "we shall be changed." The "we" here is the same as the "we" in verse 51, "we" who do not "sleep" (die) before Jesus' return! So twice in this passage, Paul has assured the church at Corinth that some of them will be living when Jesus returns. Now if the Corinthians all died before Jesus came, then Paul was a big false prophet and a fraud! That is an unacceptable option. It destroys Christianity! Either Jesus came in that "generation" as He and His apostles promised, or Jesus and His men deceived and lied to the very first Christians. What a dilemma!

Here is an additional thought regarding the resurrection. When does this passage in I Corinthians 15:51-52 say the resurrection of the dead would occur? Well, it says that some of the Corinthians would live to hear "the last trump" and see Jesus come. But once He came and before they would be "changed," the dead would be "raised incorruptible." So, where does that put the time of the resurrection? It was right there in the first century too! Amazing!

I THESSALONIANS 4:13-18

13. But I would not have you to be ignorant, brethren, concerning them which are asleep, that ye sorrow not, even as others which have no hope.
14. For if we believe that Jesus died and rose again, even so them also which sleep in Jesus will God bring with Him.
15. For this we say unto you by the word of the Lord, that we which are alive and remain unto the coming of the Lord shall not prevent them which are asleep.
16. For the Lord Himself shall descend from heaven with a shout, with the voice of the archangel, and with the trump of God: and the dead in Christ shall rise first.
17. Then we which are alive and remain shall be caught up together with them in the clouds, to meet the Lord in the air: and so shall we ever be with the Lord.
18. Wherefore comfort one another with these words.

This is another wonderful passage about the coming of the Lord. This discourse seems to have developed out of the belief and teaching in the early church that the coming of the Lord was imminent, and that many of the saints were likely to live to see His return. The saints in Thessalonica apparently became upset because some of their brothers and sisters were dying before the Lord came. Perhaps many were dying from the severe persecution of the church. Not only was the church grieved because of the loss of their loved ones, but also they seemed to fear the dead saints were going to miss out on everything the church was expecting to receive when Jesus returned. They worried that their deceased, faithful friends and family would miss "the glory [*mello*, about to be] revealed" at the coming of the Lord (Rom. 8:18). This passage seems to be Paul's effort to address this concern and to bring "comfort" to the church at Thessalonica.

What Paul told the Thessalonians in these verses is essentially the same thing he told the Corinthians in his first letter to them (15:51-52). You will remember that he promised the living, "We shall not all sleep [die]," and regarding the deceased he said, "The dead shall be raised." Now, Paul promised the Thessalonians that some of them would be "alive and remain unto the coming of the Lord," and regarding the deceased he said, "The dead in Christ shall rise first." The order of events is the same here as in I Corinthians, where Paul said that **first** the dead would be raised and then, **second,** the living would be changed.

I have included this passage in our study because it has much to contribute to our search for an answer to our question, **"When did the apostle Paul say Jesus was coming?"** I had read this passage many times, preached from it many times, and never realized that there was anything in it that could have given me any insight into the timing of Jesus' return. From these verses I preached that Jesus was coming soon, the saints of God would be resurrected, and we would all enter into eternity with Jesus. I just knew Jesus' coming had to be close by, and I hoped to be among those who would be "alive and remain unto the coming of the Lord." **But my hope was misplaced!**

I never asked all those "W" questions about this passage. You saw them earlier: who, what, when, where, and why. I never asked them because I assumed that I understood this passage. Like the passage in I Corinthians, I read and applied these verses in I Thessalonians as if they had just been written to me! Obviously, I was wrong! Yet, this is how most Christians generally read and interpret this passage today, as if it had been written to today's church!

Paul made these promises nearly 2,000 years ago. They were promises to the Thessalonians, not to us! As he had promised the Corinthians, he also promised the Thessalonians, **NOT US,** that some of **THEM—NOT US—** would be "alive and remain unto the coming of the Lord." How did I fail to see this for so many decades? Here is the answer to our "when" question! We could

VII. The Apostle Paul

end our search now! **Paul believed and taught that Jesus was coming back while some of the saints at Thessalonica were still "alive"!** They were concerned about their dead loved ones. Paul tells them not to "sorrow," for the "dead in Christ shall rise." Then he promised that "we" (Paul and the Thessalonians), who "are alive and remain unto the coming of the Lord," will be reunited with our loved ones and "together . . . ever be with the Lord." What a wonderful gathering for the faithful! What a great "reward"!

Can you grasp the obvious time frame these verses reveal for "when" the Lord would return? He had promised the Corinthians, "We shall not all sleep [die]" before the Lord comes. Then he promised the Thessalonians the same thing! He said, "that we which are alive and remain unto the coming of the Lord." Without doubt, Paul believed Jesus was coming back sometime during the lifetime of the first Christians, and even possibly during his own lifetime! **The evidence is overwhelming!** The church today recognizes this. But the church does not believe Jesus came again in the days of Paul and his fellow believers. That makes the holy apostle a false prophet and a deceiver! What a dilemma! Paul wrote more than one-half of the books in the New Testament. If his understanding of "when" the Lord was going to return was wrong, if his knowledge of such a major subject was totally inaccurate, then the apostle Paul is completely discredited! Maybe he was wrong about other doctrines too! We cannot trust any of his work, his preaching, or his writings. What a great dilemma this is for Christianity!

Paul was so sure of what he was telling the Thessalonians that he repeated his words—just as he did to the Corinthians! He wanted no one to miss his promise or fail to understand what he was saying. He had said once in verse 15, "We which are alive and remain unto the coming of the Lord." Then in verse 17 he repeated his words: "Then we which are alive and remain shall be caught up together with them [the ones resurrected] in the clouds." How much clearer could Paul have been? How much more emphatic? How much more positive? Paul used no "ifs," no "ands," no "buts," and no "maybes"! With regard to "when" Jesus was coming back, the Christians at Thessalonica could have understood only one interpretation of Paul's words:

Some of us living here in Thessalonica will still be alive when Jesus comes back!

What a great gathering day! I had always looked forward to this day. But Paul promised the people to whom He preached in the first century, that some of **THEM** would live to see His coming and the resurrection of "them which are asleep." So Jesus either came in the time of the early church or Paul misled his followers. But Paul did not mislead his people; he did not just dream up all these promises. He said in I Thessalonians 4:15 that what he was telling the Thessalonians was "the word of the Lord."

To what "word of the Lord" was Paul referring? Paul's Bible was the Old Testament. But you will remember the apostle Paul received direct revelation from God. The question is this. Can we go to the Bible and establish that what Paul promised the church at Thessalonica was something Jesus had promised? Absolutely! We can find many proofs in the Gospels. You will remember this one. When Jesus was talking about His coming and rewarding His saints He said, "There be some standing here which shall not taste death, till they see the Son of Man coming in His kingdom" (Matt. 16:28). That was "the word of the Lord" Paul was preaching! Paul said it a little differently, but it meant the same thing. Paul said, "We shall not all sleep," meaning some of them would be "alive and remain unto the coming of the Lord." Praise the Lord! **It is very reassuring to continually rediscover that Jesus' first preachers proclaimed the same messages Jesus preached.** The harmony in the Bible is beautiful!

Let us compare what Jesus taught in Matthew 24 with what Paul taught in his first letter to the Thessalonians, chapter 4:

The subject is the same, His coming!

Jesus said, "They shall see the Son of Man coming" (Matt. 24:30).
Paul said, "Unto the coming of the Lord" (I Thess. 4:15).

VII. The Apostle Paul

The timing is the same, in the first century AD.

Jesus said, "Then shall appear the sign of the Son of Man in Heaven" (24:30). "Then" was the time around the destruction of Jerusalem in AD 70.
Paul said, "We which are alive and remain unto the coming of the Lord" (4:15). His coming had to be in that first century, if some of the Thessalonians were going to be "alive and remain" to see it.

Both describe the Lord as coming from the heavens.

Jesus said, "They shall see the Son of Man coming in the clouds of heaven" (24:30).
Paul said, "The Lord Himself shall descend from heaven" (4:16).

Both refer to the clouds.

Jesus said, "They shall see the Son of Man coming in the clouds" (24:30).
Paul said, "We . . . shall be caught up together . . . in the clouds" (4:17).

Both have the trumpet of God sounding.

Jesus said, "With a great sound of a trumpet" (24:31).
Paul said, "With the trump of God" (4:16).

Both have the involvement of the angels of God.

Jesus said, "And He shall send His angels" (24:31).
Paul said, "With the voice of the archangel" (4:16).

Both have the dead being raised.

Jesus said, "And they shall gather together His elect from the four winds, from one end of heaven to the other" (24:31). The word "resurrection" is not used here, but this is not controversial. Everyone believes that whenever Jesus would come again, the gathering of His elect would include both the dead saints and the living.

Paul said, "The dead in Christ shall rise first" (4:16).

Both have their prophecies occurring in the lifetime of the people to whom they were speaking.

Jesus said, "This generation shall not pass, till all these things be fulfilled" (24:34).
Paul said, "We which are alive and remain unto the coming of the Lord" (4:15, 17).

Both have the saints being gathered together.

Jesus said, "Shall gather together His elect" (24:31).
Paul said, "Caught up together" (4:17).

This is amazing! We cannot deny that what Paul promised to the Thessalonians was indeed "the word of the Lord"! Paul was preaching to the churches the same message Jesus preached when He was on Earth! In Matthew 24:29-31, Jesus put the timing of His coming and the gathering of His saints in the SAME period of time as His Judgment on Jerusalem—the first century. Paul told the Thessalonians and the Corinthians the same thing: that since the Lord was coming in their age, some of them would be alive at His coming and at the resurrection of the dead.

If you are in the least bit doubtful that Jesus promised to come and "gather together His elect" in the first century, then listen further to the words of Jesus. In Matthew 24:30 He said they would see Him coming. In verse 31 He said He would be gathering His elect together. Then just three verses further He said:

Verily I say unto you, this generation shall not pass, till all these things be fulfilled. (Matt. 24:34)

VII. The Apostle Paul

"This generation" was the generation in which Jesus lived. It was that present generation that included the apostles and the first Christians. It included Paul, the Corinthians, the Thessalonians, and all those first believers and churches. "All these things," that were going to come to pass in that generation, included His Second Coming (Matt. 24:30) and the resurrection and gathering of His saints (Matt. 24:31). I repeat, Jesus said that generation would not pass before He came and gathered His elect, dead and alive! **No wonder** Paul went around telling the saints, "We shall not all sleep [die]" before the return of the Lord! **No wonder** he went around preaching that some of them would be "alive and remain unto the coming of the Lord." **This was the message of his Lord and Savior, Jesus Christ!**

This is very beautiful, absolutely wonderful! Bible passages that I could never reconcile now fit together perfectly! How did I miss such obvious truth for so long? Here is the reason. Whenever the Scripture did not seem to fit with what I believed, I just left it alone. I was confident that once I came to understand the passage, it would surely agree with what I already believed. I felt this way because I knew I had the truth and all the Scriptures would certainly support my positions. **I WAS WRONG!** Thank God I have been delivered from that know-it-all attitude and been given another chance to get it right!

I have dwelt on I Thessalonians 4:13-18 for a long time, but it is very important. And we have found the answer to our question, **"When did the apostle Paul say Jesus was coming?"** Paul said his Lord and Master, Jesus Christ, was coming again during the lifetime of some of the people to whom he ministered in the first century AD. How can today's church continue to proclaim a message that is totally different from what Jesus and His apostles preached? What a dilemma the church has on its hands!

I THESSALONIANS 5:1, 2 and 4

1. But of the times and the seasons, brethren, ye have no need that I write unto you.
2. For yourselves know perfectly that the day of the Lord so cometh as a thief in the night.
4. But ye, brethren, are not in darkness, that that day should overtake you as a thief.

These verses follow immediately after the previous passage in chapter 4. "The day" in these verses obviously referred to the day of which Paul had just been writing, the day of the Lord's coming. While they seemed to have had some ignorance about the deceased Christians, Paul apparently had taught the Thessalonians well regarding their readiness for the Lord's return. They must have known a lot about the signs of "the day." Paul said that they had "no need" for him to write to them about the "times and the seasons." While the coming of the Lord was going to catch a lot of people by surprise, that would not happen to them. They were not in "darkness," because they knew "the times and the seasons." While no one knew exactly when Jesus was coming, they could know from Jesus' prophecies when His return was getting close, nearby, and about to happen.

With words like those in these verses, we can continue to understand why the early church believed His coming was imminent. But think about this. If the Lord was not coming until thousands of years later, why would Paul even have had a discourse like this? That "day" and Jesus' coming were not going to catch the saints at Thessalonica by surprise! Saints and sinners alike would all be long gone! But it was because **His coming WAS GOING TO OCCUR IN THEIR LIFETIME** that they needed to watch "the times" and not allow the Advent to slip up on them "as a thief." Think a little further. What kind of signs, in "the times and the seasons" of the first century, could they possibly have seen about a day of the Lord that, twenty centuries later, still has not come to pass? The answer is "not any"! And what would have been the purpose of it anyway? Why would the early Christians need to know the signs of the Lord's coming if it was going to be thousands of years before He came? They would not need to know and it would make no sense for Paul to be concerned about it! But the truth is, Jesus was coming in their day! That is why Paul made sure they knew "the times," so that His coming would not "overtake" them "as a thief." A little reasoning makes this passage much easier to understand.

I THESSALONIANS 5:23 (KJV)

And the very God of peace sanctify you wholly; and I pray God your whole spirit and soul and body be preserved blameless unto the coming of our Lord Jesus Christ.

Continuing in the same chapter, we come to this verse. Does it tell us anything about when Paul was looking for the Lord to return? Yes, and it must have been soon, since he thought the saints in Thessalonica could possibly live to see the coming of Jesus. He prayed they might be kept "blameless" until Jesus came. If he believed it was going to be centuries before Jesus' coming, then his prayer was foolish! He should have just prayed that the saints would be "preserved blameless" until they died! But he knew the Lord was coming in his generation, and he knew the believers expected to be alive for the occasion; so he just prayed a reasonable prayer for their care and protection until Jesus arrived. Now Paul's request of God makes sense.

Paul's first letter to the Thessalonians tells us quite a lot about the Second Coming of Jesus. Before we leave his Epistle, we should note that all five chapters in the book end with a reference to that anticipated event. We have looked at those passages in chapters 4 and 5. In this study we have chosen not to highlight the closing verses in chapters 1, 2, and 3. However, if you care to read them, you will find that they also portray Paul and the Thessalonians as eagerly waiting for their Lord and expecting Him to come soon. All these passages continued to build a sense of imminence among the believers about their Master's return.

I have said it before, but I remind you again. Since the coming of the Lord was imminent in the days of the apostles, His coming cannot be imminent today, nearly 2,000 years later! Yet we are constantly being told by our twenty-first century preachers and prophets that Jesus' return is imminent today.

Somebody is wrong! You will have to make up your own mind as to who is right. I have chosen to believe Jesus and His apostles were right, and today's ministers who are still looking for Jesus to come soon are just mistaken.

II THESSALONIANS 1:3-10

3. We are bound to thank God always for you, brethren, as it is meet, because that your faith groweth exceedingly, and the charity of everyone of you all toward each other aboundeth;
4. So that we ourselves glory in you in the churches of God for your patience and faith in all your persecutions and tribulations that ye endure,
5. Which is a manifest token of the righteous judgment of God, that ye may be counted worthy of the kingdom of God, for which ye also suffer.
6. Seeing it is a righteous thing with God to recompense tribulation to them that trouble you;
7. And to you who are troubled rest with us, when the Lord Jesus shall be revealed from heaven with His mighty angels,
8. In flaming fire taking vengeance on them that know not God, and that obey not the gospel of our Lord Jesus Christ,
9. Who shall be punished with everlasting destruction from the presence of the Lord, and from the glory of His power,
10. When He shall come to be glorified in His saints, and to be admired in all them that believe.

The above passage in the King James Version (KJV) is the one with which I am most familiar, but many of the other versions make it easier to follow and to understand the text. So to help us in our study, I am including these same verses from the New International Version (NIV):

VII. The Apostle Paul

II THESSALONIANS 1:3-10 (NIV)

3. We ought always to thank God for you, brothers, and rightly so, because your faith is growing more and more, and the love every one of you has for each other is increasing.
4. Therefore, among God's churches we boast about your perseverance and faith in all the persecutions and trials you are enduring.
5. All this is evidence that God's judgment is right, and as a result you will be counted worthy of the kingdom of God, for which you are suffering.
6. God is just: He will pay back trouble to those who trouble you,
7. And give relief to you who are troubled, and to us as well. This will happen when the Lord Jesus is revealed from heaven in blazing fire with His powerful angels.
8. He will punish those who do not know God and do not obey the gospel of our Lord Jesus.
9. They will be punished with everlasting destruction and shut out from the presence of the Lord and from the majesty of His power,
10. On the day He comes to be glorified in His holy people and to be marveled at among all those who have believed.

Without any doubt, this passage is accepted by all as being about the Second Coming of Jesus. I have preached from it over the years. I proclaimed the soon coming of Jesus, the rapture of His people, and the "flaming fire" that would engulf the world, burn up the unbelievers, and burn up everything else on Earth. Now I have a better understanding of the New Testament and can see that I applied these verses incorrectly. I was correct in thinking they had to do with the Lord's coming, but my application and timing were wrong. As we shall see, these verses have nothing to do with us and our day but were all about the Thessalonians to whom Paul was writing.

Our search for "when" the apostle Paul believed Jesus was coming has brought us to this passage of Scripture. I believe these verses further support the answer we found in Paul's first letter to this church. In that first letter it was obvious Paul believed and taught that the Lord Jesus would be returning during the lifetime of some of the Christians at Thessalonica. In his second letter let us see if Paul reaffirmed this position or told the Thessalonians something different.

It is not my purpose here to try to interpret all these verses. I have included them all to help us get the big picture of what Paul was saying to the church. I am looking only for the answer to our "when" question. This passage is not difficult to understand if we will but read it and accept what Paul said. We should ask ourselves: **"What did Paul's words mean to the church at Thessalonica and how did they understand them?"** This is certainly the best starting point.

The church at Thessalonica was apparently being severely persecuted by the Jewish religious leaders and the unbelievers among the Jews. Paul acknowledges this several times:

all the persecutions and trials you are enduring (v. 4)
for which you are suffering (v. 5)
those who trouble you (v. 6)
you who are troubled (v. 7)

All this persecution and suffering likely resulted in a lot of deaths in the church at Thessalonica. You will recall that in Paul's first letter to this church, he responded to the people's concerns over their fellow Christians' dying before Jesus came.

Based on verses 3 and 4, the church at Thessalonica was made up of wonderful and dedicated people. Maybe that is why their enemies were working so hard to disrupt this church! As we have already noted above, the Thessalonians were enduring severe persecutions. Paul commended their faithfulness and acknowledged their sufferings, and then offered these faithful believers some words of comfort and hope. This comfort and hope consisted of two specific prophecies made by the apostle to the suffering church:

(1) In verse 6 he said, "God is just: He will pay back trouble to those who trouble you." Who was troubling the Thessalonians? It was their

VII. The Apostle Paul

contemporaries, Jews who would not believe in Jesus and were trying to destroy His young church. This makes it easy to see that these Scriptures are about the people in Paul's day and not about some future event, as I used to preach! Paul promised that their persecutors (the Jews) would not get away with their crimes against the Christians, but God, who "is just," would see that they "pay" for all of their wickedness.

(2) In verse 7 Paul said, "And give relief to you who are troubled and to us as well." This was surely the more wonderful promise. For their persecutors to get justice was good, but for the saints to get relief from their sufferings was better.

You can imagine that the Thessalonians read these promises with much joy and gladness. You can also imagine that they eagerly kept reading to see if Paul said when this "relief" was coming. He did not keep them waiting. Continuing in verse 7 Paul said: "This will happen when the Lord Jesus is revealed from heaven in blazing fire with his powerful angels." In verse 10 he stated again when his promises would be fulfilled: "On the day He comes to be glorified." **Paul promised their "relief" would come when Jesus returned!** This probably was not as specific an answer as they would have liked, but no one knew exactly when the Lord Jesus would return. Still, they surely took hope and comfort in their beloved apostle's promise that eventually the coming of their Lord Jesus would bring (1) relief to them and (2) justice to those who were causing them such pain.

As we try to analyze this passage, let us begin with a question. What event was going to (1) "pay back trouble" to the persecutors and (2) bring "relief" to the church? The answer is obvious—the coming of Jesus (verses 7 and 10). This means that Jesus had to return while some of the Thessalonians were living and suffering! If Jesus came after they all died, then His coming would not have brought them any relief. Death would have done that! If, as the church teaches today, Jesus has not yet come, then, whenever He does come, His coming will not put an end to the sufferings of the Thessalonian Christians. Their suffering would have ended centuries ago when they were all finally martyred or just died natural deaths! Is this not easy to see and grasp? **The Lord had to come WHILE THE THESSALONIANS WERE SUFFERING IF**

HIS COMING WAS GOING TO PUT AN END TO THEIR SUFFERING! This means that Jesus had to return sometime during the lifetime of the suffering saints at Thessalonica. This is the same answer to our "when" question that we have found in all of Paul's writings, as well as in the teachings of Jesus.

Please notice that Paul did not promise the church their suffering would end when they died. Think about that. If their only hope to end their suffering was to finally be martyred or to suffer until they died naturally, then that is what Paul should have encouraged them to do. He should have written, "Hold on, be faithful till death." But he did not do that! Paul knew, "by the word of the Lord," that Jesus was coming in their age, so he held up to the church the coming of the Lord as the hope and the answer to their suffering and misery! Paul even hoped to personally share in this "relief" from persecutions. In verse 7 he said: "And give relief to you who are troubled, and to us as well." Paul believed that Jesus was coming in his day and age. He knew it was possible that he, too, could live to see his Master's return!

If the apostle Paul misled the church, if Jesus did not come and bring the Thessalonians relief, what does that make Paul? Paul would have been a liar, a deceiver, and a false prophet! That cannot be true! **The only other option is: Jesus did come in that age and brought relief to His people, as Paul had prophesied and promised.** Yet the church today continues to maintain that Jesus did not come then and still has not come after nearly 2,000 years. If today's church is right, then Paul and Jesus were wrong. This cannot be true either! What a dilemma all of this is for Christianity today! How desperately our leaders need to come together and resolve this conflict between that which they teach and what our Holy Book says!

But let us continue our study. For most of my life I misunderstood this passage in II Thessalonians 1 because I did not apply the "W" questions in coming to an interpretation:

> Who was writing?
> When was he writing?
> To whom was he writing?
> Why was he writing to them?

VII. The Apostle Paul

About what was he writing?
Where and when was any activity to occur?
What did it mean to the original recipients?
What was the setting?
What was the time frame?

Instead of properly applying these questions I just read this passage (1) as if Paul had just written it, (2) as if he had written it to me, and (3) as if he had written about my troubles. No wonder I misunderstood it! As I said earlier, I would preach from these verses and talk about how we were suffering as Christians, and that one day soon Jesus was going to come "in flaming fire," rapture us, and then burn up this old wicked world. **I was so wrong!**

If I was ever to understand this passage, it was absolutely imperative that I come to realize that Paul was writing to a church and a people who lived more than 1,900 years ago. He was talking about **THEIR** "persecutions and tribulations," not mine! He was talking about **THOSE** who were troubling the Thessalonians, not those who are troubling you and me today! He was talking about Jesus' bringing "relief" to **THEM,** not us! Who were "those" that were troubling this church? We find no disagreement here; they were the unbelievers among the Jews. In this first chapter of II Thessalonians,

"those" to whom God was going to "pay back trouble" (v. 6),
"those" whom He was going to "punish" (v. 8), and
"those" who would suffer "everlasting destruction" (v. 9)

were "those" who were persecuting the Christians in Thessalonica! Without argument, these were the Jewish religious leaders and the unbelievers among the Jewish people in the first century—**not the enemies of Christianity today!**

What "vengeance," what punishment, what "judgment" of God have we learned was soon to come upon the Jewish people? If you have read the previous chapters in this book, you know the answer! It was the utter destruction of the Jewish people and the Jewish nation in AD 70 by the Roman legions. This was what Paul was talking about here! Jesus was coming to administer JUSTICE! This is what this passage is all about—JUSTICE! And it would come in the age of the apostles and these first Christians.

Who were "His mighty angels" (II Thess. 1:7) who would take "vengeance on them who know not God" (v. 8)? Can you recall our discussion in Chapter V about the parable of The Marriage of the King's Son in Matthew 22? You will remember in Matthew 22:7 that "the king" (God) "sent forth His armies" (the Roman legions) "and destroyed those murderers" (the unbelievers among the Jews) and "burned up their city" (Jerusalem). **This passage in II Thessalonians 1:3-10 is about the same event as Jesus' parable in Matthew 22!** Paul was teaching the same thing Jesus taught, the coming Judgment of God on His people for killing His prophets and rejecting His Son. Here in II Thessalonians, Paul calls this destroying force "His mighty angels" (v. 7) who would also come with fire, "flaming fire" (v. 8). But they are the same as "His armies" in Matthew 22:7. In both passages the Roman military forces were the messengers of God (**angels**)[xiv] who delivered "everlasting destruction" (v. 9) on Judah and Judea in AD 70, thereby bringing "relief" (v. 7) to the suffering saints at Thessalonica and to the rest of the early church. **The Jewish persecution machine was utterly destroyed!**

For decades, from II Thessalonians 1:3-10, I preached about the fiery destruction that was coming on our world, but I misunderstood the Scriptures. I am so grateful that I have finally come to understand about what event Paul was really writing! I do hope that you are also beginning to see what this and other Judgment passages are all about.

Peter said the Judge was "ready" to judge and it was "time . . . that judgment must begin" (I Peter 4:5 and 17). **James** said, "Behold, the Judge standeth before the door" (James 5:9). You will remember **Peter** said in his second sermon, "the heaven must receive [Jesus] until the times of restitution" (Acts 3:21). "Restitution" sounds like "pay back" time (II Thess. 1:6 NIV)! It sounds like justice, "destruction" for the persecutors and "relief" for the saints! "The times of restitution" had not arrived yet, when Paul wrote this letter, but they were getting closer and closer. **All the apostles agreed** with the hope and comfort Paul gave to these Thessalonians, that in the midst of their sufferings, while some of them were still living, Jesus would return and administer justice.

VII. The Apostle Paul

In AD 70 that is exactly what He did! Now, all of these Scriptures fit together perfectly!

Can you see that we must put these Scriptures in their proper setting, in their proper time frame? Can you see that this is all about the Thessalonian Christians and not about us today?

Paul is not writing to us!
He is not talking about our persecutions!
He is not talking about giving us relief!
He is not talking about Jesus coming and destroying our enemies!

This is all about the early church and their Jewish persecutors. This is all about Jesus' coming and delivering the Thessalonians from their persecutors, by bringing the wrath of God heavily upon the wicked nation that had killed His prophets, His apostles, His people, and His Son. This was the same soon-coming relief that Paul promised the Roman Christians when he said: **"And the God of peace will crush Satan [their Jewish adversaries] under your feet SHORTLY"** (Rom. 16:20, NKJV, emphasis mine). "It is a fearful thing to fall into the hands of the living God" (Heb. 10:31). But sadly, that is what happened to the Jewish nation.

When did the apostle Paul say Jesus was coming back? **In this passage, he reveals that Jesus would be returning in the midst of the sufferings of the church at Thessalonica.** This means Jesus has already come and that He came a long, long time ago. This agrees with everything else we are discovering about the timing of the Second Coming. **The harmony in our Bible is absolutely magnificent!**

II THESSALONIANS 2:1-8 (KJV)

You will remember in our study of the apostle Peter, at one time in his ministry he did not preach that the coming of the Lord was nearby and could occur at any time. In my words I said his message was that "Jesus was coming again, but not right then." This message came in Peter's second sermon in AD

30. He said the Lord would not return until "the times of restitution" had arrived. I mention this because in the passage before us we find the apostle Paul taking a similar position. Paul said some other things had to occur first and afterwards Jesus would come. Here is our text for study:

> 1. Now we beseech you brethren, by the coming of our Lord Jesus Christ, and by our gathering together unto Him,
> 2. That ye be not soon shaken in mind, or be troubled, neither by spirit, nor by word, nor by letter as from us, that the day of Christ is at hand.
> 3. Let no man deceive you by any means: for that day shall not come, except there come a falling away first, and that man of sin be revealed, the son of perdition;
> 4. Who opposeth and exalteth himself above all that is called God, or that is worshipped; so that he as God sitteth in the temple of God, shewing himself that he is God.
> 5. Remember ye not, that when I was yet with you, I told you these things?
> 6. And now ye know what withholdeth that he might be revealed in his time.
> 7. For the mystery of iniquity doth already work: only he who now letteth will let, until he be taken out of the way.
> 8. And then shall that Wicked be revealed, whom the Lord shall consume with the spirit of His mouth, and shall destroy with the brightness of His coming.

As in our preceding text in the first chapter, here also the old KJV, with its use of old English words and sentence construction, is more difficult to understand than the modern versions. So to help us get a better grasp of what Paul was saying, I am including these same verses from the NIV. As we study we can easily compare the two.

VII. The Apostle Paul

II THESSALONIANS 2:1-8 (NIV)

1. Concerning the coming of our Lord Jesus Christ and our being gathered to Him, we ask you, brothers,
2. Not to become easily unsettled or alarmed by some prophecy, report or letter supposed to have come from us, saying that the day of the Lord has already come.
3. Don't let anyone deceive you in any way, for that day will not come until the rebellion occurs and the man of lawlessness is revealed, the man doomed to destruction.
4. He will oppose and will exalt himself over everything that is called God or is worshipped, so that he sets himself up in God's temple, proclaiming himself to be God.
5. Don't you remember that when I was with you I used to tell you these things?
6. And now you know what is holding him back, so that he may be revealed at the proper time.
7. For the secret power of lawlessness is already at work; but the one who now holds it back will continue to do so till he is taken out of the way.
8. And then the lawless one will be revealed, whom the Lord will overthrow with the breath of His mouth and destroy by the splendor of His coming.

We certainly have very much to study and learn in these 8 verses. This passage is of such great importance in Christianity's doctrine of the Second Coming, that I must give it additional time and attention. However, I shall not try to deal in depth with everything here. Remember, we are just trying to find "when" the apostle Paul believed and taught that Jesus was coming back.

The first verse tells us this passage is certainly about the matter we are studying: "the coming of our Lord Jesus Christ and our being gathered to Him."

In the second verse Paul addressed a misunderstanding about the Lord's Second Coming. Apparently word had come to the Thessalonians, supposedly from Paul, saying, "the Lord has already come" (NIV). Paul implied strongly that any such report or letter was certainly not from him because he went on to teach that Jesus had not yet come.

At this point we should note a difference between the KJV and the NIV in verse 2. Look back at this passage, above. The KJV says the people's misunderstanding was that the day of Christ was "at hand." The NIV says the people thought the day of the Lord had "already come." My research indicates that the NIV is probably the correct translation, and the deception that had come in among some in Thessalonica was that the Lord had already come. Here is the translation of this passage in three other versions:

"the day of Christ had come," New King James Version (NKJV)
"the day of the Lord has come," New American Standard Bible (NASB)
"the day of the Lord has come," English Standard Version (ESV)

So the deception that Paul was trying to correct in the church was that Jesus had already come.

This brings up another observation. We know what events preachers say will accompany the coming of Jesus. Among other things, Jesus will appear in the sky, some say on a white horse. We shall see all of the graves opening and the dead rising back to life. The whole of planet Earth will be on fire and the world will be burning up, and so on. Now here is our point. If Paul taught his followers that the coming of Jesus was going to be like this, then how could any one of the Thessalonians ever have been deceived into thinking Jesus had already come? They could not have been! Paul's teachings about the nature of the coming of Jesus must have been entirely different from what is generally believed today, but this is a subject for another time.

Back to our study, Paul began in verse 3 to tell the church what I described earlier as "Jesus is coming again, but not right then." Paul named two things that must happen first, before Jesus would come. He said:

For that day shall not come, except, [1] there come a falling away first, and [2] that man of sin be revealed, the son of perdition.

VII. The Apostle Paul

Verse 4 tells us of the exalted nature of this man, even to his sitting "in God's temple, proclaiming himself to be God." Paul said this "man of lawlessness" (NIV) would be destroyed when the Lord Jesus came (v. 8).

We do not hear much about the first event, "the falling away." However, Christianity today is really looking for the second event, the coming of the "man of sin." Over the centuries "prophets" have named many men as being this person. None of them has ever materialized as being the "man of sin," so the prophets keep searching for him. Today speculation abounds and the church anticipates the arrival of this man on the world scene at any time. Recently a minister said this coming "man of lawlessness" (NIV) had already been born somewhere in Europe. We are told "the man of sin" (KJV) will soon rise to rule the world, and then be destroyed when Jesus comes. On the one hand, preachers say Jesus is coming soon and could come at any moment. But when they preach on this text, they say this "man of sin" must come first, before Jesus can come back. Which is it? What a conflict in their doctrine this is!

But we find more. Paul said in II Thessalonians 2:4 that this man would be so exalted and think so highly of himself that he would set "himself up in God's temple, proclaiming himself to be God." Today's prophets are expecting that to happen too. But, they have a big problem. No temple exists for him to sit in! The Roman army completely destroyed it in AD 70. Just as Jesus had said, not "one stone upon another" was left standing (Matt. 24:2). But that does not stop our prophets. They have found a solution. Now they are prophesying that a new temple will be built in Jerusalem, and this "man" will desecrate it with his lofty pride. It does not seem to matter that **NOWHERE** in the Bible can we find a prophecy that the temple will be rebuilt after its AD 70 demise. **NOWHERE!** It just goes to show how we preachers will virtually invent things to help support our beliefs and maintain our livelihood.

My fellowship of ministers and I were of another school of interpretation. We believed that "the falling away," meaning people leaving the true faith of the apostolic age, happened in the first few hundred years after the apostles. The truth became watered down with unbiblical doctrines and resulted in many "falling away" from the truth of the Gospel. At the same time, the Roman Catholic Church, with its popes, gradually rose to power. We saw the pope as the "man of sin." History documents the wickedness of the institution of the papacy, and some popes did rise to have dominion over most of the civilized world. They claimed to be infallible. They said they were God's representative on Earth. They seemed to fit Paul's description. **But we were wrong too!**

We should note here that this "man of sin" is also called "the antichrist" by ministers today. But as you can see from the text above, nothing in this passage mentions the antichrist. Preachers go to the book of Revelation to tell us about the antichrist that is coming. But, as hard as it may be to believe, **NOTHING** in the Revelation speaks about the antichrist. The only places in the Bible where the word is found are in John's Epistles. There John (1) defined "antichrist" as one who "denieth that Jesus is the Christ." He said that (2) the church in that day was looking for the "spirit of antichrist" to come and he further adds that (3) it had "already" come and "even now are there many antichrists" (I John 2:18, 22, and 4:3; and II John 7). That is the sum of any mention of the antichrist! **NOTHING** in the Bible supports the teaching that "the antichrist" is coming today, as we hear preached so often. **NOTHING!**

Let us go back to our text and see what else we can find. In verse 5, Paul reminded the Thessalonians that when he was with them, he had talked to them about "these things." Perhaps they had forgotten, but he said he had told them about "the falling away" and "the man of sin." So this was not new information or new revelation to the Thessalonians. They and Paul had talked about these things before! It is reasonable to assume that they knew a lot more about these matters than these few short verses tell us.

This "man of sin" had not yet risen to prominence. Something or somebody was in his way. Paul told the Thessalonians, in verse 6, that they "know what is holding him back." This confirms what we said in the previous paragraph: that the people, having discussed these matters with Paul, knew a lot more about this subject than is revealed to us in these eight verses. **They had to know who this man was because they knew what was in his way.** They knew what, or who, was keeping him from exalting "himself over everything that is called God or is worshipped" (v. 4). This is amazing and may come as a shock to you!

174

VII. The Apostle Paul

In verse 7 Paul said this "secret power of lawlessness is already at work." Whatever this "man of lawlessness" (v. 3 NIV) was up to, whatever he was doing in order to eventually come to power, Paul said he was **already at work doing it in Paul's day!** In this same verse Paul mentioned again the hindrance to this man's rise to fame and power. He identified the problem as another person, "the one who now holds it back." He then added that "one" would continue to hold back "the man of sin," "till he is taken out of the way." Wow! This certainly sounds like a situation in Paul's day, instead of something in our future!

In verse 8 we read that this wicked one would be revealed. He would exalt himself as Paul stated in verse 4, and desecrate God's temple, "proclaiming himself to be God." But it seems that his time would be short-lived for Jesus would destroy him "with the brightness of His coming."

Today, among those of us who believe the "man of sin" is history, no one knows for certain who this man was. Great scholars, whom I know, have differing opinions. I have my own opinion, but this book is not about my opinions. It is about what we can know for certain from the Word of God! From these eight verses we **can know** some things about this man! These things that we **can know** make it unnecessary for us to actually know who the "man of sin" was.

What we shall learn is that this "man of sin" is history, yesterday's news! Without any doubting, we can be certain that this text in II Thessalonians 2 was about the day and age of the early church in the first century. This is obvious from what Paul said! The following points are proof:

1. Paul knew who this man was (v. 5-6)!
2. Paul had to know who this man was because he knew "the one" that was hindering his rise to power (v. 6)!
3. Since Paul knew who these two people were, he could have named them! He did not do so, I believe, because to do so would have further exposed the Thessalonians to greater danger and suffering. Such would be the case if his letter ever fell into the wrong

hands. After all he was writing very negatively about a man who was going to have tremendous power.

4. Not only did Paul know who this man was, but the Thessalonians knew who he was too (v. 6)!

5. The Thessalonians had to know who this man was, because they also knew who was standing in his way (v. 6)!

6. This man was a contemporary figure, a matter of present concern to the Thessalonians. Paul had talked with them about him, when Paul was in Thessalonica (v. 5)!

7. Whatever kind of "lawless" activity was going on, whatever efforts were being made to bring this "man of sin" to power, Paul said it was "already at work" **THEN**, when he wrote this second letter to the church at Thessalonica in AD 52-53 (v. 7)!

8. Since this man was going to desecrate the temple, he had to do so while the temple was still standing. This means that he lived sometime before AD 70 when the temple was destroyed (v. 4)!

9. This confines this man's time of operation to somewhere between AD 52, when Paul wrote this letter, and AD 70, when the temple was destroyed!

10. All these facts leave us with no other possible conclusion but that this man of sin was a contemporary of Paul and the Thessalonian Christians!

This is all amazing! How did I ever miss all of these obvious truths for so many, many years? Is it not easy to see? The "man of sin" could not have been the pope. The man lived in Paul's day! Popes did not arise until hundreds of years later. The "man of sin" cannot be someone in our day; the Thessalonians knew who he was nearly 2,000 years ago. Our preachers and prophets say that events are happening today to bring this man to power. Just recently, I heard a famous preacher on TV say that the present economic problems (the recession) in our country and the world were "setting the stage for the rise of the man of sin, the antichrist." All my life it has been one world event, or another, that was always "setting the stage" for this man's arrival! Not any of these predictions were ever true! All of these modern-day prophets were wrong every single time and they are still wrong today! How can I be so sure? You and I can be sure because (1) Paul knew who the man was and (2) he wrote

VII. The Apostle Paul

in AD 52-53 that the process to bring him to power was already at work **THEN!** That was about 2,000 years ago! It cannot be happening today too! How can our Bible scholars read these words of Paul and then believe the "man of sin" is coming in our day? **Whoever this man was, Paul plainly and clearly portrayed him as a man of the first century, not the twenty-first century!**

Consider this! With all the problems and persecutions the Thessalonians were going through, why would Paul trouble and concern them about an evil man who would be coming to power 2,000 years later? When Paul was with this church, why would he have talked with them about something that would never affect them? He would not have done so! The truth is that Paul talked and wrote about contemporary things that concerned these first Christians! **It is obvious that this "man of sin" was a current issue in the first century AD and a present concern then of Paul and the Thessalonians!** Do not be concerned about "the man of sin" or the antichrist arising today—he has already come and he is history!

Well, I have not mentioned our "when" questions lately. People today take this passage of Scripture and say Jesus has not come yet because the "man of sin," "the antichrist," must come first. I believe we have positively shown that this man has already come. He came in the first century! Paul said Jesus was going to destroy this man "with the brightness of His coming." Well, if Jesus was going to destroy this man by His coming, then Jesus had to come while this man was living. **This man lived in the first century, which means Jesus came in the first century too!** How beautifully does this agree with all the other Scriptures we have studied! Everything is consistent. Jesus and His apostles taught the same thing about "when" He was coming! And **NOT ONE OF THEM** said He would be coming thousands of years later.

But we have not finished with these eight verses. Not only did Paul say "the man of sin" would come before Jesus returned, but also he predicted that an exodus from the church would occur before Jesus came back. He called it a "falling away." Paul said this would happen "first," before the Lord would come. Where did Paul get that information? We surely do not know the full answer to that question, but we do know Jesus prophesied the EXACT SAME THING and in the same order. Jesus said:

> And many false prophets shall arise, and shall deceive many. And because iniquity shall abound, the love of many shall wax cold. (Matt. 24:11-12)

This was Jesus' prophecy of a "falling away." Then in the verses after this prophecy, Jesus predicts His coming:

> And then shall appear the sign of the Son of Man in heaven . . . and they shall see the Son of Man coming in the clouds of heaven with power and great glory. (Matt. 24:30)

This was exactly what Paul said. A falling away would come first, preceding the Lord's return. Now if you think Jesus was talking about this all happening hundreds of years later or, as most Christians believe, in the twenty-first century, then read Matthew 24:34 again:

> Verily I say unto you, This generation shall not pass till all these things be fulfilled.

"All these things" included "many" being deceived, the "love of many" waxing cold, and Jesus coming "in the clouds of heaven." All these things would happen in the generation of the people to whom Jesus was speaking!

In our text Paul did not say "when" the falling away would occur, but Jesus confined it to that generation. Did a lot of believers give up their faith in Christ and leave the church, prior to the events of AD 70? Every Bible student knows the answer is "yes." The persecution of the believers by the Jews was terrible. But, in the mid-60s AD Nero and the Romans joined with the Jews in persecuting the Christians, and things became much worse. Under such pressure, many Jewish converts to Christianity renounced their faith and went back to Judaism. The book of Hebrews, written in AD 67 to 69, seems to have been written in an effort to encourage believers to hold on to their faith. They were assured that in "a little while" (Heb. 10:37), Jesus would come and bring them relief.

VII. The Apostle Paul

Paul warned Timothy about this problem in I Timothy 1:19, II Timothy 4:3-4, and in the following passage:

> Now the spirit speaketh expressly, that in the latter times some shall depart from the faith. (I Tim. 4:1)

Preachers today use this Scripture to declare apostasy in our day and to say we are living in the Last Days. You know when the Last Days were. Timothy was living in them and this warning was for him. **Why would Paul warn Timothy of a "falling away" in the church that was going to happen in our day, nearly 2,000 years later?** He would not! It makes no sense at all. With all that Timothy had on his young shoulders, why would Paul burden him about Christians departing "from the faith" in the twenty-first century? He would not have done so! But, this "departing from the faith" was a problem in Timothy's day, which he was going to face! Paul told Timothy, in verse 6, that if he would tell the brethren about this and warn them, then He would "be a good minister of Jesus Christ." Why would Paul caution Timothy to warn his people if this did not pertain to them and their day? It is evident—this verse was all about Timothy's day and about the possibility of Timothy's sheep leaving the fellowship of those first believers! It is not about today!

In I John 2:19, John documents "the falling away" in his day:

> They went out from us, but they were not of us; for if they had been of us, they would no doubt have continued with us: but they went out, that they might be made manifest that they were not all of us.

So a "falling away" among believers occurred in that first generation of Christians. Jesus Himself had said it would happen (Matt. 24:11-12). This should be enough for Christians to believe that it did occur. But we also have scriptural evidence that many left the faith in those days.

Paul told the Thessalonians two things would occur before Jesus came back: (1) a "falling away" and (2) the coming of the "man of sin." We have found that both of these events happened in the first century, so neither of them prevented the Lord from returning then. We further learned that the coming of

Jesus would destroy this "man." To do that, Jesus had to come in this man's lifetime. Thus Jesus had to come in the first century too! This is clear! How did I miss it for decades?

The apostle Paul made many more references to the coming of Jesus. However, they do not contribute to answering our "when" question, so we will end our study of his writings here. But, we have found the answer to our question. **Every passage we have studied has given us the same answer.** They have all agreed. Paul neither contradicted himself nor did he ever contradict what Jesus and the other apostles taught about the Second Coming. When did the apostle Paul say Jesus was coming back? **We have seen that he believed, wrote, and preached that His Master, Jesus Christ, was coming again in that first century of the church, in Paul's own generation, while some of the people to whom he preached were still living.** Why then do preachers continue to declare today, in the twenty-first century, that Jesus is coming soon? They have the same problem I used to have. They do not understand Jesus' teachings about the Last Days and His Second Coming!

As we have learned, Jesus is not coming in our day. **Absolutely no Scriptures in the Bible support such a teaching! Not any! On the other hand, everything we have found declares that He has already come!** Otherwise, the scoffers of whom C. S. Lewis wrote were right. They said: Jesus "was wrong," He "created . . . delusion," and He was a "very embarrassing" Master. What a great dilemma! These are all unacceptable options for Christians and we know they are not true! They destroy the very foundation of Christianity! Is it too difficult, for those of us who believe in Jesus, to believe that our Savior, the perfect, sinless Son of God, did exactly as He had promised and returned in that first century? The Scriptures have caused me to believe that He did! I trust that your faith is bringing you to this same conclusion.

THE APOSTLE JOHN

We come next to the apostle John and our question is the same we asked of Peter and Paul. **"When did the apostle John say Jesus was coming?"** John is credited with writing the following: the Gospel that bears his name; Revelation; and three short Epistles, I, II, and III John. We have already studied the Gospel of John and the book of Revelation in our search for "When did Jesus say He was coming?" Now we look at John's Epistles to see what his personal belief was about "when" his Master would be returning.

I JOHN 2:17 & 18 (NKJV)

17. And the world is passing away, and the lust of it; but he who does the will of God abides forever.
18. Little children, it is the last hour; and as you have heard that the antichrist is coming, even now many antichrists have come, by which we know that it is the last hour.

The precise date of this epistle cannot be determined. Apparently it was just before AD 70. The "world" of Judaism was still standing, but not for long. John believed it was in its "last hour," and that the end was near.

In verse 17 John says, "And the world is passing away." We learned in the chapter on the End of the World what "world" was passing away in those days. It was the world of Judaism and all that pertained to it. In the Jewish spiritual world, Jesus had come and had fulfilled their Law, so it was "ready to vanish away" (Heb. 8:13). As for their physical world, Jesus had prophesied its destruction in Matthew 24 and elsewhere in the Gospels. This happened in AD 70 when the Romans destroyed the people, the land of Judea, the nation, the temple, and the holy city, Jerusalem. John felt "the end" was so near that it was already in the process of happening. He said it "is passing" away. The war did last for years, but John, knowing the signs Jesus had personally given to him and the other apostles, was now sure that it was all about to be over.

I apologize for continuing to bring this fact to your attention. But we must remember that Jesus specifically **tied the time of His coming to the destruction of Jerusalem.** "Immediately" after the tribulation of those days, Jesus promised to come and gather His elect (Matt. 24:15-34). So, if this "world" of the Jews was on the verge of passing away, then Jesus Christ was on the verge of coming for His people. The two are inseparable!

In this letter the apostle John encouraged the saints, his "little children," to hold on and be faithful to the end. Jesus had said, "He that shall endure unto the end, the same shall be saved" (Matt. 24:13). "The end" was the end of the first-century world of Judaism. To renounce their faith in Jesus, and to again put their trust in Judaism, would result in their being destroyed by the wrath of God that was about to come on their nation. In contrast, John continued in verse 17, promising: "But he who does the will of God abides forever." This was the promise of eternal life to the faithful! John reaffirmed this in verse 22: "And this is the promise that He hath promised us, even eternal life." So in verse 17, John was telling the believers that the world of Judaism "is passing" away, but if they would remain true to Jesus, instead of passing away with it, they would abide "forever."

In verse 18, John continued to emphasize how very near "the end" of that "world" was, and thus how very near the coming of Jesus was. He said, "Little children, it is the last hour." John saw the end as being so near that it was no longer enough to warn the people that they were living in the Last Days. Now shortly before the overthrow of Jerusalem, John said, "It is the last hour." John believed, at the time he wrote this Epistle, that Jerusalem was in its "last hour," that is to say, very near to its end. **Since Jesus had tied His coming to Jerusalem's demise, John knew the coming of Jesus was also very near.**

Jesus had given John and the other apostles some signs as indicators for which to look, signs about "when" the end would come. In Matthew 24:11, 12 and 24 Jesus had said:

VII. The Apostle John

And many false prophets shall arise, and shall deceive many.
The love of many shall wax cold.
For there shall arise false Christs, and false prophets.

Among other signs, John saw these "false Christs," and he added in verse 18, "as you have heard that the antichrist is coming, even now many antichrists have come, by which we know that it is the last hour." John repeated himself and warned again, "It is the last hour." He KNEW this because the antichrists for which he was looking had arrived; he said, they "have come." The signs that would signal "the end" had come to pass. It was indeed "the last hour." Therefore, John was looking for the full wrath of God upon the nation at any time, at any moment, accompanied by the return of His Lord, as Jesus had prophesied. **When did the apostle John say Jesus was coming? Well, he believed the remaining time was so short that he described it as virtually being the last hour.**

I shall not repeat my discussion of antichrists. I refer you to it in the previous section (The Apostle Paul, II Thessalonians 2:1-8). But let us review **the facts.** John is the **only writer** who mentioned the words "antichrist" or "antichrists," and he said they **had already come. NOTHING** in the Bible predicts the rise of the antichrist in our world today! **NOTHING!** Is not this amazing? The church is looking for the imminent arrival today of this antichrist. Yet the **ONLY** times that "antichrist" and "antichrists" are found in the Bible, the writer says, we **"have heard that it should come; and even now already is it in the world"** (I John 4:3). Again, the rise of the antichrists was a sign to John, not us, that the Lord's Second Coming was near. So when John saw that the "antichrists" had come, **he knew** that it was "the last hour" and Jesus' return was near. Again, this is astounding! How can the church still be looking for the antichrist? (John defined who is an antichrist in I John 2:22, 4:1-3, and II John 7.)

I JOHN 2:28 (NKJV)

And now, little children, abide in Him, that when He appears, we may have confidence and not be ashamed before Him at His coming.

This verse certainly continues to show the sense of imminence regarding the coming of the Lord that we find throughout the Epistles. If we ask one of our "W" questions here it will help us to get the true feel for this verse. What did these words mean to the original people to whom John wrote this letter? It is easy to see that John's words would lead the people to believe they would live to see Jesus' return. We find no inference here that they would die, be resurrected, and then see Jesus. John said, "That when He appears, we may have confidence." The "we" is John and those to whom He was writing, and the sense of His words was "we" would be alive "at His coming."

I JOHN 3:2 (NKJV)

Beloved, now we are children of God; and it has not yet been revealed what we shall be, but we know that when He is revealed, we shall be like Him, for we shall see Him as He is.

The same things I said about the previous verse are true of this one, and more so. John really led the people to feel that they would be alive when Jesus came. In this verse John used "we" five times and closed with "for we shall see Him as He is." The promise to "see" Jesus when He returned was a promise to those who would be living at His return. **John believed he would be alive when Jesus came and he did not hesitate to instill that hope and excitement in his fellow Christians.** The apostle John surely would not have done this if he had believed it was going to be thousands of years before his Master and Lord returned.

The apostle John, **like all the other apostles,** believed Jesus would return in his own generation. It is amazing that Jesus and His chosen men never contradicted one another regarding "when" Jesus would come again! They all agreed! This was divine inspiration at work. Praise God for the unity of the Scriptures!

VIII

WHEN DID OTHER EARLY CHURCH LEADERS SAY JESUS WAS COMING?

JAMES, JESUS' HALF-BROTHER

Who wrote the Epistle of James? Apparently five men in the New Testament were named James. It is a little strange that the name was so popular, since we do not find anyone by that name in the Old Testament. Two of the men named James were the Lord's apostles. One of these was John's brother, James the son of Zebedee. He was the first of the apostles to be martyred. He was killed by Herod Agrippa in about AD 44 (Acts 12:1-2). Scholars believe he died too early to have written the Epistle of James.

We know little of the other apostle James, the son of Alphaeus. Of the remaining men named James, the Lord's oldest half-brother, is by far the most well-known. He became a leader in the church at Jerusalem. He seemed to have been in charge of the council that was held there in Acts 15. It is likely that he was an elder of the Jerusalem church. Bible scholars feel it was this James, the Lord's half-brother, who wrote the book of James. It is not possible to determine exactly when it was written. According to the Jewish historian, Josephus, it was this same James who was martyred in AD 62. So the Epistle of James was written on or before that time.

JAMES 5:7-9 (NIV)

7. Be patient, then, brothers, until the Lord's coming. See how the farmer waits for the land to yield its valuable crop and how patient he is for the autumn and spring rains.
8. You too, be patient and stand firm, because the Lord's coming is near.
9. Don't grumble against each other, brothers, or you will be judged. The Judge is standing at the door!

In verse 7 it was our Lord's half-brother who was encouraging "the twelve tribes which are scattered abroad" (James 1:1) to be patient "until the coming of the Lord." Exhortations to patience were frequent in the New Testament writings. Times were very tough. Persecutions were severe and hard to endure. In the opening paragraph, I noted the martyrdom of two of the men named James. You can understand the people wanting the Lord to hurry, to quickly come back. If Jesus was not coming soon, then it was rather deceitful for James to exhort his brothers in the faith to "Be patient . . . until the Lord's coming." But James was not being deceitful; he believed Jesus was coming in their lifetime. Otherwise, he would have encouraged them to hold on and endure the sufferings until they died or until things got better.

James used the example of a farmer waiting for his crop to mature before he harvested it. James meant that the believers must be patient until the Lord decided the time was right for the best harvest. Then He would come. This is similar to what Peter said in II Peter 3:9:

> The Lord is not slack concerning His promise [to come] . . . but is longsuffering to us-ward, not willing that any should perish, but that all should come to repentance.

So in verse 8 James said, "You too [like the farmer], be patient and stand firm, because the Lord's coming is near." Now these must really have been words of great comfort! Here was a reason for them to be patient: "the Lord's coming is near." Here was something for them to hope in, something to hang on to—**THE LORD'S COMING WAS NEAR!** Jesus' brother believed Jesus

VIII. Early Church Leaders

would be coming back soon! In this passage we are using the NIV, and as we have seen, it says that Jesus' coming "is near." Here are some other translations:

draweth nigh (KJV)
is at hand (NKJV)
is near (NASB)
is at hand (ESV)

We all know what these terms mean! We all know what they meant to the early church. What words meant to the original recipients is the first thing to consider in Bible interpretation. We all know that to them James' words meant, **"Hold on, be strong, don't give up now, our Jesus is coming soon!"** A verse of Scripture could not be clearer! **James believed the Lord was coming in the lifetime of his followers.**

It seems evident from James' exhortations that he believed the Lord's coming would bring "relief" to his suffering fellow Christians. In verses 7 and 8 he encouraged them to "be patient." The reason for patience was "because the Lord's coming is near." James was saying their persecutions would end with Jesus' arrival! This was the same thing Paul had promised to the Thessalonians: "And give relief to you who are troubled . . . when the Lord Jesus is revealed from heaven" (II Thess. 1:7 NIV).

In verse 9 **James** added, "The Judge is standing at the door." Since Jesus would be coming back to administer justice, for James to say the Judge was already "standing at the door" was another way of emphasizing how very "near" the Lord was to coming back. Jesus had promised to return while some of His original followers were still living. As the Judge, He would "reward every man according to his works" (Matt. 16:27-28), bringing destruction to the wicked nation and life eternal to the righteous. If He has not yet come, then Jesus has been "standing at the door" for about 2,000 years. That does not make any sense! **Peter** also said that Jesus "is ready to judge the living and the dead" (I Peter 4:5 NIV), and **Paul** told Timothy that Jesus was "about to judge [the] living ones and dead ones" (II Tim. 4:1, Greek text). **Fellow Christians, if the Judge has not come yet, then James, Peter, and Paul were all wrong, and**

you and I are left unable to trust anything they have said! What a dilemma!

But the dilemma is very easy to solve! **We just need to believe what the Bible says!** We need to have faith in the Word of God! Believe that nearly 2,000 years ago, His coming was "near" and "at hand." Believe that He came in that day, in that generation, and that some of the first Christians were "alive" to see Him. **The whole New Testament backs up and supports this position!** On the other hand, if we insist on holding on to our church tradition, which says "Jesus is coming soon in our day," then we have absolutely **NO BIBLE** to support our belief! **NONE! NOT ANY!**

When did James say Jesus was coming? We have found our answer; His coming was "near," "at hand," and drawing "nigh." This should not surprise you; that is ALL we have found as we have moved further from Pentecost in AD 30, and closer to "the end" in AD 70. James agrees with Jesus, Peter, Paul, and John. But that is what we would expect to find, since the same Holy Ghost was inspiring the words that each of them wrote! **THE HARMONY OF THE BIBLE CONTINUES TO BUILD MY FAITH IN GOD!** I trust and pray you are having this same experience!

VIII. Early Church Leaders

THE AUTHOR OF THE BOOK OF HEBREWS

Who was the author of the Epistle to the Hebrews? The answer to this question is not known. Many persons have been considered as possibilities, including Paul, Barnabas, Silas, Apollos, Luke, and others. My Thompson Chain Reference Bible says authorship is "commonly attributed to Paul," and it titles the letter "The Epistle of Paul to the Hebrews." Hebrews 10:34 sounds like Paul when the writer says, "For ye had compassion of me in my bonds." Paul was very close to Timothy, and in 13:23 the author mentions that Timothy had been "set at liberty," an apparent reference to his being freed from prison by his persecutors. In 13:24 the writer says, "They of Italy salute you." Tradition has Paul spending his last years in Rome, so he could have written this letter from there and included this closing greeting from the local Italian Christians. Ultimately, of course, as with all the Scriptures, the author was the Holy Spirit (II Peter 1:21)!

In this letter the temple was still standing, the Levitical priesthood was still operating, and persecutions were becoming more severe. These details cause Bible scholars to put the date of the writing of Hebrews around AD 67-69. This would be just prior to the destruction of the nation of the Jews by the Romans in AD 70.

It is generally agreed that the letter to the Hebrews was written to encourage the Jewish converts to Christianity to be faithful, to hold on to their faith in Christ, and not to turn back to Judaism. Throughout the Epistle the writer compared what the Hebrews had under the Law of Moses with what they now had in Jesus. In every instance he showed that what Christ offered was much better than the old system. He further pointed out the fact that the old system was near its end and would soon pass away. He used the superiority of the New Covenant, along with the soon-coming demise of the Old Covenant, to encourage the people to be true to Jesus. It was evident that the persecutions were severe, and all it took to stop them was to denounce one's faith in Jesus. It was very enticing to give up! This letter to the Hebrews was designed to give them reason, courage, and hope to hold on a little longer.

Can we find an answer in the Epistle to the Hebrews to our question, **"When did the author of Hebrews say Jesus was coming?"** Many verses in Hebrews contribute to the study of Jesus' return, but one lengthy passage plainly and directly addresses our question. Here it is and we shall study it:

HEBREWS 10:22-39

22. Let us draw near with a true heart in full assurance of faith, having our hearts sprinkled from an evil conscience and our bodies washed with pure water.
23. Let us hold fast the profession of our faith without wavering; (for He is faithful that promised);
24. And let us consider one another to provoke unto love and to good works:
25. Not forsaking the assembling of ourselves together, as the manner of some is; but exhorting one another: and so much the more, as ye see the day approaching.
26. For if we sin wilfully after that we have received the knowledge of the truth, there remaineth no more sacrifice for sins.
27. But a certain fearful looking for judgment and fiery indignation, which shall devour the adversaries.
28. He that despised Moses' law died without mercy under two or three witnesses:
29. Of how much sorer punishment, suppose ye, shall he be thought worthy, who hath trodden under foot the Son of God, and hath counted the blood of the covenant, wherewith he was sanctified, an unholy thing, and hath done despite unto the Spirit of grace?
30. For we know Him that hath said, Vengeance belongeth unto me, I will recompense, saith the lord. And again, The Lord shall judge His people.
31. It is a fearful thing to fall into the hands of the living God.
32. But call to remembrance the former days, in which, after ye were illuminated, ye endured a great fight of afflictions;
33. Partly whilst ye were made a gazingstock both by reproaches and afflictions; and partly, whilst ye became companions of them that were so used.

34. For ye had compassion of me in my bonds, and took joyfully the spoiling of your goods, knowing in yourselves that ye have in heaven a better and an enduring substance.

35. Cast not away therefore your confidence, which hath great recompense of reward.

36. For ye have need of patience, that, after ye have done the will of God, ye might receive the promise.

37. For yet a little while, and He that shall come will come, and will not tarry.

38. Now the just shall live by faith: but if any man draw back, My soul shall have no pleasure in him.

39. But we are not of them who draw back unto perdition; but of them that believe to the saving of the soul.

Although lengthy, it is necessary to consider it all in order to get the full picture the writer is painting and grasp the importance of the promises the author made to the saints.

Verses 22, 23, and 24 are words of encouragement to the saints to hold on to their faith in the midst of hard persecutions:

Let us draw near with a true heart in full assurance of faith.
Let us hold fast the profession of our faith without wavering.
Let us consider one another to provoke unto love and to good works.

In verse 25 the writer encouraged the Hebrews not to neglect their assembling together. In the company and fellowship of one another, the saints would find courage and strength to hold on and stay faithful to their Lord. But the writer may have been pointing the saints' attention toward the "gathering together" the church was anticipating at the return of Jesus. Either way, he said to exhort "one another" to faithfulness, and to do so even more "as ye see the day approaching." Bible scholars generally agree that "the day" here is the day when Jesus would come "the second time without sin unto salvation" (Heb. 9:28).

So, the Hebrew Christians would be able to "see the day approaching" when Jesus would come again. The Greek text says they would be able to see the day "drawing near." Jesus had said, regarding His coming and the signs leading up to it: "When ye shall see these things, know that it is near, even at the doors" (Matt. 24:33). So, the Christians could see events happening about them, and when they saw these things, they would know the day of Jesus' return was "approaching" and "drawing near." The writer encouraged the saints to exhort one another to faithfulness as they saw His coming approaching, and to intensify their exhortations as "the day" got closer and closer.

When did the writer of Hebrews believe Jesus was coming? **Well, he believed the day was so close in AD 67-69 that the saints would be able to see the day approaching!** This is amazing! Consider these questions:

1. If Jesus was not going to come for some 2,000 years, how could the early church possibly see the day approaching? They absolutely could not see it approaching!
2. What would have been the purpose of their watching for the day's approach anyway if Jesus was not coming until at least a couple of thousand years later? Absolutely none!
3. If, as we are told today, the signs of Jesus' coming are happening all around us, which of these signs occurring now could these first-century Hebrew believers have seen? None! Not any at all!

But the inspired writer of Hebrews said that they would be able to "see the day approaching." Oh! Can you see the obvious truth here? **Jesus' coming had to occur in their lifetime if they were going to "see the day approaching"!**

We can understand here how very important it is to ask those "W" questions and to keep this verse in its proper context and time setting. I used to get it all out of place. I would preach to my congregation and warn them to look for His coming. I would tell them to be sure they were "ready" as they saw His coming "approaching." **But I had it all wrong.** The author did not tell me that I would see "the day" drawing near. He told the Christians in AD 67-69 that **THEY WOULD SEE THE DAY APPROACHING.** If Jesus has not yet

VIII. Early Church Leaders

come, then this Bible writer lied to the people and deceived them! No doubt the author himself was seeing the signs of Jesus' return. He warned the people to exhort one another to faithfulness as they too saw the day getting closer. The writer's hope was that as the people saw their Master's coming getting nearer and nearer, they would be able to find the courage and strength to hold on and be faithful. As they saw the day approaching, they would know they did not have much longer to endure their sufferings. Perhaps their spirits would rise and they would say, "We can make it a little longer."

Having encouraged the Hebrews to be faithful to Christ, the writer then warned them in verse 26 of the consequences awaiting them if they "sin wilfully" after having "received the knowledge of the truth." The "knowledge" was that Jesus was their Messiah. The "sin" would have been forsaking Him and going back to Judaism. And if they did that he said, "There remaineth no more sacrifice for sins." These people had no other way except Jesus! No one else but Jesus and no other sacrifice but His could atone for their and their nation's sins! Jesus was then, and still is, the only Way!

In verse 27 the Hebrew writer warned of what would await those Hebrews who would turn their backs on Jesus and go back to Judaism. Having read to this point, you know the horrible Judgment that was soon coming upon the Jewish nation. The Hebrew believers' only escape from this wrath of God was through their Messiah. If they now turned their backs on Him, the same fate awaiting the nation as a whole would be their lot too. Verse 27 describes that fate, and for clarity we quote the NIV:

> But only a fearful expectation of judgment and of raging fire that will consume the enemies of God. (Heb. 10:27 NIV)

This was a description of what was coming upon the Jewish nation in their war with the Romans. The Jewish people had become "the enemies of God." They were the ones who killed His prophets, His apostles, His Son, and even now were persecuting and killing His servants. The war would bring terrible suffering, destruction, and death. Judea would be plundered, Jerusalem burned, and the people killed or enslaved. As for their beautiful temple, Jesus had prophesied nearly forty years earlier that there would "not be left here one stone upon another, that shall not be thrown down" (Matt. 24:2). The writer was trying to get the Hebrews to see that absolutely nothing was worthy of their turning back! NOTHING WAS WORTH THEIR FORSAKING JESUS; AND WHATEVER MIGHT ATTRACT THEM AT THE MOMENT, IT WOULD ALL SOON BE GONE.

Verse 27 also includes a time indicator that was not properly translated in the KJV. In the original Greek the word *mello* is in this verse, and we have learned it means "about to." This verse is translated in **The Emphatic Diaglott** as follows: "But some Terrible Expectation of Judgment, even of a fiery Indignation which is about to consume the opponents." This is clear! The fiery Judgment was not going to happen just sometime in the future; it was **ABOUT TO HAPPEN!** So the Hebrews who would leave Christ for Judaism would soon find themselves caught up in this wrath of God. It was **ABOUT TO HAPPEN THEN, IN AD 67-69!** It was so close, the church could "see the day approaching." The "great and terrible Day of the Lord," Judgment Day, was imminent! I do hope you are seeing this!

The Scriptures themselves plainly show that these verses we are studying were all about the first-century Christians, and all about events that would be happening in their day. Already we have found two things that make this very clear:

1. The Second Coming of the Lord was so near in AD 67-69, that the saints living then would be able to "see the day approaching."
2. The Judgment was so nearby in AD 67-69, that the author described it as being "about to" occur.

Our only hope to understand these Scriptures and others like them is to keep them in their proper context and proper time frame. It is obvious the author was writing about things relating to the Hebrews living **THEN.** He was talking about things that were, and would be, occurring in **THEIR** lifetime. He was not writing about things that would happen in our day! Besides, of what value would that have been then? How would his writing about events to happen in our day have helped these first-century Christians to remain faithful? It is obvious that these Scriptures are all about the early church. To take them out of

VIII. Early Church Leaders

this context and apply them to our day is absolutely wrong! Nothing here even hints that the writer was talking about today, about you and me seeing "the day approaching," or about our facing a "fiery" judgment!

The believers' only hope of escape would be to heed the words of Jesus when they saw "the day approaching." You remember the advice of Jesus in Luke 21:20-21:

> And when ye shall see Jerusalem compassed with armies.
> Then let them which be in Judea flee into the mountains.

Ultimately, at some point in all of this Judgment upon the nation, Jesus had promised He would come "with power and great glory" and have His angels "gather together His elect from the four winds, from one end of heaven to the other" (Matt. 24:30-31). The Hebrews' only hope was to maintain their faith in Jesus!

Verses 28, 29, and 30 continue to describe the severe nature of this "vengeance" of God. The writer said that under the Old Covenant, one who "despised Moses' law" died without mercy. In comparison "how much sorer punishment" would come upon those who had "trodden under foot the Son of God"? Again, the writer was warning the Hebrew Christians that if they rejected Jesus, they would share in this "sorer punishment" coming upon the nation. He wanted the Hebrews to realize that nothing in Judaism should tempt them to turn back.

In verse 31 he said, "It is a fearful thing to fall into the hands of the living God." The author was warning the people that they wanted no part of this Judgment! What was "about to come" on their nation would be horrible beyond description. Staying true to Christ was their only hope! As Paul told the Thessalonians, it was Jesus who "delivered us from the wrath to come" (I Thess. 1:10).

In verses 32, 33, and 34 the writer encouraged the Hebrews to remember when they were first saved, when they were first "illuminated" and their eyes were opened to "the knowledge of the truth" (v. 26). Back then, he said, they suffered too. They were "made a gazingstock" and endured "reproaches and afflictions." They suffered "the spoiling" of their "goods," but they were so happy and excited over Jesus that they did it "joyfully." They knew that "in heaven" they had something "better."

In verse 35 the author begged the Hebrews not to throw away all they had suffered for Jesus! They had come too far to lose their faith and hope in Him now! He reminded them that the "better" thing they had "in heaven" was still there! He said, in effect, "You still have a great reward awaiting you, so don't give up now!"

In verse 36 he encouraged the Hebrews to be patient! They, of course, had been patient, some for years and others for decades. The struggle was getting old and the saints were getting weary. He exhorted them, "You have done the will of God, so be patient a little longer that you might receive the promise." This is such a beautiful chapter! **Whoever wrote Hebrews, as you read his words, you can feel the love and care of a true shepherd for his sheep.**

Then, in verse 37, the writer gave the Hebrews a promise that certainly must have inspired them to muster a little more strength, courage, and patience sufficient to hold on and stay true to their Jesus. He said:

For yet a little while, and He that shall come will come, and will not tarry. (Heb. 10:37)

What wonderful news! How exciting and encouraging these words must have been to the Hebrew Christians. They were suffering persecutions every day and struggling to remain faithful. Now they have been told by a man of God that in just "a little while" their Master will come back! Just as Paul had promised the Thessalonians, they knew Jesus' return would end their suffering! Jesus would bring "relief to you who are troubled . . . on the day He comes to be glorified" (II Thess. 1:7, 10). **And the good news was that Jesus was coming again in a little while.** And to emphasize just how near His coming was, the writer assured the Hebrews that Jesus "will come and will not tarry."

VIII. Early Church Leaders

Many times I used this text to preach Jesus was coming soon, that He would be appearing in "a little while." But, if Jesus did not come **THEN,** in their day, **SOON** after this Epistle was written, then this letter to the Hebrews was just a great big deception, full of lies and false prophecies! I never talked about that possibility! I just kept preaching that Jesus was coming in "a little while" and we had better get ready. It never occurred to me that I was taking this verse completely out of its true context, completely out of its original time setting. **Again I was wrong!**

I have gone through this passage at length so we can see the proper context. Now it is easy to see that these verses were all about encouraging the Hebrew Christians in AD 67-69 to be faithful a little longer, not to turn back to certain destruction, and to find a little more patience, because their battle was almost over and their Savior was coming in "a little while." Wow!

I have written ***Christianity's Great Dilemma*** because, in spite of this Scripture that teaches Jesus' imminent appearing, the church today proclaims that He did not return in "a little while" as the Epistle said He would, and further, that He still has not come. The church attempts to get around the obvious meaning of this Scripture by saying the author meant "a little while" in God's realm where time is endless. Preachers say "a little while" in God's world could be thousands of years. So if He comes in the twenty-first century, it would still be "a little while" to God. This is pathetic! First of all, it was a man, the author of the Epistle, writing to other men and women. It was one person speaking to other people. When the writer said "a little while," he meant a little while in his world. When the Hebrews read it, they understood it as meaning whatever "a little while" was in their world. Absolutely nothing here supports the idea that the writer was talking about a measurement of time in God's sphere.

Besides, how terribly deceptive it would have been of God to promise His people He was coming in "a little while," knowing all the time that He was really not going to come until thousands of years later! God knew what "a little while" would mean to His people, and we can rest assured He kept that schedule! How deceitful it would have been of God to have done anything else! God is not a deceiver! He does not purposely mislead His people! He is a God of truth and honesty! And besides all this, the Scripture further says He "will come and will not tarry." If Jesus has not returned in nearly 2,000 years, then **HE CERTAINLY IS TARRYING** and the Scriptures are false and misleading! What a great dilemma!

How long is "a little while" anyway? Obviously it is not an exact measurement of time like a day, a week, or a year. No argument can be made that it equals three hours, ten days, six months, two years, or any other specific length of time. We think it is fair to say it is a relatively short time. But that can vary. If you cannot get an immediate appointment to see your doctor, but have to wait a little while, this little while might be a few weeks or months. Once you get to the doctor's office, if he is running behind and you have to wait a little while, this little while might be several minutes or an hour or two. If it is going to be a little while before a road construction project is completed, this little while might be a year or more.

In the Bible after Peter's first denial of Jesus, the Scripture says, "And after a little while another saw him and said, Thou art also of them" (Luke 22:58). Here a little while was probably less than an hour. John 13 begins with the Last Supper. In the previous chapter Jesus said in verse 35, "Yet a little while is the Light with you." If Jesus was talking about the time remaining until His crucifixion, then a little while was perhaps a day or a few days. If He was talking about the time remaining until his ascension, then a little while was probably about two months. What we can know for certain is that nowhere in the Bible is "a little while" portrayed as being hundreds or thousands of years! We can also know that in the general use of our English language, no one describes thousands of years as "a little while."

Bible scholars agree that the book of Hebrews was written somewhere in AD 67 to 69. By the autumn of AD 70, Jerusalem lay in ruins and the nation was destroyed. As we have learned, Jesus promised to come again sometime during this war. The writer of Hebrews said Jesus would come in "a little while." If we assume He came in AD 70, then this "little while' would have been somewhere from several months (AD 69 to 70) to as long as three years (AD 67 to 70). These are the only scriptural possibilities! In no way can this "little while" be correctly stretched out to include the twenty-first century! In no

VIII. Early Church Leaders

way can it be properly said that we are today still living in this "little while," and that Jesus is coming soon in our day! I hope and trust you can see the obvious truth here!

But we can glean more from this verse 37 in this tenth chapter of Hebrews! The King James translators did not properly translate into English what the author originally wrote. They left out two words! As we have seen, the King James Version says:

> For yet a little while, and He that shall come will come and will not tarry. (KJV)

The New American Standard Bible translators did a better job. They left out only one word. It reads:

> For yet in a very little while, He who is coming will come, and will not delay. (NASB)

For the Hebrews this made the waiting time even shorter! Jesus was not coming in just "a little while," He was coming in **A VERY LITTLE WHILE!** This was even better! They would have even less time to suffer!

But we are still missing a word! If we go back to the original Greek text, we can find it. What the writer actually said to his fellow Christians was,

> Yet for a little while very, very, the coming one will come and not will delay. (Greek text)

So the author of Hebrews was promising these hurting and discouraged Hebrew believers, not just that Jesus was coming in "a little while," not even in "a very little while," but that their Jesus was coming in **A VERY, VERY LITTLE WHILE!** And beyond that he promised that their Master **WOULD NOT DELAY, TARRY, LINGER, OR KEEP THEM WAITING!** These poor suffering saints of God would not have to be patient much longer! This is incredible!

In the Bible we find periods of time called "a while," "a great while," and as we saw above, "a little while." But, we find nothing to which we might compare this "very, very little while." We can rest assured the Hebrews took the phrase to mean a very, very short time. As events actually developed in those days, it was probably only a matter of months!

When did the author of Hebrews say Jesus was coming? The answer is in a very, very little while! How can today's church and its preachers and prophets continue to disagree with their own Bibles? How can they keep saying Jesus has not yet returned? How can they keep using this Scripture and keep saying Jesus is coming sometime in our future? The context and the time frame for this Scripture were in AD 67-69, not today. Jesus was coming in "a very, very little while" from the time this letter to the Hebrews was written! It does not mean that today, 2,000 years later, we can quote this verse and truthfully say Jesus is coming in "a very, very little while." **Jesus returned soon then, in the days of these Hebrew Christians!** Otherwise, the inspired author of Hebrews misled and deceived those to whom he was writing! Yet today's church says Jesus still has not come! What a great dilemma Christianity has on its hands!

This verse agrees with everything else that we have found about "when" Jesus was coming back! He was coming again in His own generation! He was coming while some of His first followers were still living! Paul said some of the saints to whom he preached would be "alive and remain" unto the coming of the Lord! James said the coming of the Lord was "near"! Now in Hebrews, written in AD 67-69, we find that Jesus was coming in "a very, very little while." **The whole New Testament is in agreement: Jesus was coming again in the first century AD.** How can preachers continue preaching, and how can Christians continue believing, that after nearly 2,000 years Jesus still has not come back?

Let me quickly conclude. In verse 38 the writer of Hebrews said that if the recipients of his letter "live," it would be "by faith." He added that God finds no pleasure in anyone who would "draw back." The Epistle to the Hebrews was written to the Hebrew believers in an effort to keep them faithful to Jesus and help them not turn their backs on Him and go back to Judaism.

VIII. Early Church Leaders

This is the theme of the passage we have been studying and of the whole book of Hebrews!

In the last verse (39), the writer said "we" were not of those who "draw back" unto the destruction that was coming on the world of Judaism. Instead, they were confident that belief in Jesus would be their salvation! This was the whole issue. Through faith in Jesus the Hebrews could be saved from the wrath to come. If they rejected Jesus, that wrath would fall heavily upon them. It was the same message the early church had preached since Pentecost in AD 30, when Peter said, "Save yourselves from this untoward [perverse] generation" (Acts 2:40). Now, nearly forty years later, the cup of the nation's sins was full. The end was at hand. In "a very, very little while" the Judge would come and execute divine justice. The Hebrew Christians could choose their own judgment, their own reward—stay faithful to Jesus and receive "a kingdom which cannot be moved" or leave Him and risk the wrath of a God who "is a consuming fire" (Heb. 12:28-29).

You should no longer have any question in your mind as to **when the author of the Epistle to the Hebrews believed Jesus was coming back.** It was so close that the saints living then could see "the day approaching" (v. 25). Properly translated Hebrews 10:37 says it all: "For yet in a very, very little while, the coming One will come and will not delay." The questions that may remain are:

What will you, my dear reader, do with the obvious truth that you have found about "when" Jesus was coming again?

Will you embrace this truth or hold on to erroneous traditions?

Will you continue to look for Jesus to come today, knowing all the while that we have not found one single verse that teaches such an idea? **NOT ONE!**

May God give you the courage and the strength to do the right thing!

IX

WHEN DOES THE BIBLE SAY THE COMING OF JESUS WAS IMMINENT?

At first glance it seems we need no concluding chapter addressing this question. Virtually all of today's preachers, prophets, and Bible scholars agree that the New Testament presents the Second Coming of Jesus as being imminent in the days of the early church. The apostles surely preached that message, declaring that His coming was "near" and "at hand." But the dilemma is that the church today maintains that Jesus' coming is imminent now, nearly 2,000 years later. We are told this has transpired because Jesus did not return in the days of the early church, as the first-century Christians had expected. So the message of His imminent coming has continued to be preached from generation to generation for these 2,000 years. His coming, we are told, has always been imminent and continues to be imminent in this twenty-first century. We have accepted that the combination of (1) not really knowing when Jesus is coming, and (2) realizing He could come at any moment, has been God's way of keeping His people always on their toes, prepared and ready for His return, whenever it does occur.

So, today's church continues to preach that His Second Coming is imminent. Ministers declare in this twenty-first century, "Jesus is coming soon." It is the church's message that Jesus could return at any moment on any day. We are told the time is right for His return in our age. Finally today, after nearly 2,000 years, our preachers tell us all the signs are pointing to His "soon" appearing. But they fail to point out to us that previous generations have felt the same way, but they **ALL** were mistaken! The prophets assure us they have it right this time! They are certain we who are living now are the last generation and we shall be the ones to see the Lord's coming! Today's imminence message says we are living in the Last Days, the Lord's Second Coming is imminent, and Jesus will soon bring "the end" to this world by His glorious appearing. I heard one very famous TV preacher say, "Jesus could be here in six months!" The only problem is that he made his prophecy several years ago; and like **ALL** the other doomsday prophets, he was wrong too! Yet Christians continue to buy books by the millions and to hang on to the latest revelations by our modern-day "prophets." God help us Christians to wake up, to study for ourselves, and to find the true answer to our question: "When does the Bible say the coming of the Lord was imminent?"

Of course, the great underlying problem with today's message that the Lord's return is imminent is that it lacks any scriptural foundation! Nothing in the Bible teaches that Jesus is on the verge of coming in our generation. **NOTHING!** This alone is certainly enough reason for Christianity to stop preaching this message. So let us take an honest look at today's imminence message and **three of the many problems** that make it untenable, unbelievable, unreasonable, and just plain wrong.

THE FIRST PROBLEM

Virtually everyone agrees that Jesus' coming was imminent in Bible days. As the word "imminent" implies, Jesus was on the verge of coming without delay in the days of the apostles. **The first problem** is that we are asked by the church to believe His return is imminent today too! Just as in Bible days, so also today, we are told that Jesus is on the verge of coming without delay. This is a problem! Both cannot possibly be true! We cannot have it both ways! The definition of the word "imminent" will not allow it! Either His coming was imminent in the first century or it is imminent today in the twenty-first century. It could be one or the other, but it is impossible to be both! As Christians we believe Jesus' coming was imminent in the days of the apostles. How then can we still be waiting for His arrival 2,000 years later? If the Lord's coming is indeed imminent today, then it was not imminent in the days of the apostles. But our Bibles declare it was imminent back then. What a dilemma! How unreasonable all of this is! **The fact is this! It is impossible for an event that**

IX. When Was the Second Coming Imminent?

was imminent in Bible times to still be imminent 2,000 years later! Is it any wonder today that Jews, modernists, skeptics, and atheists make a mockery of Christ and Christianity, belittling us who dare to believe in Him? This is an urgent matter! The church must quickly address its great dilemma! **Perhaps multitudes would believe if the church's teachings about eschatology were reasonable, believable, biblical, and consistent!**

THE SECOND PROBLEM

The second problem with today's imminence message is the reason we are given for this impossible scenario. We are told that for 2,000 years the coming of the Lord has always been portrayed as being imminent for a special purpose. The explanation goes something like this. Jesus wants His church to always be ready for His return. This means that at no time can His saints be slack, indifferent, or sinful. At no time can we let down our guard or lower our standard of holiness. We must always be at our best if we are to be ready to meet Jesus when He comes. To accomplish this, Jesus, through His ministers, always tells His people that His coming is imminent. He tells us He could come at any moment. He actually leads us to believe that He is on the verge of appearing. This way we Christians always feel that the Advent could occur at any minute, on any day. This keeps us on our toes and on our very best behavior. We can do no less if we want to be saved! Our Master could come today! After all, we are constantly being told by our preachers that "Jesus could come at any moment." And, we are told, this has been the message for 2,000 years and it continues to be preached today!

What a great deception at the hand of God all of this is! Jesus leads us to believe He is on the verge of coming again, yet He knows this is not really the truth! Can you believe we Christians swallow this scenario "hook, line, and sinker"? Can you believe we accept this as the solution to the imminence problem? If our God is a great deceiver like this, then we have totally misunderstood His character. If He is such a deceiver, then He is not the God of truth, honesty, and integrity that the Bible declares. All our theology is in big trouble if our God is a God of such trickery and outright lies! What a big dilemma this is! As I have said before, "Oh, to what lengths we preachers will go to try to make the Bible agree with what we already believe!" But this scenario is all wrong! Our God is not a deceiver! He is not a liar! **GOD DOES NOT PURPOSELY MISLEAD AND DECEIVE HIS PEOPLE IN ORDER TO KEEP THEM ON THEIR TOES!**

THE THIRD PROBLEM

The church tells us today that the ministry has always preached that the Second Coming of the Lord is ever "imminent" and "could happen at any moment." **The third problem** arises because the church **has not always preached** that the Lord's coming was imminent! Let us go back to the apostle Peter's second sermon in Acts 3. (See Chapter VII, The Apostle Peter.) The year was AD 30. Jesus had ascended and the Holy Spirit had come. Thousands had been saved. Peter and John had healed a lame man and a curious crowd gathered at Solomon's porch. Peter preached to this gathering of people, telling them they had "denied the Holy One" and "killed the Prince of life" (Acts 3:14-15). He called on the people to "repent" and promised them that Jesus would come again (3:19-20). But in verse 21 Peter told the people Jesus was not coming right then! Peter said Jesus would not return **UNTIL** another event arrived which he called "the times of restitution of all things." **So in AD 30 Peter was NOT preaching an "imminent" return of Jesus because at that time he knew that His return was not "imminent."**

So in the early days of the young church, "Jesus could return at any moment" was not the message being preached. They were sure He was coming back in their "generation," while they were still preaching, and before they all died. But the apostles knew Jesus had told them that He would return only after certain other events had occurred. So as the years went by they watched for the signs He had given in order to know when His return would be getting "imminent." They remembered His words: "So likewise ye, when ye see all these things, know that it [His coming] is near, even at the doors" (Matt. 24:33). While the apostles certainly always preached that Jesus would return, the Scriptures show that they waited until they began to "see all these things" before they started preaching His "imminent" appearing. **So the ministry has NOT always declared that His Second Coming was "imminent"!**

IX. When Was the Second Coming Imminent?

Two decades later, it seems that the apostles still had not yet begun to preach that their Master's coming was "imminent." In fact they were still preaching the exact opposite! Can you believe that? You may remember from our study of II Thessalonians 2, Paul emphatically declared that it was **not yet time for the Lord to come back!** (See Chapter VII, The Apostle Paul.) This was about AD 52, some twenty-two years after Pentecost! Some in the Thessalonian church were saying: "the day of Christ is at hand" (KJV) or "the day of Christ has already come" (NIV). Paul corrected them, saying that Jesus would not return until two other events happened. He said **first**, there must come "a falling away," and **second**, the "man of sin" must be revealed **before** Jesus would return (II Thess. 2:1-4). And, it was even a few more years after this incident before those first preachers said things like "the time is short" and "the coming of the Lord draweth nigh" (I Cor. 7:29, James 5:8). The apostles must have begun to see the signs for which they had been diligently watching. **It seems clear that the Second Coming of the Lord has NOT always been presented as being "imminent"!**

THE APOSTLES' IMMINENCE MESSAGE

The truth is, the apostles did not begin preaching the "imminent" return of Jesus until His coming was actually "imminent"! Now that made sense! That was reasonable! In fact, as His coming drew nearer, their preaching of Jesus' imminent appearance became more and more intense! That also made good sense and was reasonable. It is what we would have expected the apostles to do!

Having read up to this point, you know that AD 70 was the date by which all the prophecies were fulfilled. It was the time when God brought the Judgment upon the Jewish nation, destroying the people, Judea, Jerusalem, and the temple. It was "the end" so often prophesied. Jesus had promised that within the time frame of these events, He would come again and gather together His people. So sometime during these events and their conclusion in AD 70, Jesus returned as He promised.

However, the apostles did not know exactly when these things would occur or when Jesus would return. All they had to go by were the signs Jesus had given them while He was on Earth. Some of those signs are recorded in the Scriptures. Perhaps the apostles heard other signs from their Master that were never written. The point is that while they did not know the exact time of the Judgment and the Second Coming, they did know that the Day of the Lord was surely approaching as they saw signs being fulfilled. As more and more signs were fulfilled, the apostles became more and more confident that "the end" and the Lord's "coming" were near. As the evidence of Jesus' soon appearance began to mount, their message took on a new sense of urgency and they began to say things like "The end of all things is at hand" and "in a little while, He who is coming will come" (I Peter 4:7, Heb. 10:37). **It is apparent from the Scriptures that the apostles' message of Jesus' "imminent" return intensified as "the end" drew nearer.**

To help us see this important truth, we need to look at the writings of the early church leaders, accompanied by the dates of those writings. In dating the books of the New Testament, we all have to rely on the conclusions of many Bible scholars. Generally, these dates are close to one another, but for some books the well-educated opinions vary. As you will see in the endnotes, in developing the following imminence time line, I have used the work of two very highly respected Bible scholars, **Dr Adam Clarke** (nineteenth century) and **Dr. John MacArthur.** The picture that this time line brings into our view is stunning! While we know of no preaching about the imminent coming of Jesus during the early years of the church, we have much evidence that as "the end" actually approached, the message of Jesus' imminent return began to be preached, and preached with more and more intensity.

In the time line, the AD date is the approximate date the verses were written, except for Acts, where the date is the time the statements were made. In the parentheses next to each date is the number of years left until the final consummation in AD 70. When I realized what this time line shows, I was simply amazed! It supports everything we have learned in our study. I hope you will find this information exciting too!

IX. When Was the Second Coming Imminent?

INCREASING IMMINENCE

AD 30 (40 years)

Acts 3:20-21, Peter promised that God would send Jesus again, but not then!

AD 52[xv] (18 years)

II Thess. 2:1-3, Paul acknowledged that the Lord was coming again, but not then!

AD 56[xvi] (14 years)

I Cor. 7:29, "But this I say, brethren, the time is short."
I Cor. 7:31 (NKJV), "The form of this world is passing away."
I Cor. 10:11, "They are written for our admonition, upon whom the ends of the world are come."
I Cor. 16:22, "Maranatha." ("The Lord is coming.")

AD 58[xvii] (12 years)

Rom. 8:18, "For I reckon that the sufferings of this present time are not worthy to be compared to the glory about to be revealed in us" *(mello)*.
Rom. 13:11, "Now is our salvation nearer than when we believed."
Rom. 13:12, "The night is far spent, the day is at hand."
Rom. 16:20 (NKJV), "The God of peace will crush Satan under your feet shortly."

AD 60[xviii] (10 years)

Acts 24:15, "There is about to be a resurrection of the dead" (*mello*).

AD 61[xix] (9 years)

Eph. 1:21, "Not only in this world, but also in that which is about to come" (*mello*).

AD 61[xx] (9 years)

James 2:12, "So speak ye, and so do, as they that are about to be judged by the law of liberty" (*mello*).
James 5:8, "Be ye also patient; stablish your hearts: for the coming of the Lord draweth nigh."
James 5:9, "Behold, the Judge standeth before the door."

AD 62[xxi] (8 years)

Phil. 4:5, "The Lord is at hand."
Col. 2:17, "Which are a shadow of things about to come" (*mello*).

AD 65[xxii] (5 years)

I Tim. 4:8, "Having promise of the life that now is, and of that which is about to come" (*mello*).
II Tim. 4:1, "I charge thee therefore before God, and the Lord Jesus Christ, who is about to judge the quick and the dead at His appearing and His kingdom" (*mello*).

IX. When Was the Second Coming Imminent?

AD 65[xxiii] (5 years)

I Peter 1:5, "Salvation" was "ready to be revealed."
I Peter 4:5, "Who shall give account to Him that is ready to judge the quick and the dead."
I Peter 4:7, "But the end of all things is at hand: be ye therefore sober, and watch unto prayer."
I Peter 4:17, "For the time is come that judgment must begin at the house of God."
I Peter 5:1, "Who am also an elder, and a witness of the sufferings of Christ, and also a partaker of the glory about to be revealed" *(mello)*.

AD 69[xxiv] (1 year)

Heb. 6:5, "And have tasted the good word of God, and the powers of the world about to come" *(mello)*.
Heb. 9:11, "But Christ being come an high priest of good things about to come" *(mello)*.
Heb. 10:1, "For the law having a shadow of good things about to come, and not the very image" *(mello)*.
Heb. 10:25, "But exhorting one another: and so much the more, as ye see the day approaching" ("as you see the day drawing near," NASB).
Heb. 10:27, "Judgment and fiery indignation which is about to devour the adversaries" *(mello)*.
Heb. 10:37 (NASB), "For yet in a very little while, He who is coming will come, and will not delay."
(in a "very, very" little while, original Greek).
Heb. 13:14, "For here we have no continuing city, but we seek one about to come" *(mello)*.

AD 69[xxv] (1 year)

> I John 2:8 (NKJV), "The darkness is passing away, and the true light is already shining."
>
> I John 2:17 (NKJV), "The world is passing away, and the lust of it; but he who does the will of God abides forever."
>
> I John 2:18 (NKJV), "Little children, it is the last hour; and as you have heard that the antichrist is coming, even now many antichrists have come, by which we know that it is the last hour."

Now, we can see the answer to the question for this chapter, **"When does the Bible say the coming of Jesus was imminent?"** Looking at this timeline, the best I can determine is that the apostles began to preach Jesus' imminent appearing about AD 56, some fourteen years before "the end." Of course, they had always preached Jesus was coming again, but they began saying the Advent was "near" and "at hand" only in the final years before He came. **This seems to have been the only time in history when it would have been correct and appropriate to preach that Jesus' coming was "imminent."** Remember, Jesus had promised to return (1) in that generation, (2) before all of His first followers had died, and (3) while some of His apostles were still preaching and fleeing from city to city. As we have learned, AD 70 was the limit if Jesus would keep His own prophecy. So, for about a decade and a half prior to AD 70, it could truly be said, "His coming is imminent"! Then, and only then, could it be truthfully preached, "Jesus is coming soon"—and this was the time when the apostles preached their imminence message. **These years prior to AD 70 were the only time in history when Jesus was on the verge of coming the second time!** This was an amazing discovery for me! I hope you find it helpful!

To preach the "imminent" return of Jesus today is to mislead people. Jesus has already come! He came in the first century just as He and His apostles said He would. **Absolutely no Scriptures** support the teaching that Jesus is about to come today. **Not any!**

IX. When Was the Second Coming Imminent?

To summarize this chapter:

1. The coming of Jesus was imminent in the days of the early church. Therefore, it cannot still be imminent today, 2,000 years later.

2. I have tried to redeem the character of my Lord. He has not been deceiving His people for these past 2,000 years by telling them He was "coming soon" while all the time He knew it was not true.

3. The coming of the Lord has **not** always been imminent, as we are told today. For about twenty-five years after Jesus' ascension the apostles apparently did not preach that His coming was near.

4. The apostles began to proclaim the imminent return of Jesus only when His coming was actually near. Their message of His imminent arrival lasted for about the last fifteen years before AD 70.

5. These findings agree with **everything** else we have found in our search for "when" Jesus was coming back.

The harmony of the Scriptures continues to amaze and excite me and to increase my faith in Jesus and His Word! I pray that your experience will be equally elating and faith building!

CLOSING SUMMARY

Well, I have finally come to the end of my book. When I began writing, my vision was to find the answers to some important questions about "when" the Bible said Jesus would be coming again. Those questions and the answers we have found are briefly outlined below:

I. In the Gospels when did Jesus say He was coming?

    A. He would return during the time frame of God's Judgment on the nation of Judah, which reached its climax in AD 70.

    B. He would come back during the generation of people who were living when He was on Earth.

    C. He would return before all of the people to whom He preached had died.

    D. He would come while some of His apostles were still preaching and fleeing from city to city because of persecution.

    E. He would come while some of the members of the Sanhedrin, which condemned Him to death, were still living.

II. In the Book of Revelation when did Jesus say He was coming?

    A. He said that those who had pierced Him would see Him when He came.

    B. He said four times He was coming quickly, and the last time He was emphatic, saying: "Surely I come quickly."

III. When did the apostles say Jesus was coming?

    A. The Apostle Peter

        1. The glory of His coming was about to be revealed.
        2. God was ready to judge the quick and the dead.
        3. The end of all things was at hand.
        4. Jesus would come back during the times of restitution of all things, which ended in AD 70.

    B. The Apostle Paul

        1. The glory of His coming was about to be revealed.
        2. The day was at hand.
        3. The Lord was coming.
        4. The Lord was at hand.
        5. They would not all die before Jesus came. Some would be alive and remain until the coming of the Lord.
        6. His coming would not surprise them like that of a thief. They would be ready and watching.
        7. In the midst of their persecutions, Jesus would come and rescue them and take vengeance on their enemies.
        8. He would not come before the "man of sin" arose, but already that man's rise to power was developing.

    C. The Apostle John

        1. The world was passing away.
        2. Two times he said it was the last hour.
        3. They would see Jesus when He came.

Closing Summary

IV. When did other early church leaders say Jesus was coming?

    A.   James, Jesus' half-brother

        1. The Lord's coming was near.
        2. The Judge was standing at the door.

    B.   The author of Hebrews

        1. They would see the day approaching.
        2. Judgment and fiery indignation were about to devour their adversaries.
        3. In a very, very little while Jesus would come and would not delay!

V. When and what were the Last Days?

    A.   The Last Days were the days in the lives and times of Jesus and His apostles.
    B.   The time came when the end of the Last Days was at hand. The end was so near that the time left was referred to as "the last hour."
    C.   The Last Days both began and ended in the days of Jesus and the early church. We are not living in the Last Days today.
    D.   The Last Days were the final days of the Jewish nation, which met its destruction in AD 70 at the hands of the Romans.
    E.   The Last Days were the final days of Jerusalem and the temple.
    F.   The Last Days were the closing days of the Old Covenant, the priesthood, the sacrifices, the rituals, and everything that pertained to the Law of Moses. Jesus fulfilled the Law completely and it ceased to be of any further value and usefulness for righteousness.

VI. When and what was the End of the World?

    A.   The physical earth and heavens will not end.
    B.   We are not living in the End of the World today, and the world we live in is not about to be burned up by God.

C. When Jesus came the first time, He came in the End of the World.
D. The Bible never teaches and never mentions the end of time.
E. The End of the World (Age) was the ending of the age of Moses and the world of Judaism.
F. The world that ended, both naturally and spiritually, was the world of the Jewish people.
G. Jesus fulfilled the Law of Moses, so their religious world ended. The Roman armies destroyed their nation, so their natural world ended.

VII. When and what was the Judgment?

A. The Judgment was the wrath of God unleashed on the nation of Judah and the Jewish people for centuries of sin and wickedness. They had killed His prophets, persecuted and killed His servants, and rejected and crucified His Son. The nation's utter destruction by the Romans in AD 70 was the Judgment.
B. The arrival of John the Baptist signaled the nearness of the Judgment, that great and terrible Day of the Lord.
C. The coming of the Holy Spirit on the day of Pentecost likewise signaled the approaching Judgment Day.
D. The Judge was standing at the door, ready to judge.
E. It was time for Judgment to begin.
F. Bible references to the events listed below all refer to the Judgment of God on the land and on the people of Judea in the first century:

   1. The End of the World
   2. The tares being gathered and burned
   3. The wicked being cast into a furnace of fire
   4. A time of weeping and gnashing of teeth
   5. Heaven and Earth passing away
   6. The king destroying the murderers and burning their city
   7. Heaven and Earth being burned up, the elements melting
   8. The damnation of hell (*Gehenna*)

G. But as many as received Jesus, to them He gave the power to become sons of God, and they were delivered from the wrath that came upon the nation.

VIII. When was the Second Coming Imminent?

A. The coming of Jesus was imminent in the days of the apostles. An event that was imminent 2,000 years ago cannot still be imminent today.

B. Our God is not a deceiver and He has not been purposely misleading His people for 2,000 years regarding His imminent coming.

C. The imminent return of Jesus was not always taught by the apostles.

D. The apostles began to teach the imminent coming of Jesus only when His return was actually imminent. Their imminence message intensified as His coming drew nearer.

E. The only time in history when the Second Coming of the Lord has been imminent was in those final years just prior to AD 70. This is the only period of time in which the Bible says that Jesus' coming was near. **No Scriptures support the teaching that Jesus' coming is imminent today! NOT ANY!**

Let us conclude this summary. In our search for answers to our questions regarding when Jesus would be coming again, each of our sources agreed with **ALL** the other sources. Jesus, the apostles, and other church leaders never contradicted one another! They all described our Lord's return as occurring in the days of the early church, in that first century. I can honestly reach no other conclusion than to believe that Jesus came then, as He and His ministers had said He would. The church's opposite conclusion has created *Christianity's Great Dilemma.* Christianity's Holy Book, the Bible, says Jesus was coming again nearly 2,000 years ago, but today's church does not believe

He came then. Instead, the church says He is coming back in our age and that He is coming soon. **What a great dilemma the church has on its hands!**

In our study we have found no biblical support for the teaching of the modern church that Jesus is coming soon. Jesus and His disciples **NEVER** put His return far off into the distant future, occurring centuries and millennia later. It was **ALWAYS** to occur in their age, in their generation, and in their lifetime. As the end neared, His Second Coming was referred to as:

- approaching
- drawing near
- being near
- about to be revealed
- being at hand
- happening in a very, very little while
- being without delay

AND, THAT WAS 2,000 YEARS AGO! In the face of all the overwhelming evidence to the contrary, how can Christian ministers keep preaching "Jesus is coming soon"? How can we Christians keep believing and supporting this teaching? Personally, I cannot do so! I do hope you will come to see and understand the truth about "when" our Lord was going to return. I pray that having seen the light, you will then have the courage, the strength, and the backbone to walk in that light and to stand for the truth. **MAY GOD BLESS YOU!**

CONCLUSION

What a journey! Writing this book has been very exciting for me! The work required much time, but it has been most interesting and rewarding. My greatest hope is that my book will really mean something to you, my readers. However, you may be in shock, since it could easily be like no other book you have ever read. Perhaps it would be good to read it again. Maybe the second time through things will fall into place and begin to make better sense for you.

Hopefully, you just loved my book and are as excited as I was to discover the truth about the Second Coming of Jesus. If so, that makes me very happy! **Give God the glory for any light you have seen—any truth you have found!** Then please join me in spreading this wonderful understanding of His Word.

On the other hand you may be very upset with me, a little angry, even mad. I hope not! But if you do not agree with what I have written, I invite you to join me in continuing to study the subject. I have confessed all along that I am imperfect, I do not understand it all, and I still have questions about some things. I am still reading, studying, and hopefully growing in the Scriptures. I just want His truth. I do not have it all and I surely do not know it all. I remain open to new discoveries in the Bible. **I pray God will keep correcting me, changing me, and fixing me until I truly see eye to eye with Him.** I beg you to read this book again, to give yourself a little time. An idea as radical as the fact that Jesus has already come is not easy to accept, especially when all our lives we have been looking for Him to come. I urge you to pray, to study, and to be intellectually open and honest with God.

What I have learned has answered some secret questions I always had about Jesus' coming. Perhaps you may have these same questions buried deep within your own heart. As long as I can remember, the church has been declaring emphatically that our Lord Jesus was coming soon, at any moment. My secret questions were: "Why does Jesus keep waiting?" and "Why does

Jesus not come back?" My sincere searching answered those questions for me. **Now I know why!** It was not that my Jesus was keeping me waiting. The problem was that I had misunderstood His teachings about the Last Days and His Second Coming!

I began writing by opening myself to you. I confessed my frustrations at having preached "Jesus is coming soon" for nearly fifty years, yet He still had not come. I sought for an answer, and when I found it I did not want it! It would make me too different from the majority of Christians. It would likely destroy relationships, friendships, and fellowships. It would shut doors to my ministry. So I just ignored what I had found for a year or longer. But my love for the truth, my deep desire to know it, and the absolute necessity to speak the truth whenever I preached, just would not let me rest. The heartaches have come, the doors have been shut, and the pain has been awful! But the joy and gladness that come with finding His truth have sustained me and enabled me to endure. I have found new friends and discovered brothers and sisters in Christ I never knew I had. I eagerly look forward to finding more!

THANK YOU FOR READING MY BOOK! I am honored and I appreciate your time and consideration. I welcome any comments and responses you may have. If you like what I have written or if it has opened your eyes to truth, I would like to hear from you. If you feel that I have misinterpreted the Scriptures, taken them out of context, or abused and twisted the Word of God, I would like to hear from you too. Be specific and help me to see where I am wrong. I want to be right! I just want the truth! I love and live for the truth of God's Word! My contact information is below. **MAY THE LORD BLESS YOU!**

Christianity's Great Dilemma
Price: $12.00

Should you want additional books you can order them from me using any of this contact information:

Glenn L. Hill
215 Melton Road
Rocky Mount, NC 27801
glh@embarqmail.com
252-442-7087

i	THE ESSENTIAL C. S. LEWIS, edited by Lyle W. Dorsett, published by Simon and Schuster, page 385.
ii	JOSEPHUS COMPLETE WORKS, Kregel Publications, pages 580-581.
iii	JOSEPHUS COMPLETE WORKS, Kregel Publications, See Foreword by William S. LaSor.
iv	Ibid., See Foreword.
v	Ibid., page 548.
vi	Ibid., page557.
vii	Ibid., page 568.
viii	Ibid., page 568.
ix	Ibid., pages 570 & 579.
x	Ibid., page 565.
xi	Ibid., page 565.
xii	Ibid., page 587.
xiii	A NEW TESTAMENT WORD-BOOK by Eric Partridge, page 201.
xiv	According to Strong's Concordance the word "angels," in II Thess. 1:7, was translated from the Greek word "aggelos" (# 32 in the Greek Dictionary) and simply means "a messenger." The Roman soldiers were God's mighty "messengers" sent by Him to administer His Judgment on Judah. Nearly all the uses of "angel" in the KJV come from this same Greek word and all mean "a messenger." So, we should not always immediately think of some supernatural being when we read the word "angel" in our Bible. This same Greek word, "aggelos," is in fact translated many times in the KJV, not as "angel," but as the word "messenger." One example is Matthew 11:10, "Behold I send my messenger before thy face." Among other examples are: Mark 1:2, Luke 7:24, Luke 9:52, and II Corinthians 12:7. In the Old Testament it was common practice for God to use heathen kings to accomplish His will, perhaps most often in bringing judgment upon Israel. These kings became God's messengers, angels, and servants. In Isaiah 45:1 God even refers to the heathen king, Cyrus, as "His anointed." God would use him to conquer Babylon and deliver Israel from the Babylonian captivity. Considering all this information, it should be easier to understand that "His mighty angels" in II Thessalonians 1:7 were His "mighty" messengers and, indeed, were the powerful forces of Rome, which God used to deliver His Judgment upon the temple, Jerusalem, Judah, and all of Judea.
xv	CLARKE'S COMMENTARY, Volume VI, page 562.
xvi	Ibid., page 189.
xvii	Ibid., page 35.
xviii	CLARKE'S COMMENTARY, Volume V, page 875.
xix	CLARKE'S COMMENTARY, Volume VI, page 430.
xx	Ibid., page 797.
xxi	Ibid., pages 489 & 524.
xxii	Ibid., pages 582 & 636.
xxiii	THE MACARTHUR STUDY BIBLE, NKJV, page 1937.
xxiv	Ibid., page 1894.
xxv	CLARKE'S COMMENTARY, Volume VI, pages 896 & 902.

Made in the USA
Lexington, KY
12 June 2017